Paraklasis Counseling Theory

A Christian Approach Bringing Healing to Universal Loss

Sharon L. Miller, Ph.D., LCCT
Gordon S. Miller, M.A.R.Th.

Paraklasis Counseling Theory: A Christian Approach Bringing Healing to Universal Loss

CrossLink Publishing
www.crosslinkpublishing.com

Copyright, © 2014 Sharon L. Miller and Gordon S. Miller

All rights reserved. No part of this book may be reproduced in any form, except for brief quotations in reviews, without the written permission of the author.

Printed in the United States of America. All rights reserved under International Copyright Law.

ISBN 978-0-9852896-9-0

Library of Congress Control Number: 2014940606

All scripture quotations are taken from the Holy Bible, King James Version (Public Domain).

**TO GOD BE THE GLORY
GREAT THINGS HE HATH DONE!**

Contents

Introduction		vii
Chapter One	Paraklasis Counseling Theory (PCT)	1
Chapter Two	The Contribution of Loss to PCT	9
Chapter Three	PCT and the Personality Structure of Man	31
Chapter Four	PCT and the Model of Health and Illness	41
Chapter Five	PCT: Motivation, Philosophical Assumptions, and Key Concepts	47
Chapter Six	PCT: Multiculturalism and Christian Worldview	55
Chapter Seven	PCT: Terror Management Theory and Worldview	85
Chapter Eight	PCT and Crisis Counseling	107
Chapter Nine	Biblical Sources for Safety, Security, and Significance	141
Chapter Ten	Secondary Loss as Illustrated in the Book of Genesis	155
Chapter Eleven	PCT and Posttraumatic Stress Disorder	175
Chapter Twelve	PCT and Sexually/Physically Abused Children	197

Chapter Thirteen	PCT and the Homeless Population	229
Chapter Fourteen	PCT and Depression in Older Women	235
Chapter Fifteen	PCT: Cognitive Behavioral Therapy and Family Counseling	241
Chapter Sixteen	PCT and Human Sexuality	261
Conclusion		275
References		277

LIST OF FIGURES

Figure 1	The Triadic Foundation in God for PCT Counseling Presuppositions	5
Figure 2	Pre and Post-Fall Description of Adam	11
Figure 3	Psychopathology in the Context of Primary Loss	12
Figure 4	Significance	17
Figure 5	Eight Categories of Secondary Loss	27
Figure 6	Model of Good Psychological Health	42
Figure 7	Conceptualizing Illness in Paraklasis Counseling	44
Figure 8	Triads of Unhealthy Coping and Total Loss	45
Figure 9	Flexibility/Communication	111
Figure 10	Man in Crisis	118
Figure 11	The Miller Crisis Loss Test (MCLT)	121
Figure 12	Evaluation of MCLT Grading Chart	124
Figure 13	Crisis Counselor Checklist	132

Introduction

Counseling is like a war. The counselor is the ally of the client who is being attacked by himself, others, or invisible spiritual forces. During the battle, the counselor is encouraging the client to persevere. When the client feels defeated, the counselor motivates the client to refuse to accept defeat. When the client is victorious, the fruit of that victory should result in an active blessing of others with a generous spirit of good will. This process is the work of the Holy Spirit in the client and in the paraklasis counselor. It is best summed up by the prime minister of England who served his country throughout the Second World War, Winston S. Churchill. "In War: Resolution, In Defeat: Defiance, In Victory: Magnanimity, In Peace: Goodwill" (Churchill 1948, viii).

Paraklasis counseling theory (PCT) is based on the triadic foundation of the Trinity of God and the successive process of other triads, which describe man in his original pre-fallen state, man in his fallen state, and man in his redemption. Triads have an origin in the nature of God Himself. It is not surprising that triadic combinations are discovered in man and His earthly experience, as well as his metaphysical structure, and in the Bible. The personality structure of man is the image of God—body, soul, and spirit. Since man is not the original, we must go to the mold to see how the copy is made to learn about him. This is why the study of the Scriptures of the Old and New Testaments are critical to understanding God. The understanding of God in philosophy is limited, because the limits of reason are found in natural revelation. Special revelation from God is required to learn about the nature of God, and that is limited to what God has chosen to reveal about Himself. What He has revealed is sufficient for life and man's thought and behavior. Mind, will, and emotions are driven from the heart, from which motivation originates. After the Fall, man's perception of knowledge, righteousness, and holiness was skewed by sin.

The triad of life is symbolized by three aspects: the transcendental, the situational, and the existential. Adam's relationship with God transcended natural creation. His life situation before the Fall existed in the realm of nature, which consisted of experiencing relationship with God and creation. After Adam's fall, a spiritually dead heart drove man's intellect, emotions, and will. His safety, security, and significance were lost, necessitating a search for substitutes. Primary loss was the loss of relationship with God, and secondary loss was the loss in the situational and existential aspects of life. Therefore, loss is the root cause of man's profoundest psychological pain.

The believer has a primary relationship with God, and the pain of secondary loss is usually the motivation for seeking therapeutic intervention. The unbeliever has primary loss and secondary loss to deal with in therapy. The role of the counselor's psychotherapeutic actions are similar to the work of the Holy Spirit in guiding, comforting, and treating the counselee for loss and in bringing about change, both external and internal in the client's life.

The Need for a New Theory of Christian Counseling

Millon (1999) reminds us that there is nothing as practical as a good theory. A good theory provides us with simplicity and clarity. It is far better than unintegrated and scattered information. If there is unrelated knowledge and techniques based on surface similarities, then that is the sign of a primitive science.

The PCT originated from an evaluation of the current approaches to Christian counseling. It is a humbling reminder that a new perspective only comes from standing on the shoulders of the giants of the past. Jay Adams's Nouthetic Counseling approach is valuable in that it has a high view of the Scripture, which is foundational to consistent Christian counseling (Adams 1986). Larry Crabb was an early pioneer in the Christian counseling movement. His idea of man looking for substitutes for a relationship with God is excellent (Crabb 1977). Neil Anderson has contributed a great deal to the need for forgiveness while recognizing the malevolent sphere of evil that causes harm to people (Anderson 2000).

The different approaches have some surface similarities. Each of them emphasizes the process of spiritual formation from a Christian worldview in order to help people who are suffering from some kind of psychological distress. Unfortunately, there has been a lack of newer pioneering perspectives in Christian counseling. Jay Adams's

Nouthetic Counseling is helpful for Christians but is limited, because unbelievers who reject the Gospel are not considered good candidates for counseling (Adams 1986). Larry Crabb's contribution of man's need lacks the comprehensive biblical foundation found in PCT's triadic clarity and theological foundation. None are all-conclusive regarding counseling, but PCT will help the unbeliever as well as the Christian. Neil Anderson has contributed to a more divinely direct approach that has shown authentic transformation. Theophostic Prayer Counseling also shares a divinely direct approach, which also has demonstrated life-changing results with recent empirical support (Garzon 2008). There are common elements found in all of the above approaches that have helped in the formation of PCT. Although these approaches have success, there is the suggestion that the present situation in American Christian counseling is not meeting the mental, emotional, and spiritual needs of the clients in general (Clinton and Ohlschlager 2002). PCT is an attempt to take the best from previous Christian counseling theories and integrate psychology through the filter of the Scripture with empirical support, and at the same time, remain original in viewing loss as the root cause of psychological pain while embracing the person as a whole. It is the goal of PCT to be the unifying theory for all human behavior.

PCT's triadic Trinitarian foundation is not brand new. It was used in the field of Christian apologetics, specifically by Dr. John Frame of Westminster Theological Seminary. It was also the foundation for the Christian philosophy of Dr. Herman Dooyeweerde (1984). It is implicit in many Christian counseling theories but is explicit and clear in PCT. PCT develops the triadic Trinitarian foundation to include man's environment and his nature. The purpose of this book is to show how PCT can be utilized across a broad spectrum of psychopathology supported by empirical research and the insights of top Christian counselors in the field. McMinn (1996) identifies the development of a Christian counselor's spiritual formation and worldview as the bedrock for intradisciplinary integration of psychology, theology, and spirituality. A detailed and interactive theoretical map involving an accurate sense of self, need, and healing relationship is necessary. Emphasis is placed on the value of prayer, but caution is warned in the use of prayer in counseling, stressing the importance of the counselor's spiritual formation. Suggestion is made that the Christian counselor's question regarding whether prayer should be used really needs to be changed to which client it should be used with, when, and in what way. This theme is interwoven through each succeeding chapter as McMinn approaches the Scripture, sin, forgiveness, and confession in the counseling session. It is useful to understand the similarities and differences between McMinn's approach to Christian counseling and what PCT has to offer. McMinn gives great suggestions for the Christian counselor, and PCT is indebted to all that he contributes.

McMinn warns that clients can use the Scripture as a shield to keep the counselor from dealing with the real issues, underlining the importance of determining whether the counselor should use the Scripture directly or indirectly. His emphasis on the spiritual formation of counselors and their application of the Scripture to their own lives will determine how they can effectively use the Scripture to help others. For example, the *Los Angeles Times* quoted an excerpt from Ted Koppel's *Nightline*, May 27, 1987, during an interview with Jim and Tammy Baker: "Is it going to be possible for you to get through an interview without wrapping yourselves in the Bible?" (http://articles.latimes.com). It is the counselor who must be more concerned with the counselee who uses the Scripture and pious statements to avoid telling the truth, as Jim and Tammy Baker did in the interview with Ted Koppel. Particularly in Pentecostal circles, rather than making a negative confession when a person is asked how he or she is doing in the middle of a difficult life situation, the response may be a positive confession, closing the counselor out of the true state of mind, when all along the person may be having suicidal thoughts. At least when the counselor uses the Scripture, it is realistic, helpful, and in context with the rest of the Bible.

PCT uses prayer in counseling but teaches its purpose and power in relationship with God. The spiritual formation of the counselor is absolutely necessary to PCT, as well as emphasizing humility and empathy. The counselor must rely on God and walk with Him as a priority in order to help the client. PCT clearly points to primary and secondary loss due to sin as the cause of psychological harm.

Viewing emotional problems as a sickness has been overemphasized in non-Christian counseling theories. Calling it a sickness made some clients renounce taking responsibility for their sin. However, it is true that as physical sickness takes over, the person cannot control the symptoms. Symptoms of emotional problems can control people.

Clearly, there is a similarity to a sickness. PCT would not deny this, but it emphasizes the client's responsibility to change sinful and destructive habits once the loss factor is taught and the reality of false substitutes are understood by the client. In taking responsibility for behavior, PCT is similar to Glasser's reality therapy (Glasser 1965). While PCT accepts many of the commonly held concepts of Christian counselors like Dr. McMinn, it is distinctive in loss being the common culprit in psychological problems as well as the specific categories of loss. It is hoped that this book will assist Christian counselors across the theory spectrum with some additional understanding.

McMinn (1996) cites forgiveness as a powerful tool to heal relationships, using Jesus Christ as a model, and warns that applying forgiveness without biblical substance degenerates into a cold neutrality. He lays a foundation for understanding the nature and purpose of forgiveness by engaging both the mind and the emotions, reminding the reader that it is a command from God, that it reflects the character of God, and that it brings people into a deeper relationship with God and others. His discussion on guilt and its relation to confession points out that intrinsically religious people, although prone to shame-free guilt, exhibit less anger and resentment than extrinsically religious people. Shame-free guilt does not lead to maladaptive behavior. His treatment of the two common themes of confession—personal sin and one's faith—are explored, as well as the concept of connecting counseling with a caring community. PCT also connects with a caring community by including family, friends, and church fellowship.

The treatment of the biblical understanding of forgiveness uses Jesus Christ as the model and explains that forgiveness has been given to us by God to heal interpersonal relationships. Forgiveness is not denial, excusing, passive acceptance, or self-blame. McMinn stresses the importance of integrating the spiritual, psychological, and theological perspectives in forgiveness. PCT integrates the spiritual, psychological, social, and theological perspectives in its approach to forgiveness.

Elaborating on the differences between a Christian counselor and a non-Christian counselor, McMinn points out that a primary difference is that the Christian counselor's redemptive worldview is not found in techniques—but in relationship. Understanding sin gives understanding to redemption. Psychology, spirituality, and theology should be integrated into redemption in therapy, and a healthy counseling relationship must establish a healthy sense of self, need, and healing. He concludes with the reminder that the Christian counselor must multitask.

PCT does integrate psychology, theology, and also spirituality in a dynamic way. I would like to offer a concrete response to some of McMinn's opinions. He states how we need to ask the question as to which client, when, and in what way we should pray. There is counseling in the office and counseling in the marketplace. Sometimes there is no time to go through that process, or perhaps we may make the wrong choice while counseling in the marketplace. Nevertheless, when prayer is received, it is better than no prayer at all.

One day, I was faced with that very dilemma as I sat in a McDonald's restaurant with ten of our eleven children. A lady sitting at the table next to us began to say some very hurtful things about our children, causing them to become very upset. I was angry! God spoke to me in my spirit, and I knew that I should pray for this woman's healing. I did not know whether she was sick, but I told my husband that I would rather let her die. I had never said such a terrible thing before, and as soon as I said it, I knew that I was wrong. I got up, walked to the table, and asked the woman if there was anything I could pray for. She began to cry and explained that she had just been told she had an inoperable brain tumor. I sat down, took her hands, and prayed for her. She thanked me and did receive the prayer.

As we were leaving, another woman stopped me and asked me to pray for her healing. She was on her way to pre-op for ovarian cancer surgery. I stopped and prayed for her before we left the restaurant. Three weeks later, this second woman showed up in our church and asked if she could give a testimony. She explained that after that prayer in the restaurant, she continued to the hospital. After the tests, the doctor came out with new films and showed her that there were no signs of cancer. He could give no explanation except that she received a miracle. I believe that if I had not prayed for the first woman, I would have missed my opportunity to pray for the second woman. God would have sent someone else in her path, but I, instead, had the blessing of being part of seeing an answer to prayer. There was no time to question which person would receive prayer, but the Holy Spirit guided me to use the prayer of faith at the right time with the right person in the right way. PCT rests on the awareness of the providential interventions of God, even in the office.

As I reflect upon McMinn, he adequately approaches the triad of psychology, theology, and spirituality, stressing the therapeutic benefits of prayer, Scripture, sin, confession, forgiveness, and redemption as interventions. His approach would be stronger by clarifying and exposing the Trinitarian roots of these disciplines. Contrary to expectations, the repeated themes in his book do have Trinitarian roots. This is one difference that is stressed in PCT.

Beginning with the Trinity, within the theological perspective, the Scripture is normative because the Father has spoken through the Scripture. The Scripture and its principles are the ultimate schematic for man. The psychological is interested in the situation in life. The Son of God entered into the human situation, bringing forgiveness and redemption. The spiritual has to do with the existential perspective. The Holy Spirit guides into all truth, empowering and interceding. He enables us to confess personal sin and make confession of our faith in worship and praise. Father, Son, and Holy Spirit interaction is important, because it gives meaning to all these disciplines.

None of the categories in McMinn should be presented as table scraps to be fought over, as if ownership was not clear. They are all part of an indivisible whole of Trinitarian theology that belongs to, and needs to be, consciously recognized by the Christian counselor. For example, forgiveness is stolen by secular psychology and used as a clinical intervention without the Trinitarian relationship and the Christian content and context, leaving the person who forgives with cold neutrality rather than involving the emotions and the intellect. The forgiveness that belongs to the Christian counselor being conveyed to the client has the power of the Holy Spirit, the love of the Father, and the sacrifice of the Son. At this juncture, the Christian counselor will be more powerful and effective.

PCT expects that the counselor will multitask with the client, as McMinn recommends in his conclusion. Integrating psychology, theology, and spirituality, including continuously developing the spiritual formation, is necessary in order to use these interventions with sensitivity, humility, and empathy. To do this effectively in the counseling session, the PCT counselor needs to be sensitive in deciding which client, when, and how to use these interventions, while still allowing room for the Holy Spirit to direct. The client should never be taught to view prayer as a magical solution that removes all problems, but at the same time, he or she should be taught about the power of prayer and the authority that Christians possess.

Christian counselors are tempted to get caught up in the "ought" rather than the "why"—that is, making behavior changes that are in accordance with the Scripture without considering why the person had the problem to begin with. This use of the Scripture would be superficial and simplistic. PCT involves the tools that psychology has to offer and will allow the power of prayer and the Scripture to work together in bringing a needy person into a healthy sense of self, brokenness, and healing. Paraklasis counseling theory is the elephant in the room and will be difficult to ignore. There is a place for PCT that fits into the world of Christian counseling today, and it is our prayer that it will bring honor and glory to our Lord Jesus Christ and a stronger identity for Christian counselors.

Chapter One

Paraklasis Counseling Theory (PCT)

The Greek word in the title is part of two other related terms, *paraklatos* and *parakaleo*, found in the New Testament (Aland, Black, Martini, Metzger, and Wikgren 1975). They cover a fairly wide range of meanings. It appears appropriate to call this theory *paraklasis*, because the definitions fit the Christian counselor: to console, to exhort, to beseech, to encourage, to comfort, to help, to be an advocate and an intercessor. All of the above are what the PCT counselor brings to the therapeutic environment.

The Holy Spirit was sent by Jesus and the Father, along with other reasons, to address the disciples' sense of loss and grief. The Scripture uses these Greek terms to describe the Holy Spirit and also the Lord Jesus Christ (John 14:16; 1 John 2:1, King James Version) (Young 1969). The counselor's role is very similar to the Holy Spirit. The PCT counselor speaks with the authority of the Father, the love of the Son, and the wisdom and power of the Spirit. The Scripture prominently holds up the Lord Jesus Christ and the Holy Spirit as being described by these terms. In PCT, it is just as important to involve the counselor's attitude and approach, as well as the client's. Jesus never turned anyone away, Jew nor Gentile. The PCT counselor should respect anyone who comes for help, believer or unbeliever, from any denomination or religion or lack thereof. God mitigates suffering for Christians and non-Christians. He created the medicine that relieves pain, and it works for anybody with any worldview.

PCT is an original model for the counselor who has a similar role to the work of the Holy Spirit. The Lord Jesus and the Father sent the Holy Spirit after Jesus ascended to the Father. He is the other Comforter to God's people since Jesus is in heaven. He brings glory to the Lord Jesus and breathed into the apostles the Word of God, the New Testament, which represents what Jesus, the Word of God made flesh, speaks to His people. It is perfectly appropriate to use the Holy Spirit as our model for counseling since He brings glory to the Lord Jesus.

PCT is based on the presuppositions of loss. The counselee is viewed from the perspective of primary and secondary loss. Universal primary loss manifests itself in autonomy from God and originated from Adam's fall in Genesis 3. This underlying universal truth is multicultural, multiethnic, and crosses gender—as seen in sexual preference—and age. It is transgenerational loss and misery. Studies on loss demonstrate the debilitating effects that it can have on the emotions, mind, and body, far more than the limited, narrower concept found in grief (Murray 2001). Universal primary loss is also seen in defensive reactions to mortality salience in the studies of terror management theory (Arndt, Greenberg, Pysczynski, Solomon, and Simon 1997).

PCT is able to help the Christian and non-Christian, even the non-Christian who refuses the Gospel. The foundational structure of this theory moves from the triune God in PCT's core beliefs to the triads that appear implicitly in the Bible for the purpose of bringing about permanent change in attitudes and behavior.

This theory is based on a scriptural understanding of the personality structure of man and God. Man has a personality structure, because the God of the Bible has a personality structure; in fact, three personalities in one divine being. PCT affirms that mankind is in a state of universal loss—i.e., primary loss—as a result of the departure and autonomy from God, a broken relationship with God, and the transmission of a sinful nature to Adam's descendants. Secondary loss includes trauma, death entering into the world, aging, and the loss of true knowledge, true righteousness, and true holiness. The list of loss is endless. Even the creation fought against man with thorns and thistles depicted in the curse of work, which is secondary loss (Genesis 3). One way of describing this mess that has come upon the human race as a result of Adam's sin is the effects that loss can have on the body, the mind, and the emotions, not to mention the reactions to mortality salience. Loss, as a central tenet of a theory, is a newer perspective in Christian counseling from an Adamic fall perspective, although loss is often mentioned almost as an aside by many theorists. PCT attempts to use this truth as a major counseling presupposition.

Nouthetic Christian counseling approach has a practical weakness in that it has no plan for helping the unbeliever who rejects the Gospel. Since nouthetic counseling only holds to the Scripture in counseling in an ideal sense, the question for nouthetic counselors is: what will you do with the unbelieving client who rejects the Gospel? The only logical approach is either to refer the client to a secular counselor or to utilize secular psychology's interventions and techniques. In order to be true to their presuppositions, it would seem to be that referral should be the honest answer. PCT's perspective attempts to help the unbeliever from a loss point of view and at the same time utilize the Gospel. PCT does not drop the grieving person who needs interventions but helps him or her—even if he or she is not interested in the Gospel. Any other types of loss in life, grief, or disappointments are called secondary loss. Primary and secondary losses are foundational truths in PCT.

Since man is made in God's image, looking to God for understanding is logical and scriptural. Therefore, this theory originates with the triune God of the Bible and understanding the triads that appear implicitly in the Scripture regarding man, his needs, and the solutions to his many problems. This will give a basic understanding of PCT (see figure 1).

The Triadic Foundation in God for PCT Counseling Presuppositions

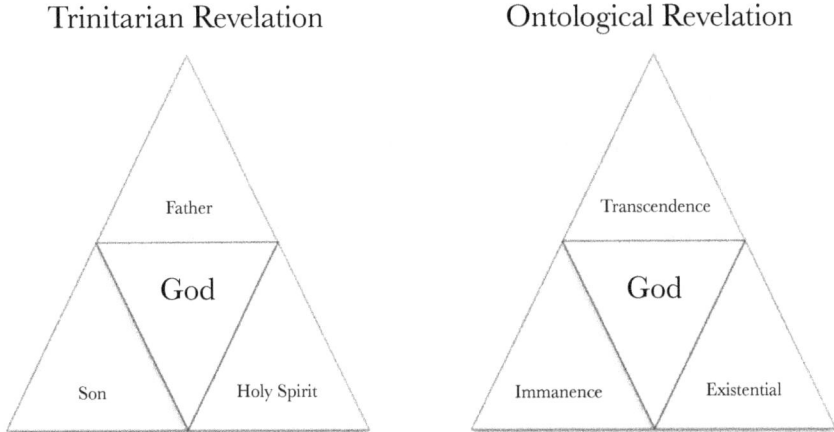

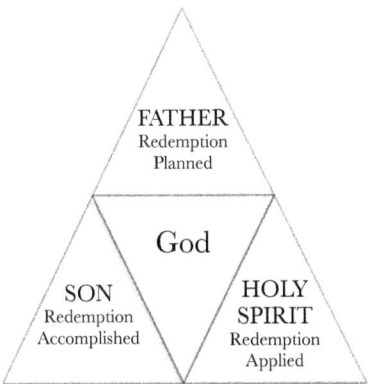

Figure 1

Notice that the individual triangles have a linkage of meaning. The Father, we have not seen, because He is transcendent and invisible. He has planned redemption. The Son became immanent by taking on human nature and entering into our life situation, accomplishing and purchasing redemption on the cross. The Holy Spirit enters into our experience by indwelling man, regenerating man, and cooperating with man in sanctification, applying the redemption that Christ accomplished for His people.

Theologically speaking, God is transcendent as well as immanent. He is infinite, eternal, and unchangeable in His being, wisdom, power, holiness, justice, goodness, and truth. God is unchangeable and eternal; therefore, His inscripturated speech has the same qualities. As a result, it can be relied upon as good counsel.

The above triadic concepts of God and His revelation in figure 1 are linked in that the God who made man in His image can communicate to man in his ontology. He makes His redemptive plans clear to man metaphysically in time, as well as man's existential/experiential, situational, and environmental/cultural aspects.

Psychologically speaking, God is willing and able to help man in the totality of his loss, primary and secondary. Man, in his social, anthropological, and individual development, as well as structural systems, can be brought to the real story to be learned and assimilated, so that brokenness and healing in man's relational and cultural milieu can occur. PCT utilizes this willingness on God's behalf to help man, which He made in His image. This is done through teaching, modeling, and being a paraklasis counselor.

Some counseling that calls itself Christian is really baptized secularism. Others simply use the Bible verses appropriate to the symptom, tell people to go home and read their Bibles more, and pray. There is nothing wrong with reading the Bible, praying, and finding appropriate verses, but very often a client's problems are much more complicated. Christian counseling should be able to go deeper into a person's life and unravel the complexities to bring about permanent change. The "why" is needed as well as the "how." PCT is a Christian counseling theory that has deep theological roots in the nature of God and the scriptural principles found in the Bible. It focuses on the "why" of the problem, as well as the "how," to solve the problem. Since all truth is God's truth, the integration of the observations of research and the Scripture must come together in a counseling theory that is comprehensive, empirically supported, and broadly applicable to the needs of the people. Yet, when it is understood, it is simple to implement. This is what PCT endeavors to offer to counseling.

Chapter Two

The Contribution of Loss to PCT

One of the first thoughts about loss that is usually considered is bereavement. A great deal of research has already been done in the area of bereavement. While grief is part of loss, it is not the only kind of loss. Everyone whom we have seen in counseling has experienced loss to some degree. It appears to be the root of everyone's problem, no matter the form it takes. If someone loses a job and goes through adjustment disorder, the root is the loss experienced. A person who has had good health and suffers a severe illness has experienced loss of health, perhaps mobility and the possibility of the loss of life. People lose loved ones through death. Even caregivers going through burnout have lost significance and freedom in doing custodial work that seems to be endless and has no reward. Clearly, divorce causes a sense of loss—the loss of significance, safety, and security. Sudden changes caused by retirement, moving, and a new environment sometimes result in the breakdown of health, panic attacks, and at bottom, loss. No longer is there the significance of a job title, the feeling of being needed. The security of a paycheck is gone. Familiar faces and knowing how to interact with fellow employees are replaced by moving to a new neighborhood and meeting new people. Loss can be a real killer. For example, the popular television show on hoarders always has the hoarder admitting that it started at a time in their lives of experiencing real loss.

The arts—including cinema, plays, novels, and television scripts, all have the central focus on loss, no matter what genre. In literature and other media forms, themes depict man against nature, man against himself, or man against God, or a combination of all three. Again, loss in some form is at the heart of it. We are curious and fascinated, and even horrified, by it as it beckons to us in entertainment or wraps its cold arms around us in life. Loss is part of life and part of death. We must all deal with it (see figure 2).

Pre and Post-Fall Description of Adam

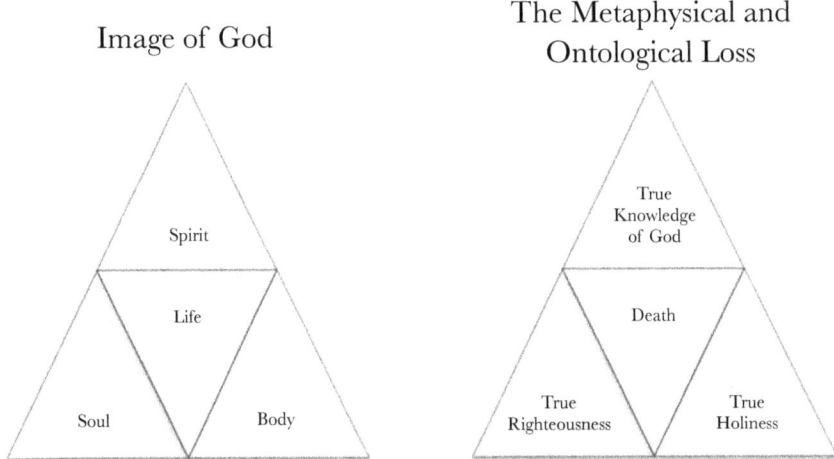

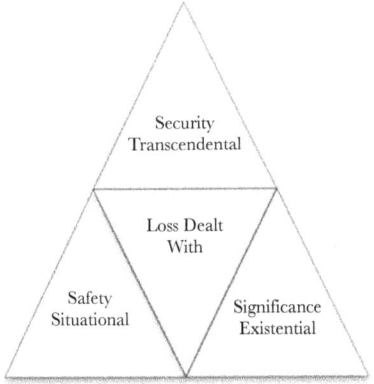

Figure 2

These triads are best understood individually. Before the fall, man was created in the image of God—body, soul, and spirit. He had life. After the Fall, he died spiritually and physically, and although he had a degree of knowledge, righteousness, and holiness, it was all marred and defaced by sin. When he lost his relationship with God, he lost a sense of security in a transcendent relationship with his Creator. His heart had not only died but motivated every other part of him with overwhelming loss. Life was no longer safe. His situation in the world was tenuous at best, because even the ground was cursed and there was a curse on all work. Healthy self-concept was lost when he came out from under the umbrella of significance with God. On his own, it was gone. His experiences in life were tainted by loss, and even in individual cases where it was not, his perception told him it was loss. Man's personality was therefore defaced by sin (see figure 3).

Psychopathology in the Context of Primary Loss

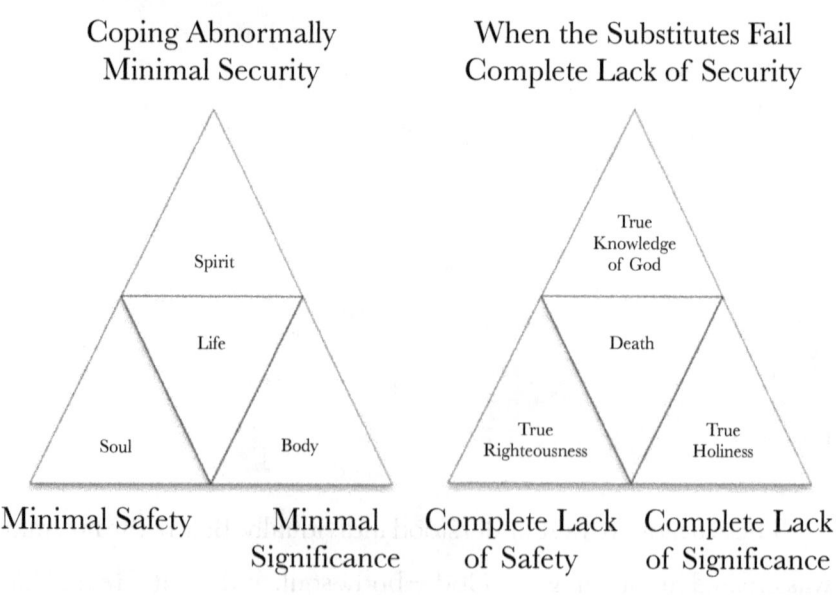

Figure 3

With a complete lack of security, safety, or significance in Christ, man seeks substitutes in this lifetime's idolatrous dance (Ephesians 5:5; Romans 1:25). Man is always looking for a better dance partner. Unfortunately, the natural man will always be dancing with death (James 1:14–15). The substitutes are like dancing partners who do not satisfy (Galatians 5:19–21). After dancing with them all—including the world, the flesh, and the devil, when the eyes are opened without grace, man perceives hopelessness, despair, and suicide, with death as his last partner. Realization of total and complete loss is the blackest and deadliest revelation of all (Acts 1:18–20; 2 Peter 2:20–22). When existentialism was initially taught in France's universities, students were asked to sign a statement that they would not commit suicide immediately after taking the class.

It is to the counselor's advantage to have this knowledge, which is also to the client's benefit. The complete awareness of total loss is similar to when Adam and Eve's eyes were opened after eating the fruit of the tree of the knowledge of good and evil. Their reaction to it was a lack of confidence, fear, and avoidance of God. This was the first incidence of attachment disorder, and, in fact, all the other ones as well.

In PCT, significance, safety, and security (the three S's) are what counselors should be aware of, so that in looking at the particular loss, the counselor can assess which of the three, or perhaps all of the three, may be applicable to treat. The importance of these three factors is that loss in one or more of these three areas creates deterioration in the psychopathology of significance, safety, and security, resulting in abnormal thinking and behavior. This occurs in the transcendental, situational, or experiential realm. The defense mechanism is to seek a replacement, and this comes naturally in the lives of non-Christians. This will be more closely looked at in the section on terror management theory.

Rationalization, compensation, repression, projection, reaction formation, identification, denial, introjection, and displacement are defense mechanisms used by someone in loss. If a substitute is harmful, it will create an insatiable desire for more to make up for the loss, creating psychological distress and other problems. The Bible says that whatever is not of faith is sin. Some substitutes are harmful and not so harmful for others. Others are very harmful. The principle "loss multiplies loss" continues to appear in psychopathology. Extreme hoarding is a good example of a harmful substitute. Addictions are also substitutes for the loss of significance, safety, or security, no matter how it was initiated.

In secondary loss, not all substitutes are harmful and therefore do not require counseling. In the case of the non-Christian, all substitutes for Christ are harmful, because in God's viewpoint, they are idolatry. Not every non-Christian is willing to approach this dividing line at the beginning of counseling. It is the authors' view to treat clients. And when they see improvement, they invite them to learn why.

For example, the loss of an expensive wedding ring replaced by a less expensive one. The substitute may or may not equal the value of the one lost, but the person does not need counseling. It still works as a substitute even if it does not have the memories attached to the original one. However, it is always harmful to the client in primary loss to seek a substitute for God in the areas of significance, safety, and security.

Sometimes Christian counseling is treating the symptoms of anxiety or depression in a proof-text method of counseling. PCT is an attempt to create a biblically comprehensive theory of Christian counseling foundational for an integrated interventional style of counseling. This is the reason for choosing significance, security, and safety as the three main areas where substitutes for primary and secondary loss are found.

Biblical distinctions demonstrate the differences between significance, safety, and security. Significance in the Scripture can be traced back to two Greek words: ψῆφος *(pseiphos)* (Acts 26:10) and ἄφωνος *(aphonas)* (Acts 8:32). In Acts 26:10, Paul states that he gave his *voice* against them. The Greek word *pseiphos* meant a small, worn, smooth stone, a pebble. In the ancient courts of justice, the accused were condemned by black pebbles and the acquitted by white; a vote (on account of the use of pebbles in voting) (Vines, n.d.). The King James Version (KJV) chooses *voice*. Other translations choose *vote*. They are the same word in Greek. It represents Saul's vote for the death penalty against the believers in Jesus. This was a significant voice. The death penalty vote is a significant one. Saul had significance here. The other Greek word, *aphonos,* found in Acts 8:32, means voiceless, without faculty of speech. To be voiceless means you have no significance whatsoever. This Scripture verse in Acts

8:32 is a prophecy from the OT regarding Jesus as the sacrificial sin offering: "He was led as a sheep to the slaughter; and like a lamb dumb before his shearer, so opened he not his mouth...." This was part of the humiliation of Jesus as a sin offering, meaning, He would not speak to defend Himself.

To feel like you have no significance means that you have nothing worthwhile to say, you have no voice, and no one would listen, because you are not worth listening to anyway. You feel like your life has no meaning. Loss has taken it away.

Some people believe that they have significance, but it may be a false significance. False significance leads to little significance. Little significance leads to no significance. It is a downhill slide. Ecclesiastes 2:9–11 tells us that the king is great in his own eyes, because he can enjoy all the pleasures of the world. He rejoices in his worldly occupation. When it did not satisfy, and loss was involved, it led to little significance. Verse 11, "all is vanity," eventually led to "hating life" (verse 17), which means no significance. Loss multiplies loss.

After man has danced the dance of life and finds no partner to satisfy him, he loses significance when he discovers that the only one who will dance with him is death. The following set of triads shows the downhill slide to no significance (see figure 4).

Significance

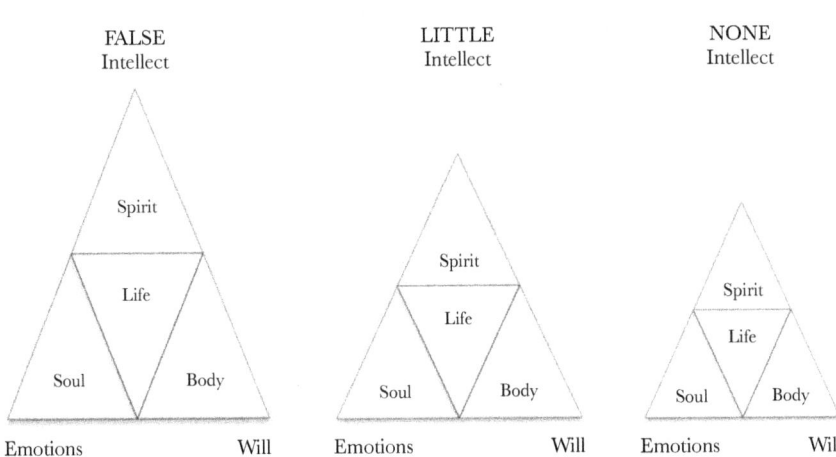

Figure 4

An influential study (Murray, 2001) has caused the authors of this book to reflect on its scriptural and counseling ramifications, which has been very influential in developing PCT. The study concludes that loss is something broader than just grief and can be a universal concept. The idea involves whatever is perceived of value that has been lost and the complex emotional amalgams of responses in behavior. This idea originates in the New Testament.

The apostle Paul had regarded what he once held valuable as actually a loss in comparison to obtaining Christ. He handled loss of the substitutes in a healthy way. A meaningful passage is Philippians 3:7–8, which is the kernel of truth for helping all people with loss and the ideal goal for assisting the non-Christian in his problems. If someone holds something as valuable and it is lost, pain is the result.

There is an instinctual need for locating a substitute. The ultimate goal of PCT is to lead the person in loss to the true substitute that satisfies, and that is the saving relationship with Jesus Christ.

Murray (2001) points out that with every change of life, there is a loss and therefore requires external and internal adjustments. She indicates that while there are many different life traumas, there is a common bond of loss that exists among those who suffered from the death of a loved one and those who suffered life traumas. She argues for a universal model of one loss, which can be applied to all, but preserves individual differences. The advantage is for the transference of clinical skills to counsel those in every kind of situation of loss. This is what PCT accomplishes. It is a universal model to treat every kind of loss for every life change.

Murray lists themes that inform us about grieving loss. The first is that grieving a loss is a normal reaction common to all human experience. The second is that the loss experience began with the earliest age of a child and that this integration into the psychological functioning of a person creates the potential for personal growth or deterioration. PCT believes that loss can cause deterioration and psychological distress when false substitutes for the object fail to satisfy. One possible intervention for the counselor is to reframe the situation into a biblical understanding of the loss and the substitute. It is important to emphasize the fact that PCT has also found that loss multiplies loss in the human experience. This must be unraveled to a certain extent for healing to take place.

Third, loss or grieving as a result of loss is a private, lonely experience. Children find it especially difficult, since they are living in an adult world. Children understand in a different dimension and intensity than adults. Their grieving will consist of unique internal influences. The meaning of the loss may be quite different than the loss interpreted by adults. The level of cognitive functioning will also influence the symptomology of loss. Therefore, the counselor must be flexible and sensitive, especially to young clients.

Another internal factor that influences loss is emotional coping or problem-centered coping. In high loss-of-control situations, actively looking to solve a problem may be less adaptive than helping to appraise the stressfulness of the situation. It appears that a variety of different coping measures may be more helpful in ensuring a positive outcome in grief and loss situations.

Murray is helpful in showing that people who are most likely to experience high levels of distress in loss are those who are apt to blame themselves or others for their misfortune, have a desire to seek revenge, or have low internal-control beliefs. PCT counselors should be aware that a loss of significance for clients can lead to feelings of shame, and, as Murray points out, research has indicated that it can affect the self-concept and lead to suicide. Guilt, on the other hand, can show that a wrong decision has been made but has no lasting impression on the self-concept, as the reverse is true of shame.

External factors that affect reactions to loss include the social context. There is a link between social support and positive adjustment to loss. Why it helps is debatable. It may be that the social context creates a more positive self-efficacy, or it may directly buffer against stress. A cultural definition of loss will determine how stressful the loss will be perceived. Multicultural sensitivity is important regarding this point for the counselor. Not only is the culture important, but the microcultural factors of the family mores and context must be considered with regard to loss. The counselor should also look at the transgenerational transmission of trauma in the loss. Communication patterns and positive adaptation to loss within the functioning of the family is important to understanding how to help the person and the family.

Murray reveals the idea that loss is a threat to someone's feelings of safety, mastery, and control in life. This strongly implies that PCT's idea of loss threatening one's safety, security, and significance is on the right track. She explains that security comes from one's assumptions about certain actions being consistently followed by particular reactions. These are learned responses. These assumptions about how the world is organized, even if the actions and responses are negative, still provide the security in their predictability. Therefore, a person can adapt to adverse circumstances and loss. A child may learn to avoid the father who comes home drunk and abusive on Friday nights. If a person has learned to believe that it is always the case, that the light at the end of the tunnel is an oncoming freight train, then there is a learned security in its predictability. That is why there is security in cynicism.

Even though loss can be adapted to, a person whose loss catches by surprise may have their security threatened, because loss can discredit important assumptions about the world and the future. Previously held assumptions do not work, and the confidence of the person is lost. Here is how it affects the person. There may be the inability to make decisions or to trust in his or her own reactions, and even lack trust in those who are in the immediate social network. This may be the experience of a pastor who is trying to comfort a couple in the sudden loss of their child. One or both parents may put up a wall to the pastor's best efforts, leaving him confused and frustrated.

Murray designates three fundamental assumptions held by people in Western cultures. First, the world is benevolent. Second, the world is just and meaningful, and third, the self is worthy. Therefore, if a person is good, then major loss can be avoided. When major loss occurs, then life is no longer meaningful or controllable, and these beliefs may be abandoned. When the loss comes and the beliefs are rigidly held, then people may make harsh moral judgments about themselves and others.

From a Christian biblical worldview, the world suffers from the curse of sin. Therefore, "just" and "benevolent" are not necessarily the best terms to describe the world. The self, whether regenerated or not, is not worthy other than being in God's image and is in need of a heart change that the Bible calls regeneration. The self is saved by grace, not by worth. Grace is a gift, not something earned. As Christians are God's children, they are loved by Him, but these people still suffer from a sin-cursed world that God permits. For example, people lose their jobs, Christians get terminal diseases, fruit trees die from disease before they bear fruit, and buildings collapse and kill people. Tornadoes, hurricanes, and tsunamis take their toll on human and animal life. Famines kill crops and people. The rain falls on the fields to water the crops of the just and the unjust. Good things even happen to bad people. In His plan of redemption, the curse of sin and its effects on man's environment will only end when the Lord Jesus returns to create a new world without the curse of sin and death. Life in this world is topsy-turvy, not very predictable.

Loss tends to make people more fearful, and the world is less predictable. The PCT counselor will try to rebuild a sense of safety, security, significance, and control in a changed environment. Murray suggests the following interventions for women affected by child abuse: resistance, reframing, mastering trauma, and controlling other areas of life. The counselor may use stress inoculation or flooding to reduce the stress of PTSD. She emphasizes the need for preventative mental health promotion. Pastors ought to teach against the idea of bad things happening only to bad people and vice versa. A Christian biblical worldview should be taught by the Church. It would help Christians in crisis mode from sudden catastrophic loss.

Murray stresses the notion that loss seldom exists alone. It is accompanied by other resultant losses. PCT also emphasizes the idea that loss multiplies loss as has been mentioned before. There may be a loss of ability as a result of loss of health. There may be a loss of independence as a result of a loss of finances. A loss of significance may cause a loss of friends. A loss of safety from a rape may cause a loss of freedom of movement because of fear. This multiplication of loss from a major loss is revealed as time goes on. Primary loss multiplies secondary loss. The sinful state in which man is born creates some of the secondary loss he is responsible for, and it gradually multiplies as a result of external factors or wrong decisions.

Both the internal factors of secondary loss and the external factors of secondary loss coming from living in a sin-cursed world can result in a pathological state. Therefore, the PCT counselor will consider both an autoplastic and an alloplastic approach in helping those in loss.

There is a danger to labeling acceptable patterns of grief with regard to a loss (Murray, 2001). The danger of stereotyping appropriate responses to a loss can cause great distress and misunderstanding of appropriate responses. The counselor in PCT must be flexible and should not fall under the cultural norms that may not be biblical after all. When a client shows anger, the counselor must not jump to conclusions that it is because of a particular loss. It may be a reasonable reaction to another's behavior or some situation not related to the loss. Someone who is terminally ill is forced to adopt the sick role when everyone who visits only interacts on one level and concentrates on the illness.

Stereotyping patterns of grief reactions can only increase the intensity of the loss. Therefore, when a counselor concentrates on the loss rather than the person, he or she might interpret that all emotions and actions resulted from the loss, and a unidimensional view of the person develops, overlooking activities that could give him or her some sense of control, thereby resulting in a lack of increased security, safety, and significance. All of this comes from the stereotyping of grief reactions and assuming that recovery will take place in a certain amount of time. PCT does not view people in a unidimensional way even though loss is examined.

Having looked at Murray's contributions to understanding loss, some recommendation to using PCT is appropriate for the counselor. PCT counselors should know themselves with regard to their own reactions to loss, considering the danger of transference and countertransference. Reconstruction of meaning, life stories, reminiscing, and appropriate biblical stories may be helpful for the client in loss. It is important to remember the uniqueness of the loss to the client. It is their interpretation and perception of the events that the counselor must try to enter into.

Some pastors tend to be very directive in their counseling, but with regard to loss, the PCT counselor ought to step back from being a director to being a facilitator who seeks the most appropriate ways to help the client in their loss to restore their safety, security, and significance in a biblical way. In PCT, although directing may be necessary, the idea of facilitating is a gentler concept than directing and is similar to the biblical idea of the Holy Spirit guiding people into all truth. The counselor is usually one of the last people that the client comes to for help. Getting permission to have facilitation of support with others who are designated by the client in their social network may be, in some cases, a valuable asset in helping the client with loss.

PCT shares many of Murray's research conclusions and has a biblical foundation for its loss concepts, from the universality of loss in the human race to the commonly shared factors, regardless of the particular loss involved. The value of Murray's study has been an empirical confirmation of what has been discovered about PCT, originating in the Bible. We can say that PCT is empirically supported.

Having delineated the difference between primary and secondary loss, it is important for the PCT counselor to determine what category of secondary loss is going on in the client. Secondary loss can be broken down into eight categories of loss. The first category is a loss by another's sinful choice; for example, the thief who steals one's money. Then there is the second category of loss by your own sinful choice, like the choice to gamble and lose your money. In the Bible, David coveted another's wife, committed adultery and murder, and then suffered loss. Repentance was the solution in that case. The third category of loss is from living in a sin-cursed world, like aging or getting cancer. The fourth category is voluntary loss for secondary gain, like the decision to not fix your car so you have more money to spend on other things, or, in a positive way, to sacrifice getting a newer car for getting a college education, or like in chess, where you sacrifice a pawn to get a queen. Then there is the fifth category of voluntary loss for Christ from a Christian worldview—losing this world to follow the Lord Jesus Christ. John G. Lake, a nineteenth century healing evangelist, walked away from an extremely lucrative business career to a life of a missionary in Africa. The choice to leave fame and fortune to become a pastor of a small church is another example. The sixth category of secondary loss is the loss of a loved one. Death and grieving is in view here. The seventh category of loss is loss caused by the actions of another. It is a loss that is not caused on purpose, or that the client was even aware that certain actions caused the loss. For example, a business has to make cutbacks for economic reasons. They have to lay off a number of employees. They suffer loss of income, which multiplies into possible depression, because houses are foreclosed and they cannot find jobs. The eighth category is loss caused by your own choice (not sinful). You buy a car that is a lemon, which consequently causes a financial loss, or you do something that is not sinful but wasn't the wisest course to take. You might obtain a degree that seemed right for you, but it does not lead to meaningful employment. These eight categories can assist the counselor in the assessment of a client's problem and how they affect a client's loss of significance, security, and safety (see figure 5).

Eight Categories of Secondary Loss

Category I   **Loss Caused by Another's Sinful Choice**

Reframed biblical thinking

1. Forgive.
2. Break off generational curses.
3. Pray for your enemies.
4. Look forward.

Category II   **Loss Caused by Your Own Sinful Choice**

Reframed biblical thinking

1. God tells us to confess our sins and to repent.
2. God will forgive us our sins.
3. Choose to forgive yourself.
4. Learn from your mistakes

Category III   **Loss from Living in a Sin-Cursed World**

Reframed biblical thinking

1. God promises a new heaven and a new earth.
2. God promises to provide for our needs.

Category IV   **Voluntary Loss for Secondary Gain**

Reframed biblical thinking

1. God promises us a future and a hope.
2. God promises to give us the desires of our hearts.
3. Walk by faith and not by sight.
4. Keep your eyes on Jesus and the goal.

> **Category V   Voluntary Loss for Christ**
>
> **Reframed biblical thinking**
>
> 1. Philippians 4:19.
> 2. Rewards in heaven.
> 3. God promises eternal life.
>
> **Category VI   Loss of a Loved One**
>
> **Reframed biblical thinking**
>
> 1. Life transcends death; no final separation from believing loved ones.
> 2. There is the comfort of the Holy Spirit.
> 3. There is comfort from the fellowship of believers.
> 4. Time will help the grief.
>
> **Category VII   Loss Caused by the Actions of Another**
>
> **Reframed biblical thinking**
>
> 1. Trust in God to give you safety, security, and significance.
> 2. Love one another.
> 3. Forgive.
>
> **Category VIII   Loss Caused by Your Own Choice (Not Sinful)**
>
> **Reframed biblical thinking**
>
> 1. Realize that you are significant in God's eyes.
> 2. Seek wisdom from God.
> 3. Do not receive false guilt.
> 4. Pray before you make future decisions.
> 5. Move on because God has given you a future and a hope (Jeremiah 29:11).

Figure 5

The above suggestions for reframed biblical thinking as shown in figure 5 are meant to give the counselor a starting point. It is not meant to be all-inclusive or in any way comprehensive. The counselor may find a different biblical approach to a category of loss that better fits with their client. The eight categories are refining the loss of safety, security, and significance to a more specific loss.

In the assessment process, the PCT counselor determines the category of loss revealed in the self-reporting of the client's history and presenting the problem. There can be more than one category of loss that contributes to the client's difficulties at any one time. The perception of the loss may be less or more than the counselor anticipates. Listening and observing the mood, emotions, verbal and physiological cues, as well as listening to the story will often reveal the weight of the particular loss perceived. The treatment plan will include reframing unbiblical thinking into biblical thinking. Bibliotherapy may be part of the educational aspects of getting well.

Under secondary loss is a subcategory of *aleph* loss (close loss) and *tav* loss (loss from the past). This assists in determining the perception of a loss. Aleph loss is the effect of loss in a personal conscious way on the individual in the present. The loss of a loved one bringing grief to the client is an example of aleph loss. Tav loss is the loss incurred from secondary loss that is a step away from being consciously realized. For example, aleph loss would be failing the job interview because of a cognitive deficit brought about by taking drugs in the past (tav loss) and not being able to answer the questions properly (aleph loss). Consequently, tav loss is the loss incurred in the past but perhaps experienced in the present (aleph loss). The passage of time is a determining factor in recognizing tav loss from aleph loss.

Aleph and tav losses are separate from the eight categories of loss, because they assist in differentiating how a particular category affects the individual, and they can be applied to all eight categories. For example, there is the category of the loss of an individual. When did it happen? Did it happen this year, or when the client was two years old? If it occurred this year, then aleph loss would apply. If it happened when the client was two, then tav loss would apply.

Tav loss can become aleph loss, and aleph loss can become tav loss. This becomes apparent through counseling. Since the client lost a parent when the client was two, we say it was tav loss. In the assessment session, the counselor discovers that as a result of growing up without a father, the client looked for a father image as a substitute for the tav loss by joining a gang and has recently been incarcerated for crimes committed as a member of a gang. Tav loss has become aleph loss. The aleph loss is the loss of his present freedom and the pain experienced from his incarceration. When the substitute for the loss has been recognized and pointed out by the counselor, treatment for loss can begin.

Joseph was sold by his brothers into slavery in Egypt. As the years went by, he rose to be second in command under Pharaoh, who probably became a father figure to him. The category of loss—loss from the sin of another—was tav loss. The tav loss became aleph loss as the pain was revived within him when his brothers came upon the scene and intruded into his life. God revealed to him that although they meant it for evil, He meant it for good, and was a revelation that enabled Joseph to forgive them; therefore, tav loss became aleph loss, which now became tav loss through the counseling of God (no longer hurting him in the present).

In relation to PTSD, the tav loss of the battlefield becomes aleph loss when it is triggered. In counseling, the reprocessing enables the aleph loss to become tav loss through desensitization of the triggers.

Another example of aleph and tav losses is in the application to addiction counseling. Assuming that the premise of loss is behind addictions, discovering whether aleph loss or tav loss is involved can assist the counselor in understanding how some of the eight categories of loss apply. Then the healing of the loss can begin.

Loss has been shown to be universal, both in its primary and secondary senses, and that man craves a substitute to bring relief from the pain of that loss. The PCT counselor can begin to move from the general to the specific in understanding the perception of that loss in the client based on the eight categories. Perception of loss is further clarified by determining the multiplication of loss by considering aleph and tav loss.

Chapter Three

PCT AND THE PERSONALITY STRUCTURE OF MAN

Secular psychology criticizes any theory that does not have empirical research behind it. Christian counseling comes under this criticism, but so does Freud. Research is concerned with whether or not the theory works, why it works, or how it works, and whether or not it can be depended on to work again with consistency and reliability. It is an area that ought to be addressed for any counseling theory. Christian counseling is unique. It uses the Bible for a great deal of empirical evidence, not in the sense of contemporary research but due to the fact that it comes from the God who made man to begin with, and shows what psychological harm can come to a man who ignores his spiritual side and his relationship with his Creator. Secularists may disagree with the Christian counselor's presuppositions and would say it rests on faith, but the Christian counselor has every right to question whether or not the secular psychologist is proceeding from faith in his own presuppositions that undergird his particular theory. There are many popular secular theories that lack a great deal of traditional empirical support.

Therefore, in order to understand man's personality structure, a biblically consistent Christian counseling theory must consider the personality structure of the God who made man in His image. Going back to the mold to consider what was molded is a first step. Therefore, we must look to the God of the Bible's personality if we are to discover the personality of man. God—as described in the Bible—has intellect, will, and emotions, as well as self-conscious existence. The Scripture describes Him as having three personality structures in one being. Man only has one personality structure but has triadic implications from God. God's Trinitarian structure of personalities is equal in power, glory, and authority, yet they are distinct from one another. The Old Testament (OT) hints of this triadic being in Genesis 1:1: "In the beginning God (Elohim), created the heavens and the earth." This is a plural ending in the Hebrew word for God. In Genesis 1:27: "Let us create man in our image, after our likeness." The pronouns "us" and "our" clearly show a plurality in the being of God. As the information concerning God increases over time within the formation of the canon of the Scripture, the NT reveals God as the Father, Son, and Holy Spirit. Yet all are fully God. At Jesus' baptism, all three are present. The Father speaks, the Son is baptized, and the Holy Spirit descends in the form of a dove. The three speak to one another from all eternity past as is revealed when Jesus prayed in the garden to the Father in John 17:5, 24 (also, refer to John 1:1, 2). Since God is love, and

Jesus' words in John 17 speak of love before time, this love implies eternal personality distinctions. God, as described in the Scripture, is a social being who speaks. God has a conscious mind, but not an unconscious mind. All things are known and are present to Him. God's personality structure is not evolving but unchangeable. The amazing thing is not that God can speak, but that man, who is made in His image, can speak. Man is the image of God, body, soul, and spirit, which are the triadic overtones passed on from God. Some of God's attributes are passed along to man and some are not.

The heart directs the overall movement and motivating factor, as described in the Bible, in life situations of the mind, will, and emotions. There is a conscious mind and an unconscious mind in man. Supernatural communication between man and God comes through the conscious mind, not the unconscious. When the NT is examined, communication from God comes from the Holy Spirit through the Scripture, the prophetic gifts, such as word of knowledge or visions, dreams, trance, and audible voice.

Man was originally created with the true knowledge of God and himself in true righteousness—that is, a perfect relationship with God in true holiness. Sin did not have control over Adam or Eve. After the Fall, mankind lost the true knowledge of God and worshiped the creation rather than the Creator. The relationship was broken between God and man, and man and man. There was a dissonance between man and his environment as a result of Adam's sin. He was clearly condemned because he was neither righteous nor holy, and it was rebellion against God. The sin of Adam was transmitted to his posterity.

He was still the image of God, although that image was skewed and defaced. That fact enabled man to be redeemable through Christ. If the biblical explanation of the personality structure is disregarded—which is body, soul, and spirit, as well as intellect, emotions and will—then there is no explanation for the core existence of spirituality in people. To put it another way, the spiritual quality and desire in man is explained by the triadic personality structure of man that is in the Bible. The triadic personality structure of man exists because of the triadic personality structure in God Himself. This triadic personality structure of God remains unchangeable. So it is with the personality structure of man. The structure of man's personality remains the same regardless of culture, age, ethnic background, or gender, because God's personality structure is unchangeable. Personality type itself may change across the lifespan of human development as people age and suffer good and bad experiences in life, precipitating change that is visible in the personality. For example, a child was a happy child until his parents died in a car accident. From that time on, he was sullen and morose. Medical reasons, such as brain tumors, can also cause personality change. If the personality can change, and it does, then there is hope for counseling.

In opposition to what has just been said about the unchangeable human personality structure, evolution-based secular counseling may be influenced by the liberal theologians' concept of an evolving God. This direction of thinking implies that since man is evolving, the image he has made of God should also be evolving. This is the desire for autonomy demonstrated in Adam and Eve's rebellion. Therefore, in the same line of thought, as the personality structure of man could evolve, the personality structure of God could as well. Even without the addition of an evolving God, the secularist counselor, if consistent with evolutionary theory, must believe in a changeable structure of human personality. Unfortunately, in a chance universe, the direction of evolution may go the other way and devolve. There are no controls. The result for the secular counselor is only a possible hope, which is really no hope, for getting better.

PCT is built on the evidence of the Scripture, which is the foundation of all ontological and metaphysical assumptions about man. The Bible does teach a personality structure of man. This personality structure is comprehensive and inclusive since every man is made in the image of God. Regardless of gender and cultural context, there are transcendental, situational, and existential aspects of the human personality that are common to all mankind.

All human beings have transcendent aspects to the personality. In other words, all people have a spiritual component. This comes out in religion—an awareness of another realm of reality that is not discovered by the senses, that is invisible. Immanuel Kant presents an illustration of the idea that man has a sense of the transcendent, a spiritual component of his personality. Kant argued that man cannot reason God's existence from empirical philosophy and he put God in the transcendent realm, essentially unknowable, to protect him against the tide of rationalistic science. According to Kant, the only thing we can know about God is in the moral realm. This is not to say that Kant has a biblical view of God, but it is useful here in illustrating the fact that man has always had a transcendent sense of the spiritual. Anthropology has demonstrated that every tribe and group of people has that transcendent sense of a spiritual realm. Western civilization is in the minority in the world, having embraced post-Enlightenment rationalism's notion that reality is only composed of what can be understood materialistically. Nonetheless, in our present day, Western culture still hungers for a spiritual component to life, whether in the interest in the occult or building some kind of confused, eclectic, spiritual worldview because of the popular film industry.

Man has a situation. Man's personality responds to his environment. Everyone has a story to tell. Everyone has a life situation with good and bad influences, gains and losses. The situation is in the culture, nation, state, community, and family in which man finds himself. The stories that reveal loss often show that loss multiplies loss. The tsunami of 2012 in Japan is an example of secondary loss in man's situation. One major loss leads to behaviors and reaction formation that creates its own loss, resulting in psychological distress that continues on after the initial trauma. Everyone comes from somewhere, whether growing up in the perfect family or being abused from childhood. We all have a situation that we have lived in and live out within our existence.

Man also has an existential component to his personality. This is the experiential component. All people have different experiences within the situation they live in. If a person finds himself or herself living in a sealed wooden barrel, the experience is the darkness and the stifling air he or she breathes, while the situation is the wooden barrel he or she is living in. The transcendent comes when he or she prays to escape it. If a person grew up inside the wooden barrel from the time he or she were a baby, with food and water supplied to him or her, he or she would think that stifling air and darkness would be normal. So it is with people who escape from abusive situations and look for another abuser to marry again; anything to maintain homeostasis. Experience and its perception may be two different things. For example, a person is depressed because he or she thinks that his boss does not like him or her, but his or her perception may not be telling him the truth. The truth is that the boss is not very outgoing or emotionally expressive and actually does like him or her.

The image of God consists of body, soul, and spirit. In counseling, this means that the influence upon one aspect will affect the other, so that thoughts will affect the body, and the body will affect the thoughts. It is always wise for the counselor to explore the medical conclusions of recent physical examinations of the clients. The same interaction involves the emotions and the will. The heart drives the overall movement in life of the mind, the emotions, and the will. The heart is the core of a person, the center of their being, according to the Scripture. PCT includes all dimensions and complexities of human life and relationships, not emphasizing one at the expense of the other (Jones and Butman 1991).

There is both a conscious and an unconscious mind. Crabb (1997) is mistaken when he believes that supernatural communication comes through the unconscious mind. Every recommendation in the Scripture for cognitive behavioral change in thinking is associated with the conscious mind (Philippians 4:8–9). If God communicated His thoughts to us in the unconscious mind, it would be sublimation, which is using deceit. According to the Scripture, God is not deceitful. This is like the newspaper advertisement that inserted the hidden word "SEX" in the content to increase sales. When schizophrenics hear voices, it comes in the conscious mind. This is not to assume that there may not be other biological reasons for hearing voices aside from demonic communication.

After the Fall, man experienced the loss of a right relationship with God and an anchoring point for cognitive thinking. Autonomy is a high price to pay. Therefore, man's security, safety, and significance will be reduced or exacerbated in people's perception without an anchoring point for cognition. Mankind was still the image of God, although this image was defaced in many ways, as has been indicated. The continuance of the image of God gives hope for man to experience permanent change with a wonderful future through the redemptive work of Jesus Christ. If the biblical structure of the personality of man is disregarded, then there is a complete lack of explaining the core existence of spirituality in mankind, and any counseling that proceeds on this basis is neglecting that which is most important: man has a cognitive anchoring point in his redemptive relationship to His Creator in Christ.

Secular psychologist Millon (1999), for example, believes that man is a bio-psycho-social being from an evolutionary perspective. What is neglected is that man is a bio-psycho-social-spiritual being whose personality is composed of intravariables from the interaction of the transcendental, the situational, and the existential perspectives that interact with the significance, safety, and security of man from a loss perspective though yet in the image of God.

Millon views the major approaches to personality theory in the field manifesting in history because of evolutionary movement. As the expressive acts domain of successors to Skinner and interpersonal conduct tradition by Keisler, Wiggins, and L.S. Benjamin, and the cognitive tradition of Beck and Freeman, the defense mechanisms of the psychodynamic school all provide empirical support for the Millon position of disorders being of the complete matrix of the person. What Millon is saying is that the opposite position of human personality and its disturbances is then a reductionism of the whole person to a part, a kind of scientific synechdoche, a part for the whole approach, whether it be cognitive, behavioral, or psychodynamic.

Similar thinking can be used to understand PCT. It encompasses the whole man as opposed to its parts, and as the other schools of thought about human personality usually focus on one aspect, they offer empirical support for PCT, just as they do for Millon. Thus, the personality theory of man as described in the Bible, as well as the personality's subsequent defacement from sin, is comprehensive and explains the pathology that affects human personality. PCT is based on a systematic understanding of the synthesis of human personality as found in the Bible.

Chapter Four

PCT and the Model of Health and Illness

Human development shows similarities and differences in human beings. The similarities are alienation from God and alienation in relationship with others. Man is the same in terms of universal primary loss. Man is different in ethnicity, gender, age, culture, religion, language, and customs. After the act of regeneration, there is a redirection of the heart and a therapeutic solution to primary loss. These are necessary presuppositions that are prolegomena to a discussion of psychological health. Problems develop when clients attempt to find unbiblical self-comfort from loss.

From a Christian worldview, optimal health is indicated by emotions, will, and mind being directed by a new heart, resulting in the signs of healthy thoughts, actions, and attitudes. After primary loss has been restored through Christ, there is a new sense of stability, because the client has true security, true safety, and true significance. The ideal is reached when the client progresses to using good self-talk, takes ownership for his or her actions, and begins to develop a deeper relationship with God through personal prayer, a high view of self, and sensitivity for others. Since Christ is the image of God, the goal for the client is to become the image of Christ and to allow a spill-over effect of psychological health in other relationships. Giving and service is part of the therapeutic healing process. Psychological flexibility is a sign of good mental health (see figure 6).

Model of Good Psychological Health

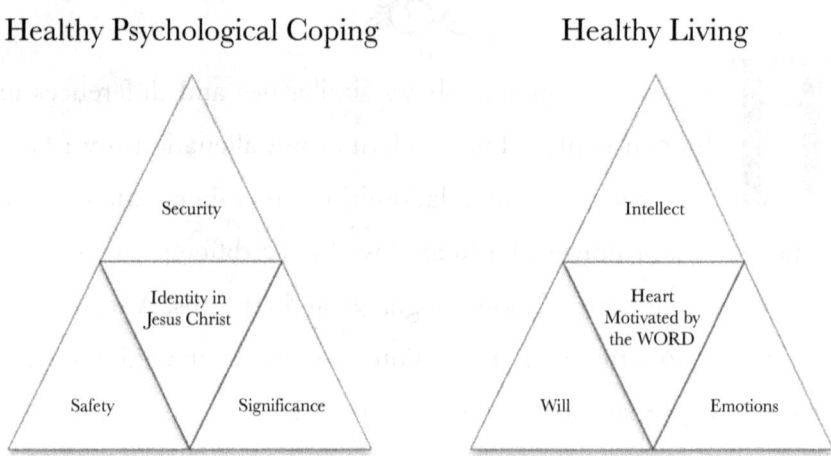

Figure 6

Sometimes the Lord taps the substitute on the shoulder and cuts into the dance of life just at the right time, changing the idolatrous dance into a dance of praise (Psalm 30:11). Man can deal with loss when he finds his significance in Christ (Romans 6). Loss cannot remove significance, safety, and security (Romans 8:1) when someone walks after the Spirit and not the flesh. The world, the flesh, and the devil are devalued by the intellect driven by a new heart. On the contrary, it values Jesus above everything (Philippians 3:7–8). As a result, the client is full of gratitude and praise (Luke 8:15; Ezekiel 36:26). Good psychological health discerns the true value of self and relationships when worthless substitutes are discarded and replaced by truth. This is accomplished only by the grace of God, not by human reasoning (Anderson 2000).

If man does not have security, safety, or significance in Christ, substitutes are sought out in this lifetime's dance of idolatry (Romans 1:25; Ephesians 5:5). Man is always looking for a better partner to dance the dance of life. The unfortunate man always finds death as his dancing partner (James 1:14–15). None of the substitutes satisfy (Galatians 5:19–21). After trying them all, the worst predicament to be in is to realize that loss is total and complete in life (2 Peter 2:20–22; Acts 1:18–20).

This may be the counselor's opportunity to help the client to see that substitutes for God always fail. People are seldom in the complete awareness state of the triangle of total loss. Sometimes their complaints are with other people, those who have become substitutes, whom they believe have let them down in some way (see figure 7). Rather than tell them to take responsibility for their actions, as Glasser would do in reality therapy, they instead help them gain an understanding of the reason they made these decisions in relation to the substitutes for loss.

Conceptualizing Illness in Paraklasis Counseling

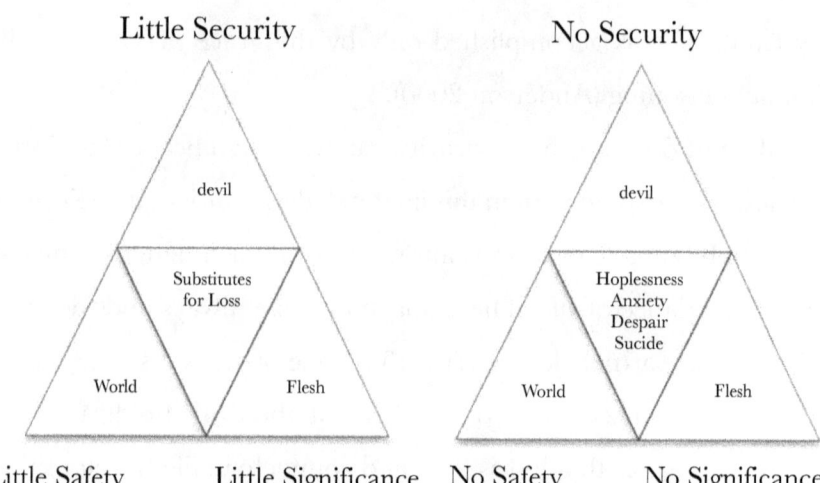

Figure 7

The following three triads represent the practical usefulness of the triads of unhealthy coping and total loss. This conceptualization distinguishes a secular diagnosis, in which the client is symptom-free, from a person who has spiritual/emotional problems (see figure 8).

Paraklasis Counseling Theory

Triads of Unhealthy Coping and Total Loss

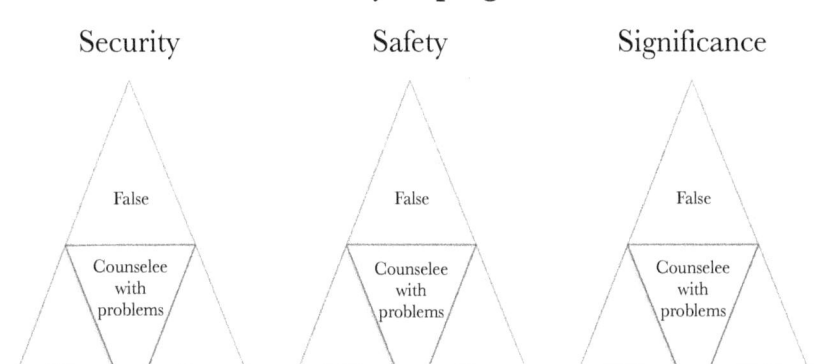

Figure 8

A person may be symptom-free yet still have the same substitutes for primary loss or secondary loss. These are not always visible. The secular counselor who ignores the spiritual component is doing the client a disservice at the very least. Without Christ, the spiritual component, even being dealt with, may get the client into more trouble.

Chapter Five

PCT: Motivation, Philosophical Assumptions, and Key Concepts

The source of motivation after the Fall was the human heart, which the Scripture describes as deceitful, desperately wicked, and cannot be known (Jeremiah 17:9). The role of motivation is based on what is provided as a substitute for the significance, security, and safety that was in God before the Fall and was lost after the Fall. The function of motivation works through the soul regarding the things of this world and the spirit concerning spirituality in man. Behavior is directed by the heart and the need to fill the primary and secondary loss that came from the Fall. That drive is powerful, affecting the behavior and the relationships with others.

The origin of motivation, the human heart, is a metaphor of a spiritual reality for the center of life. After the Fall, the heart, having been affected by sin, is described in the Scripture as stony and dead (Ephesians 2:1; Jeremiah 32:39; Ezekiel 11:19). It completely lacks spiritual life. The heart cannot be trusted, because the Scripture describes it as intensely wicked, deceitful, and unknowable in terms of clarity of motivation (Jeremiah 17:9). Heart motivation seeks substitutes for the safety, security, and significance that man lost because of the Fall. Since the heart is described as dead, it cannot even recognize the danger of replacing God with a substitute.

Motivation springs from the heart and works through body, soul, spirit, mind, will, and emotions, triggering things of the transcendental, situational, and existential domains. This results in good or bad behavior, as well as the deep need to replace the primary and secondary loss.

Man is different in terms of ethnicity, culture, religion, language, customs, experiences, and situations. Man is the same in terms of the primary loss that was brought about by his departure from God at the beginning of the human race. Present-day mankind is the same as Adam in terms of being alienated from God because of sin. Sin lies at the root of man's enmity against God and his neighbor. Therefore, sin is at the root of all of man's psychological problems. The structure of man's personality remains the same regardless of age, gender, or ethnicity. That structure is a multicultural constant. Personality may change across the life span due to experiences in life, good and bad. After regeneration, there is a redirection of love to God and others and an internal struggle for the supremacy of love or hatred, which was not present prior to regeneration.

This personality theory, based on the Bible, offers hope to the counselee, because the client is in the image of God. God is interested in the counselee and wants to see change for the better in the client's life. The counselee has hope, because God made the first man by a supernatural act. The second Adam, Jesus Christ, was also made by a supernatural act, overruling natural laws. There is no situation that is so bad God cannot do a miracle for the client and make it better.

Primary loss is always followed by secondary loss, such as the death of the provider in the family, causing financial problems to the family. The loss of a right relationship with God has produced many secondary losses in the individual's life. Empathy ought to be expressed in consolation. Comfort and encouragement can be given, bringing the hope that the Gospel brings concerning the restoration of relationship with God and man. This style of counseling invites prayer at appropriate times and in appropriate ways. The Greek word for comfort, empathy, and encouragement, *paraklasis*, was used in the Old Testament to describe the work of the prophets, bringing comfort to the people of God and also giving stern warnings to show them the outcome of their behaviors. This perspective brings hope, because it deals with the truth in love and does no harm.

Another source of hope is that, since this kind of loss is from earliest childhood, it can be—as seen in natural loss—a potential opportunity for growth. If ignored, it has the potential for deterioration. Dealing with the unbeliever from a loss perspective almost demands that external change for the symptoms of loss occurs even before internal change. A weeping person needs a tissue, not correction.

One problem with bereavement is that dealing with the challenge of loss does not make the person unidimensional (seeing the loss and not seeing the person). This means that the counselor should not view the counselee lopsided. The counselor must interact with the counselee on other levels rather than just loss. For example, the terminally ill person cannot get people to interact with him on any other level than his illness (Murray, 2001). This requires multicultural sensitivity on the part of the practitioner as well as skill. The counselor's goal is to bring about authentic transformation in the counselee and bring him to represent Jesus Christ. When internal change occurs, there will be more interest in caring for others in the client's world. He then represents Christ, as Christ represented the invisible God (Colossians 1:15).

As Christ is prophet, priest, and king, so should the goal of the counselor be to help the counselee to be prophet, priest, and king. As prophet, the counselee learns to speak healthy self-talk that lines up with the Word of God. As priest, the counselee develops his relationship with God in prayer. As king, he rules his life in the power of the Holy Spirit and learns to behave and think according to the Scripture, breaking old habits and establishing new ones.

The counselor, like the prophets of the Old Testament, would teach the counselee on how to do the will of God. The how-to is the most important part. Colossians 3:10 puts it this way: "put on the new man which is renewed unto knowledge after the image of him that created him." This has the same meaning as the word "image" when used in Genesis 1:27.

Philosophical Assumptions

The philosophical underpinnings for this theoretical model of counseling is a biblical, theistic understanding of reality, knowledge, and values, as well as the personality structure of man, who has been made like his Creator. Another way of saying it is that this theory proceeds from a consistently Christian worldview based upon the Bible.

These presuppositions have logical inferences. The first is that man, not being God but made like God, is dependent on God. Since God communicates and is Trinitarian and social, He made man to be a social being, able to have relationships with other people. God has created nature in terms of spheres of relationship and has placed man within spheres of relationships as well, family being the original structure, along with marriage.

All of created reality is dependent upon God. The difficulty for man comes in when man decides that he can live autonomously from God—in other words, to be as God. His maladaptive thinking and behavior ultimately comes from his rebellion against his Creator. In doing so, he loses that creator-creature distinction and has left behind his ability to function the way he was intended.

Knowledge has been pre-theoretically interpreted by God, and man's responsibility in theoretical exploration is to discover God's interpretation. Man has a connection with the natural world, because he was made from the dust of the earth, and a connection with the transcendent realm of God, because God breathed into him the breath of life. Therefore, man has a spiritual side as well as a connection with the earth. The Christian is indwelt by the Holy Spirit, the unbeliever is not. This has profound implications for counseling. Ontologically, Christians and non-Christians have everything in common. We share our physical beings in a material world. Metaphysically, we have nothing in common. The Christian's theory of knowledge and values will differ significantly from the non-Christian. The Christian has kept separate the creator-creature distinction. The Christian believer knows who he or she is and his place in the universe. He or she has meaning for his or her existence. The unbeliever lacks that self-knowledge and has worshiped and served the creature rather than the Creator.

Key Assumptions

Values for PCT are based upon loving God with all your strength and loving your neighbor as yourself, as Jesus sums up the law of God in Matthew 22:37–40. Assuming that the client receives the counsel, this change is to benefit others as he or she gives comfort with the comfort he or she has received. This also has implications for the counselor in clarifying the information that he or she communicates in a multiculturally sensitive way. Whether it is in the transcendental aspect of life, situational, or experiential, man has hope, because he can have his heart changed by God and have a complete cognitive restructuring by the Holy Spirit.

Although A.T. Beck uses loss as one of the four primal modes (Murdock 2009) in his cognitive therapy, to him, loss is not the overarching problem. PCT sees loss as the ultimate villain behind all psychopathology. The counselor must set the tone for a warm, therapeutic relationship with empathy, good listening, truthful speaking in love, and doing no harm (Vine, n.d.). People are uniquely individual in their responses to primary and secondary loss. The counselor, during the assessment, must determine the quality or depth of the loss in order to form a hypothesis on how the person will respond to treatment.

One of the greatest fears is separation from loved ones by death (Bath 2010). However, loss is broader than grief. Loss can be defined as "something perceived of value is lost" (Murray 2001, p. 219). There is scriptural evidence for this definition in Philippians 3:7–8. What Paul counted as lost was not objectively lost; what he lost was only the subjective value. What Paul used to think was valuable had lost its subjective emotional value to him in the light of the greater value of knowing Christ (Kittel 1976). This is actually a scriptural support for the intervention of cognitive diffusion techniques as described in acceptance and commitment therapy (ACT) (Hayes, Luoma, Bond, Masuda, and Lillis 2006).

One of the keys to making sense of the effects of loss in a person's life is to realize that man seeks to substitute. The substitute for God can become anything that becomes an absolute or has the highest value. In terms of this primary loss, the Gospel is the only answer. In terms of secondary loss, the counselor's task is to discover the substitutes and replace them with healthier and harmless ones that increase psychological flexibility and reduce pain. In that sense, PCT can eclectically use cognitive behavioral therapy concepts of the replacement of schemas.

Secondary loss always follows primary loss. There are times when primary loss is healed through the Gospel received, and then secondary loss disappears. Sometimes it is more complicated. When the client views the loss as an opportunity for growth, it can become a source of hope. If this truth is not maximized, then deterioration is the result. The counselor must identify the spheres of life that have lost their value in the client, as well as the harmful substitutes that exist in their place that result in harm to the client and the client's spouse, family members, or other relationships. In counseling people who have no interest in the Gospel, from a loss point of view, small successes in counseling bring hope. Usually, external changes that touch upon loss symptoms must be sought before internal spiritual change can be addressed. Concentrate on the client, not so much on the loss. Encouragement is absolutely important in order to restore hope to wounded people. This is what the Holy Spirit does in the believer and what the paraklasis counselor should be doing.

Chapter Six

PCT: Multiculturalism and Christian Worldview

A Christian worldview can mean many different things to different Christians, depending on how the Bible is viewed. Someone may call himself a Christian, believe in the theory of biological evolution, and believe that the Bible is just another humanly derived guide for living. In the authors' view, this is not a Christian worldview. PCT is presuppositionally based on a biblical Trinitarian worldview of creation, the fall of man, and redemption accomplished by Jesus and applied by the Holy Spirit. The Christian worldview extends from the supernatural realm to the temporal realm, and finally to the person who is made in God's image (Hawkins, n.d.; Snaith 1976).

A biblical theology combines with God-honoring psychology and with the spiritual growth of the counselor in a Christian worldview. The greatest skill of a Christian counselor is to discern what is and what is not God's truth through the integration of psychology and scriptural truth, and then apply it to the client's skewed thinking.

Integration points to the paradoxical good fruit growing from the tree of unbelief. This falls under the doctrine of common grace and natural revelation. A paraklasis counselor must have sharpened skills and ought to know biblically based theology, so that integration can take place without watering down the Bible and inadvertently offering poisoned fruit to those already sick from eating from the tree of sin and dysfunctional thinking.

The counseling session needs to be a place of hope, and the paraklasis counselor, in being like God, must connect with the client and not insist on a cold, distant relationship that hides behind the label of professionalism, an idea that is not found in the Scripture. Loss threatens people's safety and control and can completely undermine basic assumptions about how the client sees the world in which he or she lives, but an empathic counselor can bring the client hope.

As has been stated before and needs to be stated again, three assumptions are shaken by loss in the Western culture. The first is that the world is benevolent. The second is that the world is meaningful and just, and the third is that the self is worthy (Murray 2001). When these three ideas are decimated by loss, it presents the paraklasis counselor a great opportunity to bring comfort, and, in an ideal sense, it can only come from God Himself (Isaiah 57:18). The judgment of God is comfortlessness, while "comforting is God's proper work" (Friedrick, 1977). The counselor can enjoy participating in the Holy Spirit's work, or at least be like Barnabas, a son of encouragement (Acts 4:36). The counselor never needs to feel alone, because God has a better understanding of loss than the counselor. He lost His

Son on the cross, and Jesus lost His Father mysteriously when He became the sin offering.

Entwistle (2010) poses this question: "What has psychology to do with Christianity?" In the end, he asserts that the process of integration involves personal spiritual formation, an understanding of our worldview, and an open communication that allows for agreement and disagreement. Proper integration utilizes sound exegesis and clear understanding of psychology while applying intellectual virtues. In the process of answering this question, he explains the importance of a Christian worldview and discusses the assumptions and beliefs that become the windows and vantage points for understanding the world. These are qualities that are part of paraklasis counseling theory in an ideal world. It is acknowledged that not everyone who counsels has a deep understanding of the Scripture.

Historical antecedents reveal a conflict between Christianity and science, especially in counseling over differing viewpoints on how to reach the goal of helping human brokenness. Jesus claimed all of life for Himself, every part of created reality, under His Kingship as the ascended King, having accomplished redemption. Integration should be approached with redemptive goals and purposes based on the understanding that all truth is God's truth; therefore, the integration of psychology and theology must occur in order for a fully developed Christian counseling theory to exist. This assumes that what is integrated is redeemable under the authority of the Scripture.

A well thought-out Christian worldview answers the questions: "Who am I? Why am I here? What's wrong, and what is the remedy?"

The answers are clearly explained through an examination of the Bible's story of creation, fall, redemption, and consummation. Integration is only possible when intellectual virtues are combined with one's epistemological framework. PCT has a biblical epistemological framework that answers the important questions.

Secular psychology and biblical theology have antithetical anthropological views, but both are motivated by compassion. Biblical theology is not to be confused with the branch of theology that deals with time and the history of redemption diachronically through the Bible, but simply a theology built upon and submissive to the Scripture. Entwistle uses the term psychology and theology in general terms, but I would not grant the field of psychology over to the unbeliever by not distinguishing the words. The way we use words is important. Psychology is properly a domain appropriately fitted for Christians. The unbeliever is a squatter on Christian territory. It is not the other way around. That is why the authors of this book call it secular psychology.

In addition, there are unbiblically grounded theologies and biblically based theology. The latter is what the authors of this book have in mind when theology is mentioned. A lack of development of competence in theology and psychology is one of the obstacles to integration, as well as various ethical issues that need to be considered with religiously based counseling interventions.

I was brought to the "threshold of human mystery" that Pope John Paul II spoke of (Entwistle 2010, p. 220) when my daughter, adopted from a Russian orphanage at five years of age, was at the threshold of life and death due to an eating disorder. I could not find a Christian or secular psychologist who would assess her, because they claimed that because of her age, she did not fit the classic paradigm. It appeared that both the Christian and secular counselors lacked expertise in cross-disciplinary interventions. I could not find anyone with a broad enough integrationist perspective back in the 1990s.

God is the ultimate integrationist and intervenes for the sake of His people. God helped my daughter when I stepped into one of the "thin places, where the gap between the natural and supernatural worlds was more transparent than usual" (Entwistle 2010, p.95). I was at a conference, and before the meeting during my prayer time, God told me to command the demon to leave my little girl. The thought of a demon in my little girl did not fit my theological paradigm, but I obeyed. During praise and worship, my vision and hearing were shut off, and I could see a hairless, bloodless demon in muscular human form—with an arm and leg out of socket, a bashed-in head, and a silent scream of anger and fear—struggling to flee from my daughter. At that moment, for the first and only time in my life, I heard the audible voice of God saying, "Gordon's prayer, your desire, and my will have met. It is done. Your little girl is free; she is free indeed!" From that moment on, my little girl's eating disorder ceased.

God intervened when integration between theology and psychology was minimal and certainly could not help me or my daughter. What happened did not fit through my theological filter, and I had to get a new one that would let in new ideas. I was forced to reevaluate my worldview in light of new discoveries.

The quote by Jay Adams, "I've heard it said that psychology is just sinful human beings sinfully thinking about sinful human beings" (Entwistle 2010, p.12), as well as his referring to psychology as the enemy of the Church, along with Dr. Entwistle labeling him a Christian combatant, when taken together, is at the very least, evidence that would say that Adams is uncompromising and entrenched in his position. Nouthetic counseling rests on the assumption that all mental health issues are directly caused by sin and need to be handled nouthetically or confrontationally with the Scripture. In reality, in not wanting to create a straw man, the counseling is not as harsh and confrontational as his critics might make it seem.

Jay Adams's attitude about psychology contradicts the cultural mandate given to Adam to subdue the earth. Adams agrees with this in his theology, the cultural mandate being a commonly held tenet of reformed theology. But in the practice of the counseling approach, he denies it. God told Adam to subdue the earth, not the serpent. The idea of the cultural mandate is to take back what the devil stole in the arts, the sciences, politics, and every sphere of human existence that has been secularized, because God made all things good. The idea is to redeem what can be redeemed, throw out what cannot, and use it for the glory of God. Psychology, it would seem, is no exception. Integration does just that, and also PCT. In fact, it is this truth that motivated the authors of this book to attempt to find more truth in Christian counseling, and this search originated in discovering PCT. However, from Adams's perspective, psychology should all be thrown out, but his counseling center uses what they can to their advantage.

Entwistle stresses the need for dialogue and cooperation between theology and the secular disciplines. Unfortunately, he leaves out a vital spiritual component that could be an obstacle to integrational dialogue. The Christian response, coming from a Christian worldview, is to work together with others to help people where we can. The obstacle on a presuppositional level that hinders this lofty goal is the enmity that God put in the seed of the serpent toward the seed of the woman (Genesis 3). To work toward integration and ignore this spiritual obstacle makes the effort difficult where reaction to dialogue becomes unreasonably negative toward Christian counseling. Christian counselors need to be sensitive to this metaphysical roadblock. Christian counseling should be interested in dialogue with secular counseling, not defensive and reactionary in responses. Looking for truth in a humble and positive way and acknowledging it when it is observed by those who are not in agreement with Christian presuppositions is certainly a part of PCT. Christian counselors who are biblically grounded have a unique vantage point that can perceive and point out the value of theories and interventions that the secularists will not be able to accomplish.

The message that Entwistle emphasizes is to have a dialogue, so that we can learn from each other and help people in a more complete way. It is easy to read into people's positions that you disagree with and create a straw man who is easy to tear down. Labels have negative and positive effects on people. In order to be a good integrationist, judgment should be reserved on people and positions until all the facts are in.

Demographics

Demographics in the United States of America is showing a present and future shift from a White European majority of the past to a Latino, African American, Asian, and, in general, people of color majority. Counselors need training in diversity, so that they will become more sensitive and competent in dealing with the increase in diversity in their clients. Multiculturalism is a historic catch-all term covering all aspects of diversity. Diversity is discovered in the categories of spirituality, gender, age, ethnicity, and sexual orientation. Diversity training for counselors has not been added to the institutions that train for clinical practice in order to meet increasing demand. This is no longer to be treated as optional electives, but as an ethical mandate for all counselors, especially Christian counselors. The authors of the reviewed articles have made recommendations in the context of the history of multiculturalism in this country. These are evaluated from a PCT perspective to include what is redeemable and what is not, so that the Christian counselor can become more competent in implementing therapy from a biblical worldview.

Multiculturalism in counseling from a Christian worldview perspective is part of PCT. Loss cannot be properly understood apart from someone's cultural background. In 1973, the American Psychology Association (APA) conference in Vail, Colorado, emphasized training in multicultural competency for psychologists and counselors (Allison, Crawford, Echemendia, Robinson, and Knepp 1994) because of changing demographics. Progress was slow because multiculturalism was not considered to be as important as traditional training (Sue, Arredondo, and McDavis 1992). Accreditation requirements accelerated universities to include multicultural training for counselors (Fouad 2006). Some with strong ideologies studied individual differences. Three harmful models were used: the Inferiority Model—based on evolution, the Genetic Deficiency Model, and the Cultural Deficiency Model. During the decade before 1992, a better model emerged and was called by several names: Culturally Different Model, Multicultural Model, Culturally Pluralistic Model, or Culturally Diverse Model. It assumes that cultural differences are not inferior. Racial and ethnic minorities are bicultural. Biculturalism enriches the full range of human potential, and individuals are viewed in their relationship to the larger social forces (Sue et al. 1992).

In the last five years, there has been a more deeply integrated curriculum (Fouad 2006). There has also been a change of focus by leaders to utilize empirically based research (Bernal, Jimenez-Chafey, and Rodriguez 2009). Multiculturalism is important for Christian counselors because it hinders prejudice and stereotyping (Sue et al., 1992). "It is estimated that members of ethnic minority groups alone, account for one quarter or more of those utilizing public mental health facilities" (Allison et al. 1994, p. 2). Self-awareness of values, skill, and knowledge are important for the Christian counselor to avoid doing harm. Ignorance is not ethically acceptable (Allison et al. 1994). Christian counselors have a mandate from the Lord (Matthew 28:19 ff.) to communicate with other cultures effectively and sensitively if the Church is to teach all nations.

The concept of multicultural counseling is fully integrational in a Christian worldview, especially in PCT. The reason is that PCT sees commonality in ontology and commonality as well as uniqueness in the transcendental, situational, and existential aspects. The Bible was given by God in Ancient Near Eastern culture. Yet the Bible is multicultural, because its principles are designed to be communicated with every tribe and tongue. There are many different religions. The situation—i.e., the environment—and culture of man is diverse. PCT also recognizes that the existential aspect is similar yet different from individual to individual from every culture. Counselors must be sensitive to client diversity and commonality. Experiences in people are different and so are their perceptions of those experiences. The perceptions are colored by their culture as well as their unique individual perspectives. For example, families have relational problems in every culture, and that they share in common, but those problems are also unique because each culture is different. Substitutes people make to comfort themselves from loss will vary from culture to culture.

Cultures vary in the way gender is perceived. Women are not treated the same as men in many Islamic countries. Dermer, Smith, and Barto (2010) want to identify and label sexual prejudice. The terms defined are oppression, privilege, empowerment, homophobia, heterosexism, sexual prejudice, stigma, internalized homophobia, sexual orientation victimization (SOV), and minority stress. Herek and Garnets (2007) describe the sexual minority stressors, such as stigmatization, AIDS epidemic, criminal victimization, stigma, depression, PTSD, low self-esteem, drug and alcohol abuse, self-stigmatization, and institutionalized stigma. The affirmative model has replaced the illness model. The primary task of the counselor is dealing with victimization and finding integrative solutions that will provide self-acceptance and balance among the different components of identity.

The PCT counselor must be cognizant of the specific loss in victims of prejudice and be aware of the cultural prejudice depending on the nation they may originate. The question must be answered by the counselor as to whether the victim is truly victimized, or whether the client perceives that because of a difference of opinion, particularly in gay and lesbian clients. Christians should never approve of oppression that causes harm in others.

Reverse discrimination of secularists toward Christians shows up in Rainey and Trusty (2007), where certain factors are said to predict attitudes toward gays and lesbians. The subjects of the research were master's level counseling program students located in a conservative Christian region. Both were limiting factors. Results showed that religiously and politically conservative students showed negativity toward sexual minority people. Students were reminded that counselors should never push their own values on clients. It was also recommended that faculty admit their being gay or lesbian, and that bringing in gay or lesbian speakers to the college might give the students a positive experience. Yet counselors must bend over backwards in being sensitive to offending a client. Having known the subjects of the research to begin with, it should have been no surprise at their opinions of sexual minority people. To show no respect to their opinions and to totally disregard the conservative cultural environment by shoving their own opinions on them is the epitome of multicultural insensitivity and bullying. This reflects the world of secular psychology and ethics and is indicative of the behavior of the seed of the serpent that has a hatred of the seed of the woman.

The Christian counselor finds a stew pot of variation in the area of spirituality, with secular psychology crying out for multicultural sensitivity on the part of the counselor. A secular example is Cervantes and Parham (2005). Migration is a spiritual, emotional, and physical journey toward healing, and guidelines for competency in spirituality are advocated. Extreme flexibility is needed. Respecting and accepting the diverse belief systems and religious/spiritual orientations is hammered home. Beliefs, orientations, and values are fluid and dynamic. Nothing can be understood without relation to the other. Diversity is a portal to appreciate the uniqueness of people. All life is interconnected. Collaborative knowing supports community interdependence and the building of a universal humanistic agenda. Disability is a state of mind that deters meaningful dialogue. There is a supremely intelligent life force that protects, influences, guides, and instructs all life-forms. Prayer, ritual, and ceremony provide an essential ingredient in healing. Service to the community is a natural outcome of healing.

There are always principles that can be applied by Christian counselors by integrating the good from the secularists. PCT counselors, in reflecting NT values, would encourage those who receive spiritual healing to bring encouragement and assistance to others without accepting the entire belief system of the client. A counselor can show respect without swallowing the spiritual worldview of the client.

Colbert, Jefferson, Gallo, and Davis (2008) state that counselors need to realize how important religion is to African American people. They should become aware of the therapeutic benefits of religion and recognize the value of the church as supportive for African Americans. The value of demographics and statistics aids religion as a therapeutic intervention. Hage, Hopson, Siegel, Payton, and DeFanti (2006) show the need of spiritual/religious education for counselors. Counseling program leadership had minimal training in the past. In 2002, out of ninety-eight APA clinical program directors surveyed, 17 percent taught spirituality/religion in their classes; 16 percent of them, not at all.

Schulte, Skinner, and Claiborn (2002) did the only major study in APA-accredited counseling programs resulting in similar findings. This confirms the hypothesis that counseling training neglects training in spirituality. Spirituality is different than organized religion, in that spirituality may or may not believe in a transcendent being. Whatever belief brings meaning and peace should be viewed as spiritual in their opinion.

A multiculturally sensitive counselor should recognize the elderly as a unique culture in themselves. Dennis (2009) informs about depression and suicide in the elderly. Attempts are to be taken seriously. Factors are: self-isolation, alcohol abuse, anxiousness, depression, mental disorders, and poor health. Stroke and suicide appear to be coupled together. Additionally, poor visual acuity, cancer, chronic pain and disability, bereavement, retirement, and, in men, somatic illness, being recently discharged from a hospital, and hopelessness are factors not to be ignored. Increasing age in males makes them high risk for suicide. A preventative strategy is screening for depression.

Major depressive disorder in older women is examined by Goldstein and Gruenberg (2007). When women are hospitalized because of suicidal ideation, the risk percentage after hospitalization goes down to about 15 percent. Older women have lower rates of major depressive disorder than younger women. Men who outlive their wives are more prone to depression than women. Older people, after a stroke, may manifest depression for about a year. Fifty percent of patients with Parkinson's experience depression. Forty percent of people with major depressive disorder have additional psychiatric disorders. Men get more depressed from financial problems, and women, from family problems. Elevated cortisol is commonly found in older adults with depression. The loss of social support is also responsible for depression.

Treating the whole person offers a good prognosis, including drugs and exercise. Hung, Kempen, and De Vries (2010) give a comparison on views of healthy aging between older people and academic researchers. The main difference between the academic viewpoint and the older people's viewpoint about healthy aging showed that quality of life is more important than quantity. Important to the older people were family, adaptation, financial security, personal growth, and spirituality. These were not important for the academics. The hypothesis that healthy aging is a multidimensional and complex concept was confirmed.

How does this connect to PCT? The Bible speaks of having great respect for the elderly (Leviticus 19:32). The promise of God is to provide for His people through their old age. The PCT counselor is ethically obligated by the Scripture to treat the elderly who are clients, regardless of whether they have the money or not. It would seem that there is not much of an incentive to become a PCT counselor, but there is more to life than monetary reward. This is multicultural counseling at its highest level of quality.

When treating the elderly, the PCT counselor should assess whether there is primary and secondary loss, or both. Assessment of secondary loss should reveal what type of loss the counselor is dealing with—loss of significance, loss of security, or loss of safety. Since many of the oldest of old live alone, having lost their spouse through death or living as a divorced person, loss of all three areas becomes apparent in the assessment process. Financial loss may lead to loss of security. Living alone may create fear for safety, or serious health issues may create a sense of a lack of security and safety. Perhaps being ignored by adult children may lead to a loss of significance. This may not always be the children's fault. Sometimes the parents have taken steps away from building a relationship with the adult children. Work responsibilities and family needs often make it difficult for adult children to spend much time with elderly parents. The elderly parents can be encouraged to reach out and honor the children in some way, regardless of the past strains on relationships. Forgiveness issues need to be explored. The physical limitations of old age can cause a lack of significance when the person cannot do the things they used to do.

Mortality salience in the oldest of old will make some people depressed, because it forces them to face their worldview. And if it does not work for them, they will attempt to find substitutes if they are in primary loss. These substitutes are false, and the opportunity to share the Gospel is often when the client discovers this for themselves. Checking for suicidal tendencies is very pertinent in counseling the elderly. Depression can have very real issues behind it. The counselor also needs to be aware of senior community assistance programs and organizations that can be a referral source to the client.

Gender is another area of multicultural counseling awareness. Nam, Chu, Lee, and Lee (2010) examined gender in seeking psychological help and determined that females were more willing to seek counseling than males. Caucasian Americans were more willing to seek counseling than Asians. Limitations of the studies were: it did not show past trends; the studies were carried out in the United States;

and it did not consider stigma. Betz and Fitzgerald (1993) looked at gender issues in men and showed that men were less willing to be counseled than women. By 1981, studies concluded that masculine gender role conflict was dysfunctional. Yet it is idealized. It consists of "focus on control, power, and competition; homophobia; restrictive sexual and affectionate behavior; and obsession with achievement and success" (Betz and Fitzgerald 1993, p.357). Montgomery and Newman (2010) surveyed student leadership of twenty-four student organizations on college campuses and looked for gender differences. Females rated themselves higher on caring than males. Males rated themselves higher on passive leadership. Group members saw male leadership higher on the trait of vision. Females viewed their leaders as the leaders saw themselves more than males who rarely agreed with their leaders. Women showed a more participatory style of leadership, focusing on the needs and opinions of the members. Males were more confident in leading. Women desired to challenge the process for change, while men cared more about a shared vision. Women have problems when attempting to lead a male-dominated organization.

These studies have shown at least five areas where women shine and men did less. The Christian counselor, PCT or otherwise, would do well to study what the Scripture says about male gender roles, and consider what enduring principles, beyond what was local and cultural in the Bible, are what a man should be like in any culture. This assumes that the Bible trumps cultural norms. It would be helpful in marriage counseling, as well as for the single man.

Race/ethnicity is another multicultural factor for the Christian counselor to be sensitive about. Nezu (2010) indicates that recent genetic studies have found that there is no genetic phenotypical character as race. "There is far more variation within groups than there is between them" (Nezu 2010, p.2). "Ethnicity" is a better word. He warns about racial microaggressions. Intentional or unintentional, they communicate racial insults in the form of stereotyping, jokes, and insensitive ethnic comments. Counselors should inquire about a variety of diverse characteristics and about the meaning of diversity.

Cayleff (1986) is concerned about ethical issues in multicultural counseling. By not respecting the client's belief system, the counselor is not acting in a way that benefits the client, therefore, doing harm. Cayleff is assuming that respecting the client's belief system and respecting the client are the same. The Christian counselor has his own belief system and does not respect a contradictory one that the client may own. The counselor may respect the schizophrenic who hallucinates and does not ridicule the hallucinations so as not to disrespect the client. But, hopefully, the counselor does not respect the hallucinations. In the same way, a multiculturally sensitive counselor will not make the client feel foolish for his belief system, whatever that may be.

Cayleff goes on to advise avoiding preconceived notions about African American family structure. He urges counselors to recognize a female-led black household and church. African Americans have been counseled differently regarding career decisions, not always without stereotyping. A black medical student was encouraged to enter into family care because of the assumption that he would want to serve his own kind. Avoid paternalistic approaches. Cooper, Stark, Peterson, O'Roark, and Pennington (2008) deal with multiculturalism in organizational consulting psychology. Approach differences of culture, race, and ethnicity directly and in the open (Cooper et al. 2008, p.16). London and Devore (1988) conceive of layers of understanding in counseling the ethnic minority family. All counselors need a basic understanding of human behavior and must have professional values.

A competent multicultural counselor must have additional layers of understanding, such as self-awareness and knowledge of one's own ethnicity and its influence on counseling. There must be an understanding of the daily life of the client and an ability to adapt skills and modify interventions. Neville, Spanierman, and Doan (2006) confirmed the hypothesis that the greater the color-blind racial ideology, the lower the demonstrated multicultural competence as a counselor. Color-blind ideology is the newest form of racism. In other words, the person is human with their own set of problems, their own culture, and their own value system, and it must be recognized. To say that one is color-blind presents a devaluing of the person's culture. It says that it is not worth being recognized. Bernal et al. (2009) present a study confirming that adaptation of interventions to culture brought about a good outcome in spite of the universalistic argument to not tinker with proven and well-established evidence-based treatments. In contrast, adapt interventions for the contextualizing of all individuals in terms of their culture, language, values, socioeconomic status, gender, and preference.

Wong, Beutler, and Zane (2007) studied the effect of the thereapeutic relationship between Asian Americans specifically regarding the factors of credibility of the counselor and how well they worked together. Asian Americans reacted better to the direct approach rather than the nondirect approach that appealed to European Americans.

Sue, Zane, Hall, and Berger (2009) discuss the practice of competent multicultural counseling. Cultural competence is an ethical obligation. The suggested definition of competent multicultural counseling is awareness, knowledge, and skills. Studies indicate that intervention adaptations can introduce multifaceted changes in intervention philosophy, delivery, and format. Every client presents a unique constellation of background and identity as an individual. These ideas fit well with an integrational perspective and PCT.

Having considered the various perspectives on multiculturalism and worldview, it is time to critically assess their primary themes from a Christian worldview. Dermer (2010) designed a persuasive apologetic. Self-doubt, according to Dermer, manifests victimization, and it would apply to the Christian counselor if he or she is embracing the argument. This is an anti-Christian worldview, but it is helpful in understanding the way sexual minorities view the world. "The beginning of the words of his mouth is foolishness: and the end of his talk is mischievous madness. A fool also is full of words..." (Ecclesiastes 10:13). Herek (2007) attacks conversion therapy in a Christianophobic

Paraklasis Counseling Theory 75

way, indicating that conversion therapy is not empirically proven and has a negative impact. Testimonials of permanent change are not to be believed. Conversion therapy is unethical when practiced on adolescents. Ironically, there are no concerns about the minority stress model. "Since the demise of the illness model, a minority stress model has become the most commonly used framework for conceptualizing mental health among lesbian, gay, and bisexual individuals" (Herek 2007, p.5). Both the minority stress model and conversion therapy are not empirically validated, but prejudice makes the difference. Notice the spiritual macroaggression (Genesis 3:15). Therefore, a prejudiced viewpoint toward conversion therapy demands exclusion and the minority stress model utilized.

PCT is empirically supported and takes the steam out of the charge that Christian counseling is not empirically supported, and it has a positive impact on clients, no matter what their culture.

Rainey et al. (2007), challenge a Christian worldview. Conservative religious and political views are attacked in terms of their negativity toward sexual minority people. Counselors in training need to learn not to push their values upon a client. Views need to be changed through education. This is propaganda, a straw-man setup, and not valid as research, because it seeks to prove the obvious that conservative Christians find homosexuality unacceptable. Its limitation is its bias.

All ungodly behavior is counseled with the hope that it will improve. Empathy, love, and care for the person in their loss can overcome initial prejudice and tension in the counseling relationship.

When the client experiences a culturally sensitive treatment from a counselor who does not demean their relationships and views the client as multifaceted, counseling will be received. God made the client in His image and therefore has worth (Genesis 1:27) and should be treated as such.

Cervantes and Parham (2005) make suggestions that can be integrational for the Christian counselor. For example, extreme flexibility is needed for the counselor when treating someone who believes in non-Christian spirituality. People who hold on to spirituality in a non-Christian sense often borrow elements of other religious systems. Diverse belief systems are important to respect and accept only in the aspect of assessment, so as not to harm the client by being disrespectful. The client's beliefs may be fluid and subject to change. The counselor needs to look for linkage between the culture, belief system, sexual orientation, gender, and ethnicity.

Diversity is like looking through a window to appreciate individual uniqueness. The proposition that all life is interconnected (Cervantes and Parham 2005) can be interpreted to mean that from a Christian worldview, God as Creator has intelligently designed all created reality, which is interconnected and interdependent. It could also be interpreted in a pantheistic way or animistic sense from Native American tribal beliefs. Migrating into a journey (Cervantes and Parham 2005) that brings healing as a process sounds very Native American, especially as Chief Joseph and his migration and treaties are used as illustrations. The counselor must be careful that Chief Joseph is not held up as an illustration to someone whose tribe is the hereditary enemy of Chief Joseph's tribe. This would be an example of multicultural insensitivity. Communicating with spiritual leaders (Cervantes and Parham 2005) may be helpful as long as the client gives permission.

It is true that one's disabilities can become a block to meaningful communication in the therapeutic milieu. It is true that there is an intelligent life force that guides, protects, and directs the world, even apart from *Star Wars*. Christians call Him God the Father, Son, and Holy Spirit. Romans 1 indicates that all people believe there is a God even though they worship the creature instead of the Creator. Whether or not healing will be promoted depends on who one is praying to, what is said, and what rituals and ceremonies are being done, since Native American ceremonies and rituals are often directed to demonic spirits or prayer to ancestors. The powwow dancing is dancing with ancestors. The Christian counselor may not be able to stretch the mind in order to integrate these suggestions in a scriptural context without compromise. If the counselor can do it, it will take a lot of work.

We are to comfort others with the comfort God has given us. Here, it is service to the community. Colbert, Jefferson, Gallo, and Davis (2008) give general suggestions to counselors who are treating African Americans. Religion is important to the African American community. In general, this is true, but obviously not always. There is a collectivistic influence on adults. Spiritual leaders can sometimes be brought into collaboration with the client. Religion has therapeutic benefits and ministers to the whole person.

Hage, Hopson, Siegel, Payton, and DeFante (2006) reveal that spirituality/religion has been neglected in counselor training. Statistics reveal that instructors have little knowledge to teach about this subject, so that counselors have a minimal grasp of it. Religion is only mentioned in the context of emotional disorders. A Gallup poll has indicated that two-thirds of Americans with a problem serious enough to see a counselor have said that they would prefer to see one with spiritual beliefs and values integrated into the counseling (Hage et al. 2006).

Articles on the subject of age are useful integrational information, whether it is suicide (Dennis 2009), depression (Goldstein and Gruenberg 2007), or defining healthy aging (Hung, Kempen, and De Vries 2010). The striking thing about this is the radically different point of view of the academics. Elderly people have a deeper understanding of what quality of life is all about in comparison to the narrow view of the academics. Gender differences are particularly important for counselors to be competent. Betz and Fitzgerald (1993) and Nam et al. (2010) agree that males are less willing to go for counseling than women. All of these articles are integrational information. Betz and Fitzgerald (1993) describe the typical American male across all cultures in the United States as dysfunctional. Male Christian counselors need to evaluate themselves. Women still have a problem with being seen as tokens in male-dominated organizations. Males from a minority ethnicity, when placed in leadership, have great outcomes. Nezu contributes to the distinction between race and ethnicity. He recommends showing respect, not assuming, and asking questions. The universal connection between all mankind is left out of his discussion. It does not occur to him that man is made in the image of God, whatever the ethnicity, and that self-worth is more than ethnicity. One can communicate this truth from a Christian worldview in a sensitive way. Obviously, research has given us various truths that can be integrated into PCT.

Cayleff, concerned about ethics, warns the counselors against thrusting their beliefs upon the client, therefore, doing harm. As long as the Christian counselor has permission by informed consent, it would allow for sharing beliefs. Neville et al. (2006) contribute with a wise warning about not being color-blind on ethnicity. Cooper (2008) contributes to counseling wisdom by recommending that right from the beginning, there should be direct communication about ethnicity. Nezu would also agree about asking questions and encourages every counselor to take The Implicit Association Test. London (1988) and Sue et al. (2009) are in agreement that the counselor must not forget that self-awareness, knowledge of cultural ethnicity, and skills help form layers of understanding (London 1988) as the basics of competency in multicultural counseling (Sue et al. 2009).

Bernal et al. urge counselors to remember to be adaptable and use interventions according to the ethnicity and diversity of the clients being counseled, because one particular intervention does not fit every individual. This is part of the debate against the DSM. Wong, Beutler, and Zane's research indicates, as mentioned earlier, that when counseling Asian Americans, a more direct approach may be better received.

Important elements of counselor identity, function, and ethics related to multicultural counseling are very important for Christian counselors to practice in their lives, not just in treatment sessions. Most of the research can be integrated into a Christian worldview, so the counselor may be the same in professional and private life. Christian counselors who received integrative training have been instructed better and have higher standards than the secular counselor. The Christian counselor is aware of the need to glorify God in everything. Jesus is the example for identity in counseling. He interacted with the worst of people without fear of becoming defiled, reached out in love, maintained appropriate boundaries, and never compromised His ethics. The Christian counselor, more than the secular, has the responsibility to sort through research and determine if it is approved by the Scripture.

To better sort out all the above data, integrational insights from the primary themes of multiculturalism and worldview are now considered from a biblical perspective. Counseling sexual minorities requires the Christian counselor's spiritual formation to be mature, so that identity in Christ is shown in their personal and professional life, and bias does no harm. The counselor must be competent and sensitive in the functions of multicultural counseling and hate the sin and not the sinner, speaking the truth in love (Ephesians 4:15). The lack of training in spirituality and religion makes it imperative for a Christian to get instructed in a university that understands and teaches integration of theology, psychology, and spiritual formation (1 Corinthians 10:31).

The majority of what was indicated by these articles intends to do no harm to the client, whether their presuppositions are biblical or not. If the Christian counselor reinterprets those ideas through the filter of the Scripture, most can be redeemed. The Christian counselor needs to be reminded that the author of Ecclesiastes is correct in warning the elderly that there will be many "days of darkness" coming (Ecclesiastes 11:8), as well as the physical disabilities that come about in old age, along with fears (Ecclesiastes 12:1–7), but having said that, in Jesus Christ is power, love, and a sound mind, a future and a hope.

Jesus implied a multicultural competency in His followers who would introduce Him to the world (Matthew 28:19). The writers of the gospels of Matthew and Luke, in carefully choosing terminology that would not be culturally offensive, are clear in using "Kingdom of Heaven" (Matthew 13:11) to respect Jews and "Kingdom of God" (Luke 6:20) to respect the Gentiles. Both clarity and cultural sensitivity are seen in these passages. The Bible encourages counselors to be multiculturally competent, so that counselors will see the light of the Gospel shining into the cracks in their souls to reach their hearts to produce everlasting change for the glory of God.

Christian counselors ought to provide biblically grounded, ethical, and empirically based counseling rooted on the premise of 1 Corinthians 10:31, which, if practiced, will virtually guarantee that the counselor will truly care about the quality of the therapy given, because the counselor will love his neighbor as himself or herself. Then it would be counseling to the glory of God and PCT counseling at its best.

Life experience with other cultures is always a plus for a Christian counselor. The life experiences that God has given me made it necessary for me to prayerfully consider multiculturalism in every area of my life. Ethnicity and multicultural experience was gained through my own background, growing up as the only white student in an all-black school. My husband and I adopted eleven children from different ethnic and racial backgrounds, including Asian, Russian, African American, and Caucasian. We have been involved in ministries in diverse cultures, including Native American, Canadian First Nations, African American, Hasidic Jewish, Latino, Polish, and Dutch communities. Gender experience was gained through ministry with homeless men, prisoners and ex-prisoners, women's ministry, and chaplain to the VFW Women's Auxiliary. Age-related experience was received in establishing nursing home coverage in the greater Philadelphia area, dealing with death and loss, and caring for elderly parents. Rehabilitative experience was gained in working with head trauma patients and stroke victims. Sexual orientation experience was gained as I ministered to homosexuals, military families while spouses were on deployment, and soldiers in the U.S. Army chaplaincy. Continuing experience is being gained through counseling the forensic or developmentally disabled population in a southeast regional residential setting.

In the research examined, there is much to assist a Christian counselor with a biblical worldview in becoming more competent and sensitive in self-awareness, knowledge, and skills. Training or self-training in diversity is time well spent and is an ethical demand that is made by both man and God. By virtue of the counselor's calling, there is a need to intensify this effort to rise above mediocrity and to strive for excellence. Although research shows patterns of behavior, culture, traditions, language, gender, sexual orientation, age, and beliefs, people made in God's image should never be locked into a multicultural box of stereotypes from psychological research. Each individual must be regarded as the unique treasure that God has created in wonderful variety. This is true of the PCT counselor with a rich theological foundation who employs the systematic themes of the Bible in the application of counseling.

Chapter Seven

PCT: Terror Management Theory and Worldview

The following studies stimulated thinking and passion out of the box and began the journey to consider how PCT would ultimately come together, drawing together the idea of mortality salience, potential loss of life, and how both factors makes one think and feel in the context of the other premises in PCT. We saw how powerful Christianity really is when life is being threatened. The three groups of ten research articles within the framework of terror management theory (TMT) are divided into Group I – Reactions, Group II – Religion, and Group III – Age. They show the superior strength of intrinsic religiosity ("intrinsic religiosity" is interpreted as a saving, personal relationship with Jesus Christ) as a buffer against mortality salience (MS), lowering death thought accessibility (DTA) in the context of reactions, religions and age.

Some of the articles examined, represent newly discovered terror management defensive reactions. Others examine protections against mortality salience and terror defensive reactions. Current research has added to the terror defensive mechanisms that the original TMT studies uncovered in the 1990s. A key finding in the area of religion and TMT contradicts past research claiming that religion is nonsignificant in the light of MS. Now, it is shown that religion is a significant factor in MS response and identifying the reason for the change. Correlations are indicated at the end of each grouping, concluding with connections between the articles as an entity.

To better understand reactions and protections from mortality salience in religion and age in the context of TMT, current concepts of mortality salience and TMT are grouped according to reactions to MS, religion and MS, and age and MS. This organizational grouping allows for a broader picture of TMT. This grouping shows similar findings in multinational and multicultural contexts. The articles have to do with MS reactions and demonstrating MS protections.

The importance of intrinsic religiosity is shown to be a dominating force in buffering MS and mitigating DTA, as well as diminishing other terror management reactions. The overview indicates that death and dying is far more complex than was once considered. It is multidimensional, not unidimensional. Proximal and distal connections occur at the end of each group, and practical implications are discussed. In relation to PCT, the intrinsic versus extrinsic religious worldview demonstrates the power of an intrinsic Christian worldview as seen within the context of TMT.

GROUP I – REACTIONS

The first article in this group has to do with "Being present in the face of existential threat: The role of trait-mindfulness in reducing defensive responses to mortality salience" by Niemiec, Brown, Kashdan, Cozzolino, Breen, Levesque-Bristol, and Ryan (2010). It consists of seven studies completed in the U.S.A., postulating that trait-mindfulness reduces defensive responses to mortality salience. Mindfulness is something that has shown good results in behavior management and interpersonal relationships (Brown, Ryan, and Creswell 2007). Trait-mindfulness is a receptive state of mind where the person, aware of the present experience, simply observes what is taking place. In dangerous situations, it reduces emotional reactions (Arch and Craske 2006). It enables a tolerance of unpleasant states (Eifert and Heffner 2003), reduces habitual responding (Wenk-Sormaz 2005), and gives the ability to adaptively respond in threatening situations (Barnes, Brown, Krusemark, Campbell, and Rogge 2007). It builds self-esteem and responds negatively to neuroticism (Brown and Ryan 2003). It is an observant stance toward experience. Mindfulness is not a worldview, but in the mindfulness mode, all "the contents of consciousness, self-relevant thoughts, images, and identities—and overt behaviors are simply on display" (Niemiec et al. 2010, p. 5). Since mindfulness creates an unbiased processing of threat, the hypothesis is that it would moderate both proximal and distal defensive responses to MS (Niemiec et al. 2010).

The first three studies within this article reveal that trait-mindfulness mitigates defensive responses to MS when the cultural worldview is attacked. The results of Study 4 show that those more mindful report less worldview defense. The hypothesis that this moderation would generalize to a related though distinct form of defense, specifically, self-esteem striving, is supported. Study 6 found an explanatory mechanism that accounted for the inverse relation of trait-mindfulness to pro-U.S. bias. Study 7 shows trait-mindfulness in relation to proximal defense suppressing death thoughts. This also supports the hypothesis (Niemiec et al.). These findings point to an inner resource that reduces proximal and distal defense and can be developed (Kabat-Zinn, 1990).

The second article, whose title is tersely cogent, gets to the hearts of the matter: "Is death really the worm at the core? Converging evidence that worldview threat increases death-thought accessibility." Schimel, Hayes, Williams, and Jahrig's research (2007) consist of five studies conducted in Canada. They are built around the hypothesis that if cultural worldview buffers thoughts about death, when the worldview is attacked and weakened, DTA increases. Another hypothesis is if the threatening worldview literature could be discredited by argumentation, then DTA will remain low. Both hypotheses are supported by the research (Schimel et al.). Results agree with prior studies. Whether the worldview was nationalism or even creationism, the same results occurred. This present research is built upon the research of TMT. These studies demonstrate that attacks on cultural values increases DTA. It is shown that if the worldview threat can be reduced by cognitive means, DTA does not increase (Schimel et al.). This fact alone is encouraging for counselors.

In the third article, "Separation from loved ones in the fear of death," Bath (2010) did an exploratory study conducted in Australia to examine the fear of the death of self and the fear of the death of others. The relationship to fear is determined by using the CLFDS (Collett-Lester Fear of Death Scale, 1969). Results are consistent with past research. Those high in fear of their own dying were also high in fear of other people dying. The people who came out low in fear of their own death were also low in the fear of others dying (Bath 2010).

Common themes are the event of death and the pain of dying. Some participants were frightened about the uncertainty of knowing when they would die. Others were frightened about the certainty of knowing when they would die. Other common themes are the unknown afterlife, the finality of death, the unfulfilled life, and the pain of dying. The one that stands out is the loss of loved ones and the separation that death brings (Bath 2010).

Men and women who were high on the fear of death were equally anxious about the unfulfilled life, the unknown afterlife, and the uncertainty of death. The unfulfilled life appeared in all categories of men and women. The second least common fear was the finality of death, but the most prevalent fear was the loss of loved ones. This agrees with prior research and is the key finding in this study (Bath 2010).

Therefore, one of the most important themes in literature on bereavement is continuing the bond between the living and the dead. Some degree of attachment is normal, but sometimes it can be maladaptive. The most difficult time is when those who grieve cannot make sense of the loss of a loved one (Neimyer, Baldwin, and Gilles 2006). One possible reason is that the situation may be influenced by the person's own fears of death. This shows the need for future studies (Bath 2010). When there is a strong Christian worldview, there is at least the element of faith that strengthens people in the uncertainty of why a loved one dies. This mitigates the difficult time that people go through when nothing makes sense.

The fourth article, "From the grave to the cradle: evidence that mortality salience engenders a desire for offspring" by Wisman and Goldenberg (2005), hypothesizes that MS creates a desire for offspring. The four studies are conducted in the Netherlands.

Following the September 11, 2001, destruction of the World Trade Center, there was a baby boom. In 2005, the current literature in psychology had not explained this reaction to a terrorist attack or disaster (Wisman and Goldenberg 2005). TMT shows that people want a symbol of immortality after MS. Therefore, this need can be best met by having children who can carry a part of the person in life after he or she dies (Solomon, Greenberg, and Pyszczynski 1991). TMT also shows that people look at themselves in an abstract, symbolical way (Sedikides and Skowronski 1997). Therefore, having children can become a symbol of one's immortality. This calms the fear of death (Wisman and Goldenberg 2005).

Symbolism is, therefore, an important part of people's significance. PCT would add that the need for children after 9-11 would show that loss of significance is a reaction to MS and DTA, and the response is having more children, which would increase personal significance. As the studies were done in the Netherlands, quite far from New York City, it would suggest that the world was not as safe a place as was previously thought, and the MS and DTA would give them a perception of the loss of safety and security that their worldview could not give them. The need to find a substitute in having children is a PCT way of looking at the results of the study. Another example of the fact that people look at themselves in an abstract, symbolical way are tombstones in a cemetery. They are also symbols of immortality.

The first study reveals that males under MS want more children than males in the control group. Women show equal results in the control group and the experimental group and do not seem to be affected by MS in the same way. The findings show that MS increases the drive of men to have more children than women. Further testing shows that relationship is not a factor in men wanting more children after MS (Wisman and Goldenberg 2005). The second study replicates the results of the first and demonstrates that the desire to procreate is a buffer of anxiety. The results find that under MS men want more children than women. The third study agrees with the findings of studies one and two, that in the face of MS, more men want children than women.

When God created Adam and Eve, they got the mandate to multiply and fill the earth. The many genealogies in Genesis mention only the men and not the women. That there is a cultural reason for this is clear enough; however, there could also be an underlying desire that may be related to the above study, which implies that men under mortality salience, by living in a dangerous world, desire children to carry on and replace them as they live under MS. It is an interesting thought that may require future investigation. Loss is very much involved in people's reaction to possible impending death.

The factor of career ambition is included in study three. Women want more children as they show less interest in career ambition (Wisman and Goldenberg 2005). The fourth study shows similar results. When there is a mutual desire for children and career, MS causes women to not want children. Yet, when women think they can balance career and children, even after MS, a stronger desire to have children is more than likely in the women in the control group. In conclusion, the evidence supports the hypothesis that males and females, when not inhibited by conflict with careers, show an increased desire for children after MS (Wisman and Goldenberg 2005).

The fifth article, "Terror management and attributions of blame to innocent victims: Reconciling compassionate and defensive responses" (Hirschberger 2006), is conducted in the U.S.A. and Israel, hypothesizing that reminders of personal death affects the normative attribution process and increases the motivation to blame severely injured, innocent victims. When victims are injured in a disaster, there is a tendency to place distance between the observer and the victim, so that emotional dissonance is not felt. Some people say, "I am glad it's not me" (Bennett and Dunkel-Schetter 1992; Pyszczynski, Greenberg, Solomon, Sidaris, and Stubing 1994, p. 832).

A method of distancing is to stigmatize the victims, ignoring and shunning them (Bennett et al. 1992). This is motivated by a need to justify behavior. There are two psychological benefits from this behavior. The first is to shield the observer from awareness that a similar fate could happen to the observer. Second, the observer can ignore the victim with no feelings of guilt since they believe that they probably deserved it. This is interesting because it reminds us of how readily the German people accepted Hitler's propaganda, blaming their economic problems on the Jews. However, much literature states that observers can go completely in the opposite direction in their MS response with care and compassion (Carver, Glass, and Katz 1978; Katz 1981; Scheier, Carver, Schulz, Glass, and Katz 1978). Explanations for this ambivalent behavior can be found in the attribution theory (Kelly 1955). Some people feel very intense about the need to live in a just world. As a result, blame may be given to the victim, because the observer needs to feel safe (Lerner and Miller 1978).

TMT indicates that people live in paradoxical situations. They cherish living but they know it is only temporary. Instinctual drives push people to live, but, unavoidably, it is ultimately going to fail. This inability to escape could cause people to feel helpless and full of terror. Symbolic defense mechanisms remove thoughts of death from the conscious mind. Two constructs let this happen. They are validation of a cultural worldview and drive high self-esteem (Greenberg et al. 1997). Primary loss contributed to the need to seek a substitute for a good relationship with God as death entered the world at the time of the Fall, resulting in a loss of significance, safety, and security. TMT's research has reinforced PCT.

When there is an encounter with someone (a victim) who, by what has happened to him/her, denies their worldview, the reaction of the observer can lead to distancing, derogation, and even aggression when death is salient. The Jews had a completely different worldview from others. The Germans jumped at the opportunity presented by Hitler to blame their economic suffering on these strange people.

A proximal defense is initial and tries to remove death thoughts from awareness. The distal defense emerges when people are distracted from death-related thoughts, when the thoughts start to resurface but are not in primary focus (Arndt et al. 1997; Greenberg et al. 2000). This needs explanation. The defense of cultural worldview is both proximal and distal. The more severe the injury is, or more innocent the victim, the greater the blame. This is the just-world hypothesis (Burger 1981; Rabbenolt 2000) (Lerner and Miller 1978). Sometimes the greater the severity of the injury to the victim, the greater becomes the sympathy (Weiner et al. 1988). The unpredictability of people and their responses depends on their worldview.

Four studies show that MS induces attribution of blame toward severely injured victims, particularly when the injuries are irreversible. One result is when circumstances surrounding an injured victim are under the victim's control, such as clumsiness; there is much more blame given to the victim (Weiner et al. 1988). The presence of MS leads to greater blame, because terror management defense mechanisms kick in. This is true even to those victims who have physical disabilities.

All the studies replicate one another. If innocent victims are injured, observers are reminded of the fragility of life. As a result, the observers move to a just-world theory (Landau et al. 2004). In the presence of MS, this reaction of blame is focused on the more severely injured victims more than the moderately injured victims. This holds true only if the moderately injured person is clearly innocent of all blame. Findings indicate that MS moderates the connection between outcome severity, victim responsibility, and attributions of blame. This concurs with the findings of Hirschberger et al. (2005). The current research unifies the dichotomy between compassion and blame because of the relationship with MS and TMT. TMT provides an effective framework to explain why people act inconsistently and beyond rational thinking (Hirschberger 2005).

The research of the five articles in Group I-Reactions all deal with reactions to MS as a common theme, confirming the TMT. One of the greatest and most prevalent anxieties is fear of being separated from loved ones (Bath et al. 2010). Terror defense mechanisms are shown to have an irrational side in the blame of innocent victims by observers (Hirschberger et al. 2006). This confirms the idea that the severe loss of one's safety, security, and significance can cause one to leap into irrational thinking that results in attributional thinking. Two of the articles show that by attacking the cultural worldview, no matter what kind of worldview, results in increased DTA, as well as attacks on others (Schimel et al. 2007; Hirschberger et al.).

A protection from attacks on worldview is demonstrated in trait-mindfulness (Niemiec et al. 2010).

GROUP II – RELIGION

There are some interesting surprises for Christian counselors in this group of research articles. Article one in this group, "Mortality anxiety as a function of intrinsic religiosity and perceived purpose in life" by Hui and Fung (2009), showed that intrinsic religiosity is protection from MS, not reaction from it. The hypothesis that intrinsic religiosity, not extrinsic, lowered anxiety toward the dying and death of self and someone close through fostering perceived purpose in life was supported by the findings. The limitation of the research was a question of whether the findings would apply to other cultures since the participants were Chinese Christians in Hong Kong (Hui and Fung 2004).

This research is an eye-opener for Christian counselors and supports the supposition that a Christian worldview is very strong and a buttress against the negative effects of MS and DTA, while those who are simply churchgoing people who lack the Christian worldview—not having a relationship with God through Christ—are prey for MS and DTA. This research supports a historical Christian worldview that has roots going back to the beginning of the Church. This supersedes any denominational perspective, revealing the power and grace of being a Christian.

There has been controversy in the literature between religiosity and DTA, because death and dying is multidimensional and the various dimensions are related to each other in complex and also inconsistent ways. For example, a unidimensional perspective showed a nonsignificant association between death and dying anxiety and religiosity. The reason for this is because, in past research, religiosity was never separated into the categories of intrinsic and extrinsic dimensions (Hui and Fung 2009). Additional support comes from Frank et al. (1990–1991), whose research indicated that extrinsic people showed no connection between death anxiety and religiosity. Here is the important reason: extrinsically religious people do not consider religion important enough to satisfy their basic needs (Hui and Fung 2009). Merely attending church services is not going to work when the going gets tough.

Extrinsic religiosity describes participants who have no commitment to religion and who have not internalized beliefs. As a result, there is no buffering ability to defend against the effects of MS. On the other hand, intrinsic religiosity is positively connected to purpose in life. One significant finding of this study shows that intrinsic religiosity exerts buffering power against death and dying anxiety, as well as lowers DTA, by its influence on perceived purpose in life (Hui and Fung 2009).

Is it not great that God protects our minds and hearts when danger comes our way and has strengthened us by giving us purpose to live? The various metaphors of the Scripture come to mind about God protecting us by putting us on a high place that cannot be reached by destructive things, or the Shepherd who protects His sheep with the rod against their enemies, or even how the Lord Jesus stops the wind and the waves that threaten to sink the boat with His disciples onboard. Being hidden in the secret place of the Most High and how the Lord will not break the bruised reed nor quench the smoking flax are just some of the thoughts of God toward His people who live in a sin-cursed world. These are just some of the benefits of a Christian worldview that protect us when extremely bad things threaten our very existence. Hui and Fung have given Christians evidence, through their research, that can be understood as God taking care of His people even when perceived loss is the greatest loss.

We can trace back in time confirming the same lines of thinking as Hui and Fung (2009); for example, Jonas and Fischer's (2006) research supporting their own hypothesis that intrinsic religiosity is a protection against death issues brought by MS, and that extrinsic religious beliefs do not prevent worldview defense. These were research studies conducted in Germany and Turkey. The need for this research came at a time when there was no empirical evidence to show how religion defuses existential terror that MS brings to the individual's cognitive system. Studies show that intrinsically religious people are protected by internalized religious beliefs. They protect because they provide a basis for cultural worldview and culturally derived self-esteem, giving meaning to life and promising transcendence from death. Intrinsic means striving for meaning and value, while extrinsic means a utilitarian use of religion (Jonas and Fischer 2006). We are seeing the same results in China, Germany, and Turkey.

Other researchers have also indicated differences between intrinsically religious people and extrinsically religious people. Jonas and Fischer (2006) report the findings made by Donahue (1985) and cite Saroglow's (2002) research findings indicating that religious beliefs are more important for intrinsic than extrinsic people. Commitment to religious beliefs were also stronger for intrinsic as opposed to the extrinsic. Jonas and Fischer also cited a prior research by Maltby and Day (2000), reporting that intrinsic people showed emotional stability as opposed to extrinsic people who showed neuroticism. Intrinsic people showed a strong religious coping ability, a more secure relationship with God, and a more positive outcome for mental health, as well as demonstrating a negative relationship with psychoticism. The research keeps piling up as Jonas and Fischer report (Baker and Gorsuch 1982; Bergen et al. 1987; Maltby, Lewis, and Day 1999; Sturgeon and Hamley 1979) findings showing that extrinsically religious people had poor religious ability to cope with problems, had a pattern of neuroticism, and had an insecure relationship with God. Not surprisingly, intrinsically religious people had lower levels of anxiety than their counterparts. The previous studies by Bolt (1977), Minton and Spilke (1976), and Spilke et al. (1977) are all reported by Jonas and Fischer to have shown that intrinsic people had lower levels of various fears of death. Genia (1996) is also cited by Jonas and Fischer, and that research concluded that intrinsic religiousness is a strong predictor of psycho-spiritual health. In addition, the sense of a personal relationship with God appears to make those people less susceptible to existential angst. Jonas and Fischer summarily reported that these studies have pointed out that intrinsic religiosity becomes a buffer against existential terror and, most importantly, does not trigger terror management defenses. The very opposite reaction occurs in extrinsic religiosity. In PCT interpretation, these findings revealed that believers in Christ have stronger safety, security, and significance, because God is not only with them in the transcendental but also in the situational and the existential when MS occurs.

After terrorist attacks in Istanbul, Turkey, people who were highly intrinsic in terms of religious practice did not react with worldview defense. The opposite was true of the low intrinsic. The higher the intrinsic orientation, the more people went to church and prayed, believing in God to help them cope with MS. The extrinsic were the opposite. The intrinsic people were less prone to think about possible future terrorist attacks, while the extrinsic were the antithesis of that. The conclusion is that intrinsically religious people cope with the fear of terrorist attacks by an increased tendency to affirm their religious faith (Jonas and Fischer 2006).

The affirmation of religion is the necessary precondition for finding less terror management reactions among intrinsically religious people. Intrinsic religiousness was effective in managing terror, while the extrinsic was not capable of buffering existential anxiety. Highly intrinsic religious people did not indicate a heightened DTA, although those who were low intrinsic did show heightened DTA. The bottom line of this is that an active commitment to religious beliefs reduces the fear of death. MS does not induce DTA as it does in low intrinsic and nonreligious people. The value of this study is that it adds similar findings to previous studies regarding TMT and religion. In addition, religious belief plays a protective role in terror management and makes a distinction between the quality of belief rather than the quantity (Jonas and Fischer 2006).

The correlation of all this research makes it very clear that during times of danger, when one's death could be likely, the Christian worldview and internalized belief system trumps what the world has to offer. For counselors who know the Lord, a client without primary loss (that is, who does know the Lord) who survived dealing with the possibility of secondary loss (a possible death) have a very good mental health prognosis. On the other hand, the breakdown of substitutes may or may not be harmful in secondary loss. Often they take the shape of behavior that looks for symbolic immortality or, possibly, attributional blame and hostility toward another group of people or individuals.

MS does not induce DTA and other terror defense mechanisms in people who have a close relationship with God. Those who do not have that close relationship with God will have a fear of death and dying that brings on great anxiety in the face of their possible death. The studies in Hong Kong, Germany, and Turkey indicate this. Here is the amazing thing. The stronger the MS threat became, the stronger the worldview became of the intrinsically religious. Here is why: their belief system was internalized.

These studies disprove the conclusion of older studies that religion had no significance in relation to MS. The more current studies have indicated that unidimensional thinking about death and dying is too simplistic, that death and dying is multidimensional.

Christians have heard the criticism from secularists that to believe in God is simply a crutch to lean on for weak people. These studies, at the very least, debunk this idea completely. In reality, Christians have an all-around better mental health than the unbelievers. They have a worldview that gets stronger when attacked with the possibility of death. So who has the crutch? Who is the weak when it comes to facing up to the reality of DTA? Who frets the most? Who suffers from anxiety? It is definitely not the Christian.

PCT also rests on the empirical research from the studies discussed in this chapter and comes against anxiety and loss with power and authority, unapologetically standing for Christian counseling as having real answers to real problems. It offers a worldview that refuses to crumble under the most fear-inspiring terror the world has to offer. Like Rocky Balboa, this worldview gets hit and comes back stronger. PCT brings hope and healing to hurting people.

GROUP III – AGE

The three articles in this group reflect on protection against death and dying anxiety in the aged. The aged is a growing population in most nations, and many researchers are doing studies on them. Particularly relevant are death and dying studies (Azaiza, Ron, Shohom, and Gignini 2010). Most have been done in the West on mainly Christian populations (Fortner and Neimeyer 1999; Neimeyer, Witkowski, and Moser 2004). This study was done on an elderly Arab population living in a nursing home in Israel. The hypothesis that the residents of the nursing home would have higher levels of DTA than those who lived in the community was confirmed. Anxiety of the process of dying was also higher in the nursing home than in the community. It is interesting, in the light of what was previously written, that religiosity was not a factor. It produced nonsignificant results. Religion among these residents was probably taken for granted, and the issues of death and dying in a fatalistic Islamic religion may be responsible for this nonsignificance of religion (Azaiza et al. 1999).

Social support and self-esteem were also higher for the elderly living out in the community than in the nursing home. The nursing home residents who had family support had less anxiety about death and dying than residents with no support (Azaiza et al. 1999).

The research in the second article in this group was conducted in Turkey. They found support for their hypothesis that the anxiety of death motivates people to do health-promoting behaviors. Results indicated that the elderly under the anxiety of death did more health-promoting behaviors than did younger adults. The odd thing is that when death anxiety is not present, younger adults do more health-promoting behavior than the elderly. One reason may be the older adults' view of death as normal (Bozo, Tunca, and Simsek 2009). They are not as affected by it as much as younger people. They support these findings from Greenberg, Pyszczynski, Solomon, Simon, and Brues (1994). Young adults feel that they have their whole lives ahead of them and that death is far away. However, when confronted with death reminders, younger adults do take health-promoting behavior seriously. In general, older adults take stress better and care about good health more than the youth. This study shows that the presence of death reminders did not make any difference in older adults who did health-promoting behaviors. In conclusion, death anxiety and age are important predictors of health-promoting behaviors. More research is apparently needed in this area (Bozo, Tunca, and Simsek 2009).

A study was conducted in the U.S.A. among people in late adulthood. It revealed that people who scored high in the belief of a rewarding afterlife and at the same time scored low in religiousness turned out to be high in the fear of death. Those who scored high on a belief in a rewarding afterlife and also high on religiousness had a lower DTA. It also turned out that moderately religious people were more afraid of death and dying than the highly religious and the nonreligious. The apparent reason is that the disjunction between faith and practice brings about the fear of death. Lukewarm religious engagement in late adulthood shows a high fear of death. The reason they feel this way is that they know they are not living up to the standards of their religion and are afraid of punishment. In late adulthood, the self becomes fragile with chronic anxiety, which manifests when people are without a strong philosophy regarding death, whether secular or religious. When someone is in this condition, there is usually a lack of connection with social institutions. It would appear that clinical interventions ought to be applied to this group.

People in their sixties had more fear of death and dying than people in their seventies, because older people had more experiences of sickness and death. If a person is not religious in their forties, more than likely, they will not be religious in late adulthood, with a lower level of the fear of death than a moderately religious person. Again, the fear of death is lowered in cases of intrinsic religiousness, while the opposite is true of the extrinsic. This study was limited in that the participants were white and mainline Protestant (Wink and Scott 2005).

The correlation in Group III – Age shows three studies done in Israel, Turkey, and the U.S.A. with ethnically and religiously diverse people. DTA motivates health-promoting behaviors among the older adults, but when not reminded about death, the older adults do not go out of their way to do health-promoting behaviors, since they believe that death is normal. This last study among oldest of old in the U.S.A. again reminds us that those who have a moderate interest in religion and who have a weak philosophy of death yet have a belief in the rewarding afterlife have the highest anxiety about death and dying. It proves that a little knowledge can be dangerous. These are probably the ones whom the unbelieving critics of the Church speak about when they complain that the Church is full of hypocrites. The high in religiousness are the lowest in fear of death and dying, as the intrinsic and extrinsically religious come up again. It is not really surprising that religion played a nonsignificant role in the fear of death and dying with the elderly Arabs in the Israeli nursing home since Islam is a fatalistic religion, and acceptance is a given in that culture.

This is where Christian counseling can shine the brightest. What other kind of clinical interventions can bring the comfort toward death that the Gospel can bring to the aged who suffer from DTA? The section Group I – Reactions presents the variety of responses to MS, which reveals the importance of intrinsic religiousness. In relation to age, intrinsic religiousness is successful in lowering DTA, especially in the framework of TMT. These articles bring out a broader understanding of the value of intrinsic religiousness.

Without repeating all that has been said about intrinsic religiousness, its value works as a protection against MS, because it has strong purpose in life, and this transcends death (Hui and Fung 2009). Internal religiousness lowers the DTA because of the belief that death does not permanently separate loved ones, which is one of the most prevalent fear of death and dying (Wink and Scott 2005; Bath 2010). This is what Christianity has to offer to a mentally unhealthy world—a powerful coping mechanism (Jonas and Fischer 2006). Finally, the three groups of researches I, II, and III show that intrinsic religiousness is both transcultural and transnational. This is more of a testimony to the idea that man possesses a common personality with a spiritual component. Theologically speaking, he is the image of God. PCT has the view that intrinsic religiousness, being universally demonstrated, reflects the universal loss and universal grace to meet the needs of so many who suffer from emotional pain.

Chapter Eight

PCT and Crisis Counseling

The need for crisis counseling in the United States of America has never been greater. Although there are many effective forms of crisis counseling coming from a Christian worldview, there is always room for improvement. The application of PCT to crisis counseling is shown to be broadly applicable to a variety of crises. It is not based on one or two verses of the Scripture, but a deeper systematic biblical understanding of the nature of man, his primary loss due to sin, and the universal secondary loss due to living in a sin-cursed world. The root of man's inability to handle crises is due to the failure of safety, security, and significance to maintain his defenses against tension and stressors.

PCT replaces cognitive distortions of safety, security, and significance with true ones that are found in man's relationship with God, the world, and others in applying biblical principles for living. It is comprehensive yet simple enough to apply in a crisis counseling situation and useful for both the believers and unbelievers in Christ.

Since the World Trade Center collapse on September 11, 2001, the need and importance of crisis counseling in the United States has increased not only because of terrorist attacks, but also of natural disasters, such as hurricanes and tornadoes. There are times when a crisis counselor is called to intervene very soon after the crisis, but the real need for crisis counseling may actually be in the months after the event (Sohn 2011). To underscore the need for crisis counseling assistance in the aftermath of hurricanes alone, nineteen million dollars was awarded to seven states for counseling aid by the Substance Abuse and Mental Health Services Administration in 2006 ("Seven states share," 2006). Over the past ten years, there has been a profound need for development and evaluation of crisis counseling strategies and interventions in the field of disaster mental health (Watson and Ruzek 2009).

Some police departments are using a mental-health-based response to people in crisis not limited to domestic violence or mental health issues alone (Young and Brumley 2009). Financial loss is also the source of crisis counseling because of a loss of security (Miller 2008). This fits with the thinking of PCT. There is also a need for a fresh approach to crisis counseling from a Christian worldview. PCT for crisis counseling is a biblically comprehensive approach internally consistent and empirically grounded in the Scripture and research, and views primary and secondary universal loss as the root cause for the inability to withstand crises in an emotionally healthy way.

A Christian counseling theory must have internal consistency and be rooted into the ontology, metaphysics, epistemology, and etiology of the Bible in order to be consistently Christian and be a good theory. PCT is rooted in the areas concerning the nature of man and is consistently a theory grounded in a biblical model, which serves as its psychological framework, to help hurting people in crisis (Thomas and Sosin 2011). Dr. Larry Crabb (1977) stated that security and significance are two of man's basic needs. The concept of safety is a third basic need. Safety is paramount for crisis counseling and is at least as significant as the other two needs of security and significance. According to *Webster's New World Dictionary* (1988), crisis is defined as "a time of great danger or trouble, whose outcome decides whether possible bad consequences will follow." For counselors and victims involved in a crisis, this uncertain outcome is what feeds the emotions and unravels a person's sense of control, making a crisis worse in terms of perception. Sometimes the perception is worse than the actual crisis. PCT can help the counselor get an understanding of the perception of the crisis in the client's mind.

A crisis is determined by tension and stress (Greenstone and Leviton 2002). But tension and stress are not the cause of the emotional response to the crisis; they are symptoms of the real cause, which is primary and secondary loss. As tension and stressors increase to high proportions, coping skills that normally work become ineffective (Greenstone and Leviton 2002). In a family crisis situation, tension and stress can wear down the family's coping abilities. Family resources consist of effective communication, flexibility, and cohesion. When a stressor event cannot be dealt with by these three characteristics, the family enters a state of crisis.

The book of Philippians consists of powerful examples in handling stress and tension to deal with a family crisis. The book is addressed to the church family as Paul considers them brothers. If the family can reframe the stressors, then the outcome would be positive. For example, in Philippians 4:6, it is written: "Be careful for nothing; but in everything by prayer and supplication with thanksgiving let your requests be made known unto God" (KJV). The word "careful" means anxious. All resources for dealing with stress originate from God, who gives grace through the supply of the indwelling Holy Spirit (1:19) or changes the circumstances and brings about safety.

Cohesion of family members is important in order to handle stress properly. This involves shared values. An example is the connectedness in the church of Philippi, revealing the same values, love, and support that is given to Paul (4:10, 14; 1:5). It has been shown that a family worldview that responds to stress effectively includes optimism and religiousness. Philippians 1:6, 25–26 and 4:19 reveals Paul's optimism, faith, and relationship with a powerful, benevolent God, giving him personal significance. When a family is led by the counselor to reframe harmful thinking by biblical principles, their safety, security, and significance diminishes a crisis and can turn it into an opportunity for growth (Wilmoth and Smyser 2009).

When these family resources cannot deal with a stressor event, then the family is in a crisis or aleph loss. Stress and tension can sometimes wear down a family's ability to cope with the situation, pointing to the secondary loss of safety, security, and significance. The three resources—communication, cohesion, and flexibility—work when there is little loss, or no loss of the three S's. The resources are symptoms that tell when the family is in homeostasis or not.

Reframing the perception of the loss according to Philippians can help the situational, the existential, and the transcendental aspects in spite of whether the stressor event is gone or not (see figure 9).

Flexibility/Communication

Families not in Crisis   **Families in Crisis (Aleph Loss)**

Effective Communication   No Effective Communication

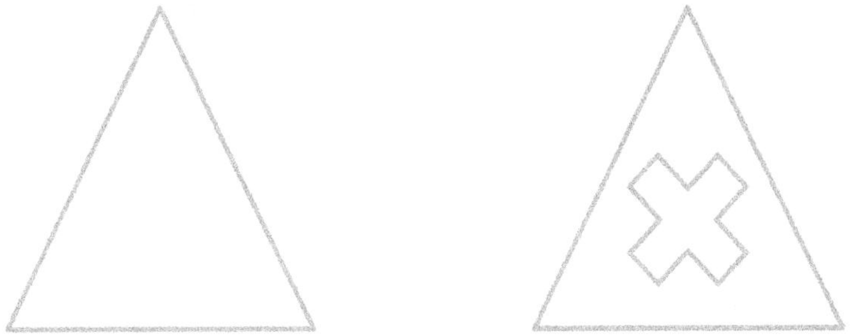

Flexibility/Cohesion   Inflexibility/Lack of Cohesion

Figure 9

PCT recognizes that tension and stress are factors in causing a crisis, but this is only the surface of what is visible in a crisis. It is the tip of an iceberg. Underneath this lies the universal of loss (Murray 2001). PCT is grounded in the primary relational loss of man and God and the secondary universal loss, which is the experience of all mankind. This theory proposes that the counselor should be as the Holy Spirit, a paraklasis counselor. This means being an advocate (1 John 2:1), to stand by the side of, to comfort, to guide, to direct, to encourage, to exhort, to console, to beseech, to edify, to help, to empathize with the client, and to intercede with God and man (Young 1969). Jesus' disciples entered a state of crisis when Jesus told them about His going away in John chapters 14 and 16. This was when He said He would send them another comforter, the Holy Spirit. The disciples in that crisis had a problem rooted in the loss of Jesus, and Jesus had to do crisis counseling. He strengthened their significance, safety, and security by reminding them that He would send the Holy Spirit who would comfort them and guide them into all truth. He let them know all was not coming to an end and that they must love one another. Receiving love from others builds a support base that strengthens significance to receive the hard truths that come along. Jesus handled the situational, the existential, and the transcendental with excellence, giving them just what was needed for the moment.

Loss affects man who is made in God's image (Genesis 2:26–27). Original loss occurred when Adam sinned against God and lost true righteousness, true knowledge, and true holiness. This was the first relational loss in the human race. As a result of sin and its effects in the world and mankind, a derivative loss continues through creation and in every event that can precipitate a crisis. Loss is not always the same as grief, although it can be grief. It is loss that creates the tension and the stress, not the other way around, as mentioned in Greenstone and Leviton (2002). Loss in a crisis affects three areas of the victim: the areas of safety, security, and significance. The PCT counselor involved in crisis counseling looks at the eight categories of secondary loss and determines which category is part of the presenting crisis (see p.30).

The Father, Son, and Holy Spirit have created man to think and behave in a normative way when God meets the needs of significance, security, and safety. As counselors are to be like Christ, Christ to His people is Prophet, Priest, and King. As a prophet, the counselor must always speak the truth to the counselee. As a priest, the counselor intercedes to God for the counselee in prayer. As a king, there are times when the counselor must speak in a direct manner.

PCT declares that the Bible does teach a personality structure of man. God has personality, and all that is communicable in terms of His attributes were given to man who is created in His image. Man has cognitive functioning, a will, and emotions, with an integrated body, soul, and spirit. God speaks, therefore man speaks. Even unsaved man is still in the image of God after the Fall and has a spiritual sense that is part of his personality. If a biblical structure of the personality is denied, then there is no explanation for the existence of spirituality in mankind. Man is motivated from the heart, which, after the Fall, is sinful (Jeremiah 17:9). Good and bad behavior is directed by the heart, which is the ultimate schema that manifests through the cognitive, volitional, and emotional aspects of human personality.

Loss can be defined as "something perceived of value is lost" (Murray 2001, p. 219). Paul, in Philippians 3:7–8, reveals the perception and the subjective value of his loss and contrasts what he once held as valuable to what he has gained in knowing Christ (Kittel 1976). As Saul the persecutor, he trusted his security, safety, and significance in his racial background, education, and position as a Pharisee. As a Christian, these three basic needs are met in Jesus Christ.

In crisis counseling, especially when a counselor is called to the location where the crisis is occurring, the counselor may have to be an advocate for the family on behalf of the client, to the client on behalf of the family, and even to the law enforcement. The goal of paraklasis crisis counseling is to help the counselee to devalue harmful substitutes for significance, security, and safety as quickly as possible. The counselor must always be on alert to help the counselee avoid using negative self-talk, which devalues the counselee.

In a crisis, people sometimes feel confused, surreal, strange, and often out of control. This cognitive dysfunction is fed by the emotions. As the spiral goes downward, the confused cognitive functioning creates impulsive behavior, because it feeds the will, which results in maladaptive behavior. In order to stop the downward spiral leading away from normative behavior, biblical principles need to be applied in the areas of safety, security, and significance.

As emotions are the controlling factor in the victim in a crisis, they need to be addressed first. However, it is important to remember that the thinking controls the emotions and not the other way around. Physical safety must be considered, as there might be harm to the client or to others. The client should be led to a safer location, and that must be evaluated on a case-by-case basis. Nonverbal communication of listening, building trust, and showing empathy can speak to the emotional aspect of a victim. The cognitive cannot be initially reached, because the emotions rule. That is the reason why some people must go to a short-term mental health facility, where the emotions can be calmed down through medication before the cognitive domain can be treated, but only if they are a danger to themselves or others.

The counselor must be able to deal with outbursts of emotion, anger, frustration, and tears without feeling overwhelmed. The actual presence of the counselor, even without saying anything, can bring comfort to the victim. That God is present with His people in times of trouble, in crises, is a common biblical principle. The ministry of presence is a valuable fact of help for victims in a crisis.

In addressing the emotions in times of loss, prayer for God's presence is useful. He can bring peace without the counselor's understanding, or, for that matter, apart from the client's understanding. If possible, it should be done before anything else. Prayer sets the emotional tone for what follows and implies that there is a God who cares and is in control of all things. It builds trust and shows empathy from the counselor.

Providing structure assists in helping someone who feels they have no control in their crisis (Greenstone and Leviton 2002). Jesus had thousands of hungry people to deal with, and so He had them sit down in groups. As food was passed out, we think that it was for convenience's sake, but He may have wanted them to realize that He was in control. There are times in a crisis when a counselor, in order to bring about confidence in the client regardless of cultural factors, must show that they are in control even though the client does not feel in control.

At this time, asking what started the crisis is appropriate. The counselor is looking for a recent trigger, not something way back in the past. The Psalms are rich with people who are pouring out their complaints to God, who listens with empathy and is interested in their plight. The perception of the event that precipitated the crisis is important for the counselor to understand.

Restating what the counselee said can be important for confirmation and clarity. After calming the emotions, interaction on a cognitive level is possible. Open-ended questions can be asked to allow the counselee to express their feelings (Kanel 2007), as well as their perception of the crisis. For example, in the book of Jonah, God asked Jonah some heart-revealing questions, so Jonah could more accurately perceive his crisis when he despaired of life itself (Jonah 4).

The counselor must listen for cognitive distortions in the domains of safety, security, and significance. They must be replaced with truth in the Scripture. Hopelessness, anxiety, and despair can be attacked with faith, hope, and the love of God. Psalms 40, 91, and 121 reveal a heavenly Father who gives security and safety as a refuge in times of trouble. If the counselee is a Christian and a victim, the person can be reminded that he or she has significance in God's eyes, because He adopted the victim as His child and into His family (Romans 8:15).

Obtaining significance is crucial for a victim of sexual abuse. This has been robbed from the victim. They need to be reminded that they have value, because they are in God's image. The Holy Spirit was sent to be the other Comforter, who guides us into all truth and will assist the counselor in correcting cognitive distortions (John 16:13). "Where no counsel is the people fall: but in the multitude of counselors there is safety" (Proverbs 11:14). (See figure 10.)

Man in Crisis

The natural man finds crisis when his substitutes for God fall apart.

Spiritual Safety

Spiritual Autonomy characterizes the natural man.

Loss of control in these three domains leads to acting out to attempt to regain control. They combine to create the worldview. The crisis event may result in impulsive behavior that can harm the one in crisis or others.

Volitional Security
He seeks security in life situations: Career, social involvement, family, etc.

Emotional Significance
He derives self-esteem from the perceptions about his life situations.

Counseling treatment is time constrained, and reframing these substitutes into a biblical perspective is of life-saving importance. The self should no longer be god and autonomous.

Man in Crisis

The natural man finds crisis when his substitutes for God fall apart.

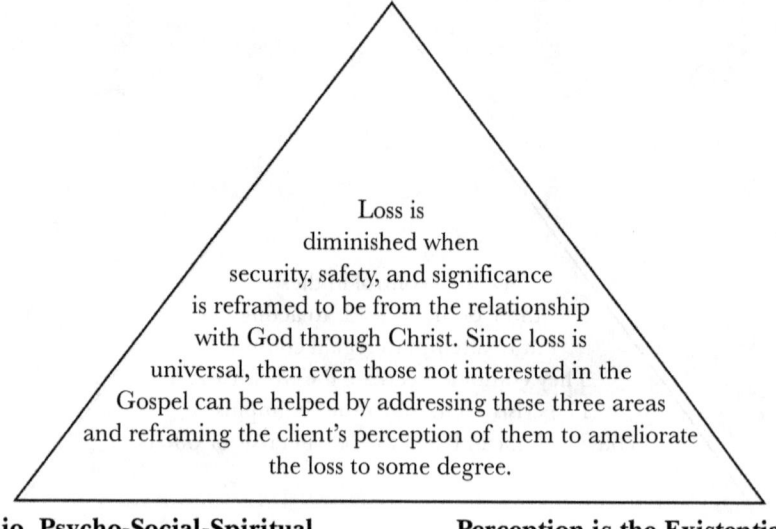

Figure 10

PCT is applicable to believers as well as unbelievers since they are all created in God's image and are ontologically the same. Believers and unbelievers suffer from loss, which is the root of all mental disorders. Many people, when confronted with their mortality or a serious crisis, view prayer as acceptable, especially if the counselee believes that the counselor appears to know the "man upstairs." The Bible shows that God will answer prayer from unbelievers, sometimes doing miracles, faith or no faith (Matthew 8:16–17). It is important for the counselor to tactfully discover the religious point of view of the person in crisis. It is important to discover what the counselee can believe God is able to do for them while in crisis to ask God to do only what their level of faith can receive. In this way, the three S's can be enhanced in the client's life, while the emotional damage of the crisis can be relieved to some degree.

Man lives in a transgenerational loss condition, having lost fellowship with God because of Adam's sin. A derivative condition of death and the misery of living in a sin-cursed world is the place where crises occur—man's situation. Therefore, loss is a common factor in human personality and is also the determining factor to discern the perception of the counselee to their crisis. The counselor needs to discover the degree of loss in the counselee's perception. When the word "loss" is articulated in counseling sessions, whether it is relational or another category of loss, people often shed tears when it is recognized. Much of counseling is very subjective, and it is difficult to determine how deeply the client perceives the crisis.

The Miller Crisis Loss Test can help assess this level of loss. This is a twelve-question self-reporting test that the authors created to help a counselor deal with a counselee in a crisis once the person is calm enough to utilize the tool. This can give an idea of the perception of loss the client is feeling and will impact a person's life in crisis. The foundational concept is that everything that causes a crisis, including tension and stress, is based on loss. The degree of loss felt is the perception of the impact of the crisis. Perceptions of what is a crisis may vary in the counselee. Even the observations of the counselor may not pick up the internal perception regarding the crisis that is within the client.

What may appear to be a crisis to the counselor, and even the counselee's family, may be life as usual for the person going through the crisis. The alleged crisis may not have any impact on the person's life. For example, a counselor is called by family members to help a husband who has been notified that his wife has been killed in a car accident. The husband is assumed to be in a severe crisis as the counselor meets him. However, he seems calm, reserved, and not as upset as would be expected, and the counselor, through questioning, finds out that he has been planning on divorcing her, because he has someone else in mind to take her place. In addition, she has a life insurance. There are many other reasons why a person is not in a severe crisis but by every apparent reason should be in crisis. The perception can be ascertained through the Miller Crisis Loss Test (MCLT) (See figure 11.)

The Miller Crisis Loss Test (MCLT)

Circle the answer that most applies: YES (Y) NO (N)

1. Do you have a personal relationship with the Lord Jesus Christ?   Y   N
2. Are you presently having thoughts of killing yourself?   Y   N
3. Are you presently having thoughts of killing or harming others?   Y   N
4. Do you have a plan for killing yourself?   Y   N
5. Do you have a plan for killing or harming others?   Y   N
6. Do you see this crisis as an opportunity for growth?   Y   N
7. Can you see any light at the end of the tunnel?   Y   N
8. Do you have no hope (NH), or are you optimistic (O) that with counseling you may get help to deal with this crisis?   NH   O
9. This crisis has negatively impacted my life:
    (0 being the least, and 10 the most)   0 1 2 3 4 5 6 7 8 9 10
10. This crisis has made me feel angry.   0 1 2 3 4 5 6 7 8 9 10
11. I feel out of control.   0 1 2 3 4 5 6 7 8 9 10
12. This same or similar crisis has occurred before.
    Never   Once   2×   3×   more than 3×

Figure 11

Judith Murray, in discussing internal factors that influence loss, points out that problem-centered emotional coping in high loss-of-control situations may be less helpful than appraising the stressfulness of the situation. This concept makes the MCLT important. If the crisis is high level, Murray (2001) reminds the counselor to look for self-blame or others for the crisis, revenge, and low internal control beliefs. Shame has a lasting impact on the self-concept and can lead to suicide, while guilt does not have a lasting impact on how the person views their self-concept.

Interpretation of the Miller Crisis Loss Test (For the Counselor Only)

If all the answers are Y, NO HOPE, and NEVER, the level of perceived crisis loss is the highest (160 on a 0–160 scale). If all the answers are N and 0, OPTIMISTIC, and MORE THAN 3×, the level of critical loss is 0, the lowest on a 0–160 scale. This is based on the presupposition that in a crisis, loss is the common denominator and is universal. In a crisis, the counselee is desperately feeling the loss and impulsively seeking a substitute for the loss of safety, significance, and security. The impulsiveness can lead to acts of revenge or even suicide. The substitutes can be dangerous. This opens the door for the counselor to offer substitutes for this loss that is fitting with a Christian worldview. Depending on how interested the person is in spiritual things, those substitutes may not be intrinsically religious in nature, but much less harmful than the impulse of the client. The data that can be derived through this questionnaire determine the depth of the perception of that loss. What appears to be a debilitating crisis may not turn out to be as bad as how the counselor may initially view the situation. This gives the counselor direction in how to proceed, as well as how the person in crisis perceives the loss.

Projected Outcome of the Crisis Counseling Based on Answers in the Questionnaire

If the counselee has a personal relationship with Jesus Christ, then the outcome is highly positive functionality—scores are 0. If the counselee is suicidal and does not have a personal relationship with Jesus Christ, scoring 30 points, the outcome could be negative functionality. Functionality is getting through the crisis and living without or with maladaptive behavior. The client may repeat the suicidal ideation at another time. If the client is suicidal and homicidal, the outcome could be highly negative functionality, suggesting that even if the client is put into a residential treatment program, there is a strong possibility of repeated maladaptive behavior. If the client is not suicidal or homicidal and does not have a relationship with the Lord Jesus Christ, has no hope, and scores a 10 for negative impact on the life, a 10 for anger, and a 10 for out of control even if the crisis has a positive outcome, there could be positive functionality.

A first-time event can be more destructive than a repeated one, because the person in crisis has already had the opportunity to utilize some way of coping to get through it even if it may be by using maladaptive behavior. Positive functionality means that the counselor's skills and the client's reception to the treatment can help the client change, live a productive life, and get through the crisis, even if the person in crisis is not in a saving relationship with Jesus Christ. The goal should be to reduce the maladaptive behavior and seek substitutes that fit in with a Christian worldview, even if the client does not understand that. When the outcome is beneficial to the client, and there is still no spiritual interest, the client does not care what philosophical viewpoint there is behind it. It would be good if they were seeking the Lord, but if there is no desire, they can still be helped. The Lord Jesus still helped the nine lepers who did not thank God (see figure 12).

Evaluation of MCLT Grading Chart

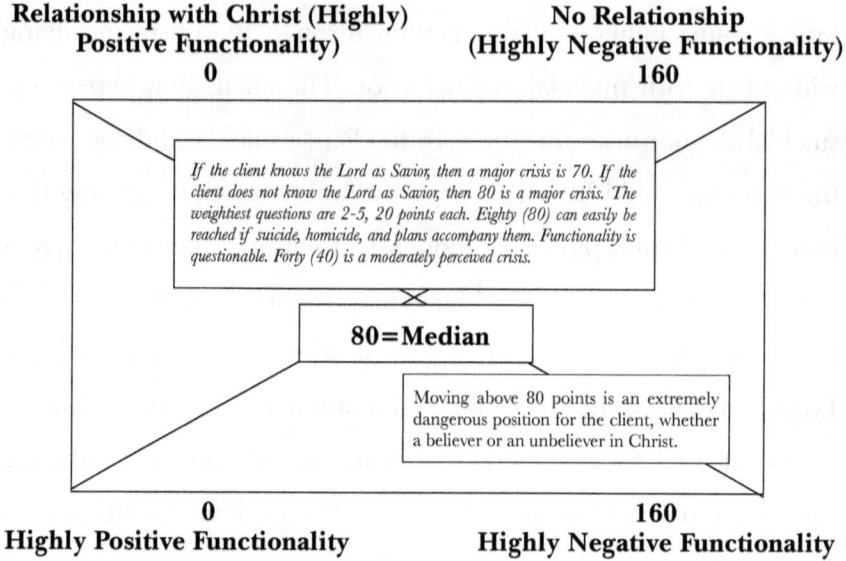

Figure 12

Point Scoring the Miller Crisis Loss Test (MCLT)

In evaluating the test, the highest score is the most serious and indicates that the crisis is perceived as bad as it could be. The median is 80, and the best is 0; worst cumulative score is 160.

1. Y=0, N=10
2. Y=20, N=0
3. Y=20, N=0
4. Y=20, N=0
5. Y=20, N=0
6. Y=0, N=10

7. Y=0, N=10

8. NH=10, O=0

9. On a 0-10 scale, the number chosen corresponds to the points.

10. The number chosen corresponds to the points.

11. The number chosen corresponds to the points.

12. Never=10, Once=8, 2×=6, 3×=4, more than 3×=0

Interpretation of the Miller Crisis Loss Test (MCLT)

In evaluating the test, the highest score is the most serious and indicates that the crisis is perceived as bad as it could be. The median is 80, the best is 0, and the worst is 160.

1. If the client has a personal relationship with the Lord Jesus Christ, the outcome is highly positive. Y=0, N=10.

2. Are you having thoughts of killing yourself? Y=20, N=0.

3. Do you have a plan? Y=20, N=0.

4. Question Three: Are you having thoughts of killing or harming others? Y=20, N=0.

5. If answer is Y, do you have a plan? Y=20, N=0.

6. Do you see this crisis as an opportunity for growth? Y=0, N=10. If the client does, it is 0 points.

7. Can you see any light at the end of the tunnel? Y=0, N=10.

8. Do you have no hope, NH= 10, optimistic, O= 0.

9. This crisis has negatively impacted my life: Points are from 0 to 10 (0=the least and 10= the worst). Say that the client circles 10, then the point score is 10.

10. This crisis has made me feel angry. Again, the choices are 0 to 10, with the points corresponding to the choice.

11. I feel out of control. The choices are 0 to 10. If the client chooses the 10, it is the most out of control, meaning 10 points; choice 9 would mean 9 points and so on.

12. The event has happened two times in the past. Often a one-time event can be more destructive than 2× (never=10 pts., Once=8 pts., 2×=6 pts., 3×=4 pts., more than 3×=0). If more than 3×, the client has worked out some defense mechanisms (dysfunctional or not) to survive in that environment, therefore 0 points are given.

If the client knows the Lord as Savior, then a major crisis is 70. If the client does not know the Lord, then the cumulative score is 80. The weight is on questions 2, 3 and 4. Suicide and homicide would shoot the score up to 160 if there was a plan; no plans 140. Functionality is questionable.

PCT is efficacious with regard to victims of rape. According to the National Violence Against Women survey, one in six women has experienced rape or has experienced an attempted rape (Carlyle and Roberto 2007). A victim of rape needs an advocate, and this is exactly what a paraklasis counselor does when the model of the Holy Spirit is followed. The rape crisis advocate is responsible to support the victim, make sure the rights are maintained, that her voice is listened to, and no further harm occurs. Reducing anxiety is the challenge of the crisis counselor. Self-efficacy and sensitivity of the counselor to cultural issues, awareness of values, and in overall communication with the victim will lower anxiety (Carlyle and Roberto 2007). Sexually abused persons often feel invalidated and full of shame, as well as unsafe, making it difficult for trust and healing to take place (Wise 2007). Traumatic events do not happen in a box but within a social and cultural context that defines the perception of an event as a crisis (Silva and Klotz 2006). According to PCT, these victims of sexual abuse suffer from the category I of secondary loss, which is, loss from another's sinful choice.

Paraklasis counseling theory can assist in lowering anxiety, because it understands the root problem, which is loss. Rape destroys the victim's three basic needs: the need for safety, the need for security, and the need for significance in category I of loss—loss from another's sinful choices. The presence and activity of a gentle, confident, crisis counselor carrying out the Holy Spirit's work of empathy and advocacy can understand where the hurt is originating while providing, through interventional skills, the support of others, prayer, and the comfort of the Scripture, a restoration of the loss with a biblical schema. A verse that applies to hope and significance is Joel 2:25. Psalm 54:4–5 is appropriate for security. Psalm 55:16–18 is appropriate for safety. Not only is PCT appropriate for rape victims in crisis, but also for the elderly.

Elderly people often find themselves involuntarily losing weight, having a susceptibility to falling, physical weakness, and general frailty. This combination of factors can reach a crisis state, a panic at the closing of the gate, as they are unable to project themselves into the future and only see their impending death (Fillet and Butler 2009). Frailty identity crisis can lead to depression and even suicide.

Paraklasis counseling theory views this as a loss of safety, significance, security for the present as well as the future. It has been generally recognized that elderly people usually respond well to counseling. This is probably because during counseling, they become significant, at least in the eyes of the counselor. When there is recognition of frailty by caregivers, there is usually an accompanying acceptance and adaptable dependency rather than depression.

PCT can help the frail counselee who is a believer to project into the future of heaven. When an older person has reached acceptance, they take on an active putting-the-house-in-order attitude. Emphasizing the significance of the person to family and having life experience that is useful to others is one intervention (Proverbs 16:31). It is good to point out that our safety and security is in God, and that He regards us as important and will protect us as the pupil of His eye (Psalm 17:8). We do not have to fear dying, because that day is appointed by God and we will be watched over to get there (Hebrews 9:27).

Fillit and Butler (2009) make recommendations for care management, and aside from responsible dependency, the pleasure of reminiscence, and learning to accept one's coming death, there was no sign of hope for the future. It was just adapting to the present. This is where a biblical theory of counseling for spiritually receptive elderly people can prevent a frailty crisis, as significance, security, and safety are focused upon from a scriptural perspective.

Crisis counseling is psychological first aid. A list of eight core psychological first-aid actions are listed in Sandoval, Scott, and

Padilla (2009): making contact, providing safety, stabilizing effects, addressing needs and concerns, providing practical assistance, facilitating connections with social supports, facilitating coping, and creating linkages with needed collaborative services. Sandoval, Scott, and Padilla (2009) credit this as originally listed by the National Child Traumatic Stress Network and National Center for Posttraumatic Stress Disorder (PTSD) (2006).

Paraklasis counseling theory is in full agreement with these actions. Considering that any therapy for children is normally fine-tuned and sensitively worked out, this should apply as an overview of crisis counseling to include adults as well. Sapp (2006) argues that adolescents need to be counseled with an emphasis on identifying their cultural and individual strengths, rather than their deficits. The advantage that PCT possesses is that it encourages the potential of growth and also connects loss in life to the spiritual foundational components, so that emotional healing may take place.

Self-mutilation is a pathological behavior that is truly a crisis. The triggers can be varied, but impulsive behaviors during a crisis are typical of people who perceive a crisis. Whatever is the trigger for this kind of behavior, when someone hurts himself or herself, he or she perceives a crisis. Ross and McKay (1979, 43–75, pp. 43–75), lists explanations of this behavior: ritual and symbolism, psychobiological determinants, sex, archaic biological reflexes, death wish, regression, existential statement, plea for help, manipulation, risk-taking, attention-seeking, iatrogenic, retaliation, frustration, coercion/contagion/conformity, depression, tension relief, escape, drug related, deprivation, response to the body, conditioning, and self-esteem. The authors call it a "mind-boggling array of explanations." They say that there is a "distinct lack of coherent theory" (p.75), and no attempt to integrate the explanations. What is interesting is the authors' comment that they do have one thing in common.

What is common to all of the explanations is "deficiency" (p.75). The creators of the explanations indicate that they come from hereditary malfunction or psychopathology. Another word for "deficiency" is the word "loss." The authors have pointed out that no matter what explanation is offered, how true it is, or how not empirically supported it is, the bottom line is that the behavior is coming from loss. Knowing how powerful loss is in creating many varied responses, as has been already explained, it appears that a satisfactory explanation is that no matter what the trigger, as is pointed out in the various explanations, the loss has put the client on a trajectory where the loss of significance, safety, and/or security creates a cutting, carving substitute. The loss may be categorized and treatment narrowed down to finding a less harmful substitute, and dealing with that loss is a way that supports hope and healing.

Approximately 23 percent of professional counselors have had individuals who have committed suicide and describe it as the most deeply disturbing experience in their professional careers (Granello 2010). Therefore, a crisis counselor needs to work on self before counseling a suicidal person. Specific factors that resulted in clients who committed suicide while under a counselor's care were the counselor's inability to cope with the release of strong emotions, a toleration of client dependency, the counselor assuming that suicide was inevitable, and a failure to confront the suicidal decision.

It is absolutely imperative that in a crisis, the counselor quickly makes a working connection to the counselee, because it has been established that a positive, therapeutic relationship and the counselee's expression of feelings prevents people from committing suicide. The most significant cluster of factors for ending suicidal ideation was when the counselor dealt with helplessness and despair. This involved dealing with suicidal thoughts and feelings, working through pain, connecting feelings to experiences, acknowledging feelings, resolving feelings of helplessness, and resolving feelings of despair.

Emotions serve two purposes: motivation and giving meaning-making function to a person's information processing. The crisis counselor can assist the counselee in perceiving significance to their life by helping the client confront painful, negative experiences and feel personal validation as they challenge self-destructive behaviors. If the counselee does not feel acknowledgement of these powerful and overwhelming feelings, they cannot move beyond them. Suicidal people have a rigid, negative view of self that an emotionally connected supporting crisis counselor can break through (Paulson and Worth 2002). (See figure 13.)

Crisis Counselor Checklist

Evaluation:
1. Discover the triggering event.
2. Evaluate the category of loss (I-VIII) and the three S's
3. Evaluate family/friends and determine if the client needs to be separated from them during the crisis counseling.
4. Check for distorted thinking.
5. Discern observers and counselee's agreement or nonagreement of the perception of the event/Miller Crisis Loss Test.
6. Look for maladaptive behavior.
7. Look for suicidal/homicidal ideation.
8. Evaluate religious orientation.
9. Determine coping resources and family resiliency.
10. Consider risk vs. protective factors.

Treatment:
1. Lower emotional tension and stress by prayer.
2. Introduce structure.
3. Give hope; suicide contract if necessary or seek immediate help.
4. Reframe for safety, security, and significance into biblical perspective.
5. Prioritize goals with the counselee to deal with the crisis.
6. Enable counselee to recognize the crisis trigger.
7. Help counselee to know what to do in the future to prevent a similar crisis.
8. Establish support through collaborative services.
9. Set up follow-up counseling.

Figure 13

Confronting a suicidal decision is the counselor's responsibility. Being sensitive and a good listener, the paraklasis counselor will recognize the rigid, negative view of self by acknowledging the depth of the feelings, and then attempt to replace the loss of significance, security, or safety with true biblical significance in a warm therapeutic environment. If there is a spiritual willingness, then a biblical reframing of the trigger event can proceed. If there is no interest in spiritual things, then the three S's must be found in something else.

PCT is broadly applicable to most crisis situations. It can reach the objective of changing people through Jesus Christ by attainable goals, which include replacing the maladaptive substitutes for safety, security, and significance for these three basic needs of man to be found in God alone. Primary loss can be met in receiving God's invitation through the Gospel for restoration of relationship with Him. Secondary loss in whatever category can be restored to true safety, security, and significance found in the Scripture by replacing poor substitutes.

Demonstration of Effectiveness of PCT and Crisis Counseling

Consider what happened to a policeman who was injured at the World Trade Center on 9-11. Six weeks in an induced coma to undergo twenty-seven surgeries followed by two years of rehabilitation brought John McLaughlan—one of two Port of Authority police officers who were rescued out of the rubble of the World Trade Center—to the place where he needed counseling for posttraumatic stress disorder (PTSD). The disillusionment phase of overcoming his psychological and physical consequences left him facing the difficulties of rebuilding his shattered life. The reconstruction phase has been ongoing through his two years of rehabilitation, bringing him to counseling due to intrusive thoughts and images, distressing dreams, reliving the trauma, and difficulty sleeping (Kanel 2007).

Prior to the terrorist attack on the World Trade Center, John was looking forward to retirement after twenty-one years on the force. He acknowledged that he had been very careful all of those years in a very dangerous job. He had been on the job in the 1993 bombing of the parking garage under the Twin Towers and was said to have known the buildings better than anyone else, causing him to be the officer called upon to lead the rescue team.

As a first responder, he entered the building with the intention of saving lives but instead became a victim needing to be rescued. Upon entering the building, he was suddenly confronted with the possibility that he might be approaching his own death in the process. Fear was written all over his face as he heard the sounds of bodies falling to the ground—but in an instant, his fears became a reality as he and the other officers were buried under tons of concrete and metal. John tried to save his team by shouting an order to run to the elevator shaft. The entire building collapsed around them, and only John and two others were still alive, although they were severely injured. One of the men described their plight: "It is like being alive in hell." There was fire, smoke, and pain, and the overall similarity was to *Dante's Inferno*. One police officer, having been crushed and pinned by tons of concrete, drew his revolver and shot himself, to the pain of the other two policemen who begged him not to take his life.

The horror of John's injuries and fear of dying may have been relieved after he was rescued, but the traumatic event was continually present. Persistent symptoms that were not present before the trauma robbed him of restful sleep, and recurrent nightmares and disability due to serious injuries contributed to difficulty in other areas of functioning (Kanel 2007).

In an attempt to solve his problem without counseling, he refused going into buildings other than his own home, manifested avoidance by refusing to talk about the trauma, and remained in denial when confronted with how he felt. He stayed in a chronic state of stress as he relived the horror over and over, whether sleeping or awake. Physical rehabilitation efforts were his only solution, assuming that as his body grew stronger, it would all go away. He thought that retirement would help, but instead it was only another form of avoidance that brought no relief. The strains on his marriage made it difficult for him to function effectively as a husband and as a father of four children. He consistently withdrew from pleasurable activities of the family under the pretense that he was just not feeling very well physically—but, in reality, he was depressed.

His perception of the crisis was tainted with survivor and leader's guilt, because he felt responsible for the well-being of his team, and he failed them. Even in his relationship with his wife, he felt that he had let her down, because, all these years, he had been careful, and now he screwed up. The pictures that were etched in his mind kept reinforcing this faulty perception of his responsibility for the deaths of his team members and haunted his thoughts both awake and asleep. Increased episodes of intense emotions that fluctuated from tears to anger were dismissed as something he would almost welcome, because it helped him remember he was alive. He thought of the other survivor who reminded him to "see pain as a friend, because it means that you are alive."

The following scenario is presented as a demonstration of the effectiveness of PCT in crisis counseling. The DSM Code 309.81, posttraumatic stress disorder (PTSD), is considered appropriate in diagnosing this client due to his exposure to such an extreme traumatic event that involved serious injury and possible death to him and those close to him (Criterion A1). The sense of helplessness (Criterion A2), the reexperiencing of the event in recurrent thoughts and dreams (Criterion B), and the increased arousal (Criterion D) continued for two years, leading to his difficulty to function in many areas of his social life, as well as his occupational pursuits (Criterion F). This client is having recurrent and intrusive images of the event (Criterion B1) and nightmares (Criterion B2), and his normal functioning is impaired by flashbacks that bring distress and arousal that are heightened at each reminder of the traumatic event, creating intense psychological distress (Criterion B4). The criteria for PTSD (309.81) have been met for this diagnosis as evidenced by his exposure to a traumatic event in which actual and threatened death to self and others, as well as intense fear and helplessness, are being experienced. He is reexperiencing the event through images, dreams, and thoughts, creating intense psychological distress.

Further criteria have been noted: his avoidance of reminders of the trauma, avoidance of places and people who are associated with the event, and his diminished interest in former activities. Presenting problems that were not present prior to the trauma are difficulty in sleeping, hypervigilance, and an exaggerated startle response. The client's symptoms have continued for two years and have greatly interfered with his ability to maintain social connections, as well as other important areas of functioning (Kanel 2007; American Psychiatric Association [DSM-IV-TR] 2000).

The client needs to have the crisis alleviated and be taught coping skills through the application of biblical principles related to PTSD. John expressed the fact that he feels guilty for surviving when so many of his team members perished. After actively listening to his story, empathizing with him, and respecting his need to grieve, he should be encouraged to elaborate on his feelings of guilt and given support and validation about the intensity of this traumatic event. As he further elaborated on his guilty feelings, he stated that "God must have a reason." This opened the door for him to explain and explore the spiritual side of his life. God's Word supports what the client just stated and creates a natural opening for bringing spiritual comfort through Psalm 91:7: "A thousand shall fall at thy side, and ten thousand at thy right hand; but it shall not come nigh thee." The client may raise the question as to why God spared him. Comfort can be given through Psalm 91:15–16: "He shall call upon me and I will answer him: I will be with him in trouble; I will deliver him, and honor him. With long life will I satisfy him, and show him my salvation." Obviously, the PCT counselor is not just going to parrot words without explanation that is contextually and systematically demonstrated in the whole of the Scripture, but the verses are starting points.

John explained that during the trauma, he called on God and found himself repeating the Lord's Prayer, and then he was saved. In our simulation of the counseling session, he wanted someone to show him how to feel safe and secure, and to explain how he could turn his life around to live for God, because he could not change anything. The counselor explained the Gospel message, and, at his request, he prayed and sought forgiveness and asked Jesus Christ to be his Savior and Lord. The counselor then prayed for the healing of his mind and asked that God exercise His power and set him free from the bondage he was experiencing. God reaches the heart when the counselor can only dabble with it.

As this virtual counseling session continues, cognitive behavioral techniques are introduced to help him with future anxiety by deep breathing techniques. A rubber band is given for him to wear on his wrist, with instructions to snap it at the first sign of reexperiencing the event, and is encouraged to thank God for his deliverance to fulfill his purpose on the earth to his wife and his children. A homework assignment is given so he can write down specific things that he can do to be a better husband and to value his wife. The following week, the homework assignment for him is to write down what specific things he can do to be a better father. His responses will be discussed at future sessions, and plans to carry out new thought patterns are explored. The emphasis here is to give John a sense of significance that he lost in the tragedy. John had suffered category I loss, which is loss by another's sinful choice. That sinful choice was from the terrorists who flew that plane into the Twin Towers.

Working on John's safety, security, and significance that he lost in the 9-11 attack and determining what category of loss he suffered from, coupled with recognizing the triggers of PTSD and teaching coping strategies supported by prayer and Bible education to help him reframe his thoughts, would be a PCT counselor's general clinical strategy.

Chapter Nine

Biblical Sources for Safety, Security, and Significance

Safety, security, and significance are the three major aspects of life that loss deteriorates. The Scripture reveals human nature in and out of relationship with God. The counselor may find it helpful to have some of these verses at hand to use as appropriate in the context of counseling. Christian counseling is far more than looking for proof texts to support good behavior or a symptom. Often it is wrongly used as a club to point out the error of a person's ways. The counselor can never be the Holy Spirit. Rather, the counselor should bring out judgment unto truth in such a way that the person is encouraged and built up, not harmed. Isaiah 42:3 says, "A bruised reed shall he not break, and the smoking flax shall he not quench: he shall bring forth judgment unto truth." Notice that God does not club the person into submission. When He brings about judgment, it is always truth that comes out, blowing the winds of God's breath upon faith that is about to be extinguished by the suffocating trials of life. A bruised reed is bent and can fall off at the slightest pressure. People who are emotionally hurting are fragile. They can easily be pushed beyond repair by judgment from a harsh counselor. Truth in the mouth of the Holy Spirit heals, comforts, and looks at the situation with truth, accuracy, insight, and in teamwork with the counselor to strengthen, not destroy. *Strong's Concordance* numbers were left to make word references and meanings easier for anyone with the inclination to look them up.

Safety

For the OT Israelite, God's promise of safety was primarily from the enemies of Israel—from Egyptians to the Canaanites and the Amalekites. The importance of the depth of safety in relation to the human soul will be seen as one reflects upon these verses. So, not only is physical safety involved, but spiritual and emotional safety as well.

(Leviticus 25:18–19) Wherefore ye shall doH6213 (H853) my statutesH2708, and keepH8104 my judgmentsH4941, and doH6213 them; and ye shall dwellH3427 inH5921 the landH776 in safetyH983. And the landH776 shall yieldH5414 her fruitH6529, and ye shall eatH398 your fillH7648, and dwellH3427 thereinH5921 in safetyH983.

(Deuteronomy 12:10) But when ye go overH5674 (H853) JordanH3383, and dwellH3427 in the landH776 whichH834 the LORDH3068 your GodH430 giveth you to inheritH5157 (H853), and when he giveth you restH5117 from allH4480 H3605 your enemiesH341 round aboutH4480 H5439, so that ye dwellH3427 in safetyH983.

(Deuteronomy 33:12) And of BenjaminH1144 he saidH559, The belovedH3039 of the LORDH3068 shall dwellH7931 in safetyH983 byH5921 him; and the LORD shall coverH2653 H5921 him allH3605 the dayH3117 long, and he shall dwellH7931 betweenH996 his shouldersH3802.

(Deuteronomy 33:28) IsraelH3478 then shall dwellH7931 in safetyH983 aloneH910: the fountainH5869 of JacobH3290 shall be uponH413 a landH776 of cornH1715 and wineH8492; alsoH637 his heavensH8064 shall drop downH6201 dewH2919.

(Job 3:26) I was notH3808 in safetyH7951, neitherH3808 had I restH8252, neitherH3808 was I quietH5117; yet troubleH7267 cameH935.

(Job 5:4) His childrenH1121 are farH7368 from safetyH4480 H3468, and they are crushedH1792 in the gateH8179, neitherH369 is there any to deliverH5337 them.

(Job 5:11) To set upH7760 on highH4791 those that be lowH8217; that those which mournH6937 may be exaltedH7682 to safetyH3468.

(Job 11:18) And thou shalt be secureH982, becauseH3588 thereH3426 is hopeH8615; yea, thou shalt digH2658 about thee, and thou shalt take thy restH7901 in safetyH983.

(Job 24:23) Though it be givenH5414 him to be in safetyH983, whereon he restethH8172; yet his eyesH5869 are uponH5921 their waysH1870.

(Psalm 4:8) I will bothH3162 lay me downH7901 in peaceH7965, and sleepH3462: forH3588 thouH859, LORDH3068, onlyH910 makest me dwellH3427 in safetyH983.

(Psalm 12:5) For the oppressionH4480 H7701 of the poorH6041, for the sighingH4480 H603 of the needyH34, nowH6258 will I ariseH6965, saithH559 the LORDH3068; I will setH7896 him in safetyH3468 from him that puffethH6315 at him.

(Psalm 33:17) An horseH5483 is a vain thingH8267 for safetyH8668: neitherH3808 shall he deliverH4422 any by his greatH7230 strengthH2428.

(Proverbs 11:14) Where noH369 counselH8458 is, the peopleH5971 fallH5307: but in the multitudeH7230 of counsellorsH3289 there is safetyH8668.

(Proverbs 21:31) The horseH5483 is preparedH3559 against the dayH3117 of battleH4421: but safetyH8668 is of the LORDH3068.

(Proverbs 24:6) ForH3588 by wise counselH8458 thou shalt makeH6213 thy warH4421: and in multitudeH7230 of counsellorsH3289 there is safetyH8668.

(Isaiah 14:30) And the firstbornH1060 of the poorH1800 shall feedH7462, and the needyH34 shall lie downH7257 in safetyH983: and I will killH4191 thy rootH8328 with famineH7458, and he shall slayH2026 thy remnantH7611.

(Act 5:23) SayingG3004, TheG3588 prisonG1201 trulyG3303 foundG2147 we shutG2808 withG1722 allG3956 safetyG803, andG2532 theG3588 keepersG5441 standingG2476 withoutG1854 beforeG4253 theG3588 doorsG2374: butG1161 when we had openedG455, we foundG2147 no manG3762 withinG2080.

(1 Thessalonians 5:3) ForG1063 whenG3752 they shall sayG3004, PeaceG1515 andG2532 safetyG803; thenG5119 suddenG160 destructionG3639 cometh uponG2186 themG846, asG5618 travailG5604 upon a woman with childG2192 G1722 G1064; andG2532 they shall notG3364 escapeG1628.

Security

The scriptural context for the idea of security includes much that is relevant for the PCT counselor. All of the phobias are fears. Fear produces anxiety and depression. Man's shelter and preservation does not come from the limited security of the things of this world, but in the attributes, character, and transcendent promises of God. He even gives security to the person appointed to die, perhaps even those on death row. The loss of safety, as we have seen, and the loss of security can be devastating in a client's life.

(Psalm 61:3) For thou hast been a shelter for me, and a strong tower from the enemy.

"For thou hast been a shelter for me." Observe how the Psalmist rings the changes on "Thou hast," and "I will" (Psalm 61:3, Psalm 61:4, Psalm 61:5, and Psalm 61:6).

Experience is the nurse of faith. From the past, we gather arguments for present confidence. Many and many a time had been the persecutions of Saul, and the perils of battle put David's life in danger. He escaped only by a miracle, yet he was still alive and unhurt. This he remembers, and he is full of hope. "And a strong tower from the enemy," as in a fort impregnable, David had dwelt, because he was surrounded by omnipotence. It is sweet beyond expression to remember the loving kindness of the Lord in our former days, for he is unchangeable and therefore will continue to guard us from all evil.

(Genesis 19:32) ComeH1980, let us make(H853) our fatherH1 drinkH8248 wineH3196, and we will lieH7901 withH5973 him, that we may preserveH2421 seedH2233 of our fatherH4480 H1.

(Genesis 19:34) And it came to passH1961 on the morrowH4480 H4283, that the firstbornH1067 saidH559 untoH413 the youngerH6810, BeholdH2005, I layH7901 yesternightH570 withH854 my fatherH1: let us make him drinkH8248 wineH3196 this nightH3915 alsoH1571; and go thou inH935, and lieH7901 withH5973 him, that we may preserveH2421 seedH2233 of our fatherH4480 H1.

Here is an example of category I loss, suffering loss from the sinful choices of another. In addition we see the daughters of Lot choosing a sinful substitute in their father, when they lost their husbands. They were also suffering from the loss of a loved one, category VI. They chose a false substitute for trusting in God, and would therefore suffer from category II loss, the loss from one's own sinful choice. All of these categories of loss would be wrapped up in the loss of significance, security and safety. They were in incredible emotional pain.

(Genesis 45:5) NowH6258 therefore be notH408 grievedH6087, norH408 angryH2734 with yourselvesH5869, thatH3588 ye soldH4376 me hitherH2008: forH3588 GodH430 did sendH7971 me beforeH6440 you to preserve lifeH4241.

(Genesis 45:7) And GodH430 sentH7971 me beforeH6440 you to preserveH7760 you a posterityH7611 in the earthH776, and to save your livesH2421 by a greatH1419 deliveranceH6413.

(Deuteronomy 6:24) And the LORDH3068 commandedH6680 us to doH6213 (H853) allH3605 theseH428 statutesH2706, to fearH3372 the(H853) LORDH3068 our GodH430, for our goodH2896 alwaysH3605 H3117, that he might preserve us aliveH2421, as it is at thisH2088 dayH3117.

(Psalm 12:7) ThouH859 shalt keepH8104 them, O LORDH3068, thou shalt preserveH5341 them fromH4480 thisH2098 generationH1755 foreverH5769.

(Psalm 16:1) MichtamH4387 of DavidH1732. PreserveH8104 me, O GodH410: forH3588 in thee do I put my trustH2620.

(Psalm 25:21) Let integrityH8537 and uprightnessH3476 preserveH5341 me; forH3588 I wait onH6960 thee.

(Psalm 32:7) ThouH859 art my hiding placeH5643; thou shalt preserveH5341 me from troubleH4480 H6862; thou shalt compass me aboutH5437 with songsH7438 of deliveranceH6405. SelahH5542.

(Psalm 40:11) WithholdH3607 notH3808 thouH859 thy tender merciesH7356 fromH4480 me, O LORDH3068: let thy lovingkindnessH2617 and thy truthH571 continuallyH8548 preserveH5341 me.

(Psalm 41:2) The LORDH3068 will preserveH8104 him, and keep him aliveH2421; and he shall be blessedH833 upon the earthH776: and thou wilt notH408 deliverH5414 him unto the willH5315 of his enemiesH341.

(Psalm 61:7) He shall abideH3427 beforeH6440 GodH430 for everH5769: O prepareH4487 mercyH2617 and truthH571, which may preserveH5341 him.

(Psalm 64:1) To the chief MusicianH5329, A PsalmH4210 of DavidH1732. HearH8085 my voiceH6963, O GodH430, in my prayerH7879: preserveH5341 my lifeH2416 from fearH4480 H6343 of the enemyH341.

(Psalm 79:11) Let the sighingH603 of the prisonerH615 comeH935 beforeH6440 thee; according to the greatnessH1433 of thy powerH2220 preserveH3498 thou those that are appointedH1121 to dieH8546.

(Psalm 86:2) PreserveH8104 my soulH5315; forH3588 IH589 am holyH2623: O thouH859 my GodH430, saveH3467 thy servantH5650 that trustethH982 in theeH413.

(Psalm 121:7) The LORDH3068 shall preserveH8104 thee from allH4480 H3605 evilH7451: he shall preserveH8104 (H853) thy soulH5315.

(Psalm 121:8) The LORDH3068 shall preserveH8104 thy going outH3318 and thy coming inH935 from this time forthH4480 H6258, and even for evermoreH5704 H5769.

(Psalm 140:1) To the chief MusicianH5329, A PsalmH4210 of DavidH1732. DeliverH2502 me, O LORDH3068, from the evilH7451 manH4480 H120: preserveH5341 me from the violentH2555 manH4480 H376.

(Psalm 140:4) KeepH8104 me, O LORDH3068, from the handsH4480 H3027 of the wickedH7563; preserveH5341 me from the violent manH4480 H376 H2555; whoH834 have purposedH2803 to overthrowH1760 my goingsH6471.

(Proverbs 2:11) DiscretionH4209 shall preserveH8104 H5921 thee, understandingH8394 shall keepH5341 thee.

(Proverbs 4:6) ForsakeH5800 her notH408, and she shall preserveH8104 thee: loveH157 her, and she shall keepH5341 thee.

(Proverbs 14:3) In the mouthH6310 of the foolishH191 is a rodH2415 of prideH1346: but the lipsH8193 of the wiseH2450 shall preserveH8104 them.

(Proverbs 20:28) MercyH2617 and truthH571 preserveH5341 the kingH4428: and his throneH3678 is upholdenH5582 by mercyH2617.

(Proverbs 22:12) The eyesH5869 of the LORDH3068 preserveH5341 knowledgeH1847, and he overthrowethH5557 the wordsH1697 of the transgressorH898.

(Isaiah 31:5) As birdsH6833 flyingH5774, soH3651 will the LORDH3068 of hostsH6635 defendH1598 H5921 JerusalemH3389; defendingH1598 also he will deliverH5337 it; and passing overH6452 he will preserveH4422 it.

(Isaiah 49:8) ThusH3541 saithH559 the LORDH3068, In an acceptableH7522 timeH6256 have I heardH6030 thee, and in a dayH3117 of salvationH3444 have I helpedH5826 thee: and I will preserveH5341 thee, and giveH5414 thee for a covenantH1285 of the peopleH5971, to establishH6965 the earthH776, to cause to inheritH5157 the desolateH8074 heritagesH5159.

(Jeremiah 49:11) LeaveH5800 thy fatherless childrenH3490, IH589 will preserve them aliveH2421; and let thy widowsH490 trustH982 inH5921 me.

(Luke 17:33) WhosoeverG3739 G1437 shall seekG2212 to saveG4982 hisG848 lifeG5590 shall loseG622 itG846; andG2532 whosoeverG3739 G1437 shall loseG622 hisG848 life shall preserveG2225 itG846.

(2 Timothy 4:18) AndG2532 theG3588 LordG2962 shall deliverG4506 meG3165 fromG575 everyG3956 evilG4190 workG2041, andG2532 will preserveG4982 me untoG1519 hisG848 heavenlyG2032 kingdomG932: to whomG3739 be gloryG1391 for ever and everG1519 G165 G165. AmenG281.

Significance

The notion of self-esteem, as used in psychological terminology, is really a misnomer. Self-esteem has to do with self-importance and can be a very self-centered concept. Significance differs from self-esteem. Significance, in biblical context, comes from the work of the Holy Spirit within and the work of the Trinity from without. The significant person is the one who has knowledge of his earthly status or role as the apostle but approaches others as an infant among them. Significance comes from being adopted (Romans 8:15) into the royal family of God, as well as the comfort that comes from the new birth and the filling of the Holy Spirit. In the book of Philippians, the apostle Paul shows the heart of true significance, as it does not come from pharisaical success but from his significance in relationship to Jesus Christ, which gives him confidence in the present and a sure hope for the future. Even though the word "significance" itself is used sparsely in the Scripture, the concept is clearly there. It is very much like the word "trinity," which is not found in the Bible at all. But the word "godhead" is there, as well as a clear description of who God is in His ontology.

God has significance. Man, who was made in His image, should have significance. In Genesis 22:16, God swears by Himself. This is a healthy self-image. The word "myself" is revealing. David shows personal significance, demonstrated in withholding the emotions of revenge and trusting God in 1 Samuel 25:23. Job, in spite his troubles, still showed healthy significance, and that significance was expressed by the fact that God was his hope and strength (Job 6:10–11). A biblical significance is found in the person who delights in himself or herself; comforts himself or herself; quiets himself or herself as a weaned child in God, His Word, and His judgments; gives himself or herself unto prayer; and behaves wisely. He or she is the person who keeps himself from iniquity (Psalms 18:23; 101:2; 109:4; 119:16, 47, 52; 131:131:2). It is not pride, but an awareness of self-identity in relationship to God, which governs relationships with man. A healthy significance keeps one from pride and is more related to humility. Again, significance comes from God. The Lord Jesus is our example (John 8:54). He is not concerned with honoring

Himself, but finds His significance from God. True significance places all of life under God's ownership (Acts 20:24) as the Apostle Paul puts his coming death in its proper place—under the call of his life. A healthy significance is also expressed in a conscious desire to avoid offence to God and man (Acts 24:16). To possess a biblical sense of significance is to reflect in life the servant heart that we see in Jesus and shown by the apostle Paul (1 Corinthians 9:19). Healthy significance is not arrogant, nor does it grab hold of the idea that one is perfect here in this world. But it focuses on forgetting all the good things he or she did for Christ in the past, not being satisfied or trusting in them. Significance is not selfish nor focused on self. For example, in marriage counseling, a spouse might say, "After all the good things I have done for him, he did this to me?" Paul keeps his hand on the plow, looking forward—like a runner—to the finish line. Significance involves looking forward with hope for the future (Philippians 3:13–14). The above descriptions of a true biblical significance show that it is not just inward, but it has practical purposes in serving God as love is expressed to our neighbor.

(1 Thessalonians 2:7) Although we could have insisted on our own importance) as apostles of Christ, yet we became infants in your midst, like a nursing mother cherishes her own children.

We do not have to strive for our significance in life. Rather, to reframe it biblically, let God raise us up and be gentle, not allowing an angry defensiveness be our attitude; be a servant instead.

(1 Corinthians 14:10–11) "There are, it may be, so many kinds of voices in the world, and none of them is without signification.

Therefore if I know not the meaning of the voice, I shall be unto him that speaketh, a barbarian, and he that speaketh shall be a barbarian unto me."

The word for importance or the idea of significance is from the Greek word *dunamis,* or "power." It is the same word for the power that raised Jesus from the dead. A lack of significance is meaninglessness or being voiceless. No one will listen to you. Significance means having meaning in life, being important enough that you are listened to.

Chapter Ten

Secondary Loss as Illustrated in the Book of Genesis

Genesis is the book of beginnings. It is the beginning of all created reality: all galaxies, planets, stars, and the structure of the heavens; on earth, all biological life, the geological world, and most importantly, for our interests, the creation of man. Genesis makes it plain that man did not stumble on aeon after aeon in an evolutionary progression upwards, until he reached the status of modern Homo sapiens. On a molecular level, and in every other way, natural selection did not result in modern man. In fact, natural selection, and even the law of gravity itself, cannot be counted on to exist one more day, let alone millions of years in a chance universe.

The Genesis story tells us that God created man in His own image, after His likeness, and, as a result, we have a human being made with an intelligent design, a plan, from the molecular level on up. This is an extremely important fact that undergirds Christian counseling, for it gives man a natural value that supersedes any debilitating upbringing. Genesis also describes a cataclysmic fall of all God-made reality into the effects of sin. Especially significant is the effects of Adam's sin on all of his posterity.

The first fact of importance is the creation of man into God's image, and the second most important fact is the fall of the entire human race into Adam's sin. These Genesis-given presuppositions tell the counselor that man, as descended from Adam without God's supernatural intervention, has a natural tendency to hate God and his neighbor. These tell the Christian counselor volumes about the client. These presuppositions offer hope and explain dysfunctional human thinking and behavior. They give the counselor a starting point.

Genesis also offers the prospect of God's intervention in the client's presenting problems. Genesis 3:15 looks into the future of the history of redemption by pointing to the coming of the Son of God who was pierced by Satan upon the cross, but gave Satan a mortal blow as indicated by the words, "bruised his head." Those who look back to the cross in faith have the promise of deliverance from sin and Satan, and receiving the gift of a blessed life here and on forever into eternity.

Paraklasis counseling theory holds to the idea that all mankind suffers from primary loss that came with the fall of man, described in Genesis 3. This was a loss of relationship, of security, safety, and significance with the Creator God. As a result, all of Adam's progeny suffer in the same way, producing a desire for complete autonomy from God and a tendency to hate God and others. This is called original sin in theological terminology. There is also a spiritual bondage to

Satan. As far as man's personality and behavior go, this has completely affected his motivation, unhealthy thinking, and actions.

The loss of safety, security, and significance has been attempted to be replaced by the things of this world without the ability to have a right relationship with God. That only happens when God intervenes with redemption through Christ. The replacements for God will fail.

Secondary loss is the prime mover for all of the behavior and thinking that is done in order to be a substitute for the safety, security, and significance that should be found in God but is no longer. The book of Genesis is a continuous narrative of the stories of men and women who have suffered and dealt with secondary loss. Primary loss is not referred to in this study since the entire Bible deals with that in terms of God's plan of redemption.

The examples show that loss is universal. People suffer from it, not just in terms of grieving for loved ones who die, but it is at the heart of all of man's emotional and behavioral issues and problems. This is a problem for man today, even as it was in the days of the beginning of the human race, and is demonstrated in the lives of the prominent people found in the Bible.

(Genesis 4:2–7) When God accepted Abel's offering and rejected Cain's offering, a simmering rage led to an encounter with God, a rejection of God's suggestions, and a fatal outbreak of emotion that was the first murder in recorded history. God stepped in and tried to reason with him, but Cain would have none of it. Cain terminated the counseling, and God did not refer him to anyone, except the devil. The problem can be traced back to loss. Cain lost prestige, or significance, when his younger brother was accepted and he was rejected. This was category VII, loss caused by the actions of another. In this case, Cain's perception of God's acceptance of Abel's sacrifice meant that Abel's offering is different. The loss he experienced led to overwhelming jealousy, which then resulted in the killing of his brother Abel.

Cain was not a victim of a racist society, nor a victim of an abusive upbringing. It was not the fault of the primary caregiver. He did not make a mistake. He expressed his authentic self. He was fully responsible for his actions. The root of Cain's problem is loss, and the sinful choices he made after that recognition came to his conscious mind. The principle for counseling is that loss must be taken seriously, because it can lead to violence. In this case, loss of significance led to jealousy and, eventually, to fatal aggression.

(Genesis 9:11–17) After the flood of Noah's time, his family and their children were probably worried that the same state of affairs that led to the first flood would lead to a second horrible deluge. This could be looked at as a fear of the loss of life. God steps in and intervenes by giving comfort with the appearance of the rainbow, signifying that safety and security could be found, at least in this case, in His promise never to destroy the world again by a flood. The principle found here is that God is concerned about the fear of the loss of life and is willing to bring comfort, even to those who reject Him and His sign.

Counselors should realize that comfort is one way of dealing with perceived loss. As God comforts the unbeliever, so should Christian counselors, even if people reject the Gospel. The fear of loss would fall under category VII, loss caused by the actions of another. In this case, anxiety was caused by the possibility that God might send another flood. This fear of loss was, of course, ameliorated by the rainbow promise.

(Genesis 12:12) A famine provoked Abraham and his entourage to move his flocks and herds into Egypt. He and his wife agreed to say that she was his sister, so that no one would kill him. After Pharaoh began to desire for her, Abraham lied to him. God plagued Pharaoh's house, and Pharaoh realized she was really Abraham's wife. So, Abraham is summarily sent out of Egypt. This was a case of perceived loss. Abraham was afraid of losing his life. The perceived loss caused him to act out of character. The principle here is that perceived loss can cause people to act in such a way that they would not normally act. It can lead to unhealthy thinking, resulting in wrong actions. The counselor needs to take the time to explore what perceptions and fears a client has about loss. In Abraham's case, it was a loss of safety, which would be, again, category VII, loss caused by the actions of another.

(Genesis 16:10–6) Sarai was barren, and she sought to have a child through her handmaid Hagar, whom she gave to Abraham. Hagar despised her, and she responded by treating Hagar harshly. Superficially, a counselor would recommend anger management or focus on the actions toward Hagar. The real root of the problem in her relationship with Hagar is how she regards her barrenness. This was the loss at the bottom of all the turmoil. This was a loss of significance as a woman. It was also a loss of security on how she perceived herself in the eyes of her husband. She needed to come to terms with that, and it would have helped her to give a better response to a mean woman. The point is that loss comes in a myriad of disguises, but the astute counselor can root it out.

Several categories of loss exist here. It was her idea for her husband to get her a child through Hagar to begin with, which is category II, loss caused by your own sinful choice. It is also category I, loss caused by another's sinful choice, Abraham and Hagar. It also involves category IV voluntary loss for secondary gain. Sarai sought to obtain God's promise of a son by her own shrewd efforts. If Sarai were a client, her loss of significance and security would be caused from three categories of loss. This gives the counselor a point of embarkation in counseling her.

(Genesis 19:26) The story of Lot's wife is known by everyone and reminds us of what happens when you disregard God's specific instructions. Lot and his unnamed wife were leaving Sodom when it was in the middle of being destroyed by flaming material coming down from the sky. She stopped and turned to look back upon the burning city, and she was turned into a pillar of salt. The substance that fell from the sky on the city fell on her, and where she was standing was a pile of salt. The point is that she was told not to look back by the angels. She completely ignored what they warned her about, and she died as a result. Disobedience killed her. Underneath it was a longing for what she could not have anymore. There was a real loss, not a perceived loss. This probably was a loss of significance. God wanted a complete break with the past and the sinful city. It did not happen in her case, and she was destroyed. The principle for the counselor is that there may be a loss discovered in counseling that should not be comforted, because it is sinful. There must be a parting of the ways with it, not looking back with longing. The counselor must be directive at times. Her loss of significance resulting in maladaptive behavior (premeditated disobedience to God) would be more accurately defined as category II, loss caused by your own sinful choice.

(Genesis 19:30–38) After the destruction of their home in Sodom, Lot and his daughters sought refuge in a cave. The girls had no husbands, because they were killed in the city. They feared for the future and thought that they would not be able to find a husband to take care of them, or have children who would take care of them in their old age. They carried out a plan for their futures by making their father drunk and having sexual intercourse with him, so that they could get pregnant. They succeeded.

What can be learned through this story is that, again, it is seen that loss can cause people to act in ways they normally would not act. They were suffering from the loss of losing their husbands, which is category VI, loss of a loved one. They also suffered from perceived loss that they would not be able to find other husbands. This was category III, loss from living in a sin-cursed world. Who would take care of them in their old age? They must have children. They looked to Lot to be their provider. This would be a loss of significance, security, and safety. Trauma, grief, and perceived loss are at the bottom of this situation.

Studies on mortality salience have shown that loss from living in a sin-cursed world results in a desire for having children. This was evidenced by the 9-11 attacks in New York City. Afterwards, the marriage rate increased, and there was a baby boom all over the country. The desire for children after a mortality salience experience is a terror management defense mechanism (Wisman and Goldenberg, 2005). This reaction by the daughters of Lot brings up the question of what worldview they really had and questions whether they trusted in God at all. They were in covenant relationship with God because of Abraham.

Counselors should remember that just because a client professes to be a Christian and belongs to a church does not automatically mean they view life from a Christian worldview. Worldview needs to be examined for its specifics. The trauma, crisis, and perceived loss of the daughters resulted in impulsive maladaptive solutions that they would not ordinarily do in normal life situations. The loss of significance, security, and safety were powerful motivators for the behavior that the Scripture bears witness to, and perhaps we can take the three S's more seriously in people who are counseled.

(Genesis 20:1–18) Abraham went to the land of Gerar, and Abimelech desired to have Sarai for himself. Abraham then lied and said that she was his sister. Abimelech took her into his house but did not touch her. Fortunately for Abraham and Sarai, God intervened and spoke to the king in a dream, warning him not to touch her, because she was Abraham's wife. His household women had their wombs shut up; he was made sick; and Abraham prayed for him, and he was healed. He had given many expensive gifts to Abraham for Sarai. The king gave her back to Abraham.

This was the second time Abraham had done the same thing. He admitted that this was the arrangement he made with his wife (half-sister) to save his life. After the experience with Pharaoh, it might have occurred to him not to do this anymore, because it was a bad idea. He did not learn and did it again. Why did he do it? The answer is the perceived loss of his life. As a result of the perceived loss, he entered into deception. God, in His great mercy, got Abraham out of this trouble again. Perceived loss is the culprit causing Abraham, who was normally a man of integrity, to slip into deceiving the king. He should have trusted God to protect him and walked in faith as he normally did. The counselor should encourage people to walk in faith in the face of perceived loss, even of life. Abraham had a perceived loss of safety, which would be category VII, loss caused by the actions of another.

Terror management theory's understanding of mortality salience is that when confronted with the possibility of dying, people fall back upon their worldview for support. If unbelievers, they will look to join some organization to make a lasting name for themselves. If believers, they will fall back upon the comfort and trust in their relationship with God through Jesus Christ. It is a Christian counselor's duty to encourage a hurting believer who suffers from the anxiety of the potentiality of dying—of perceived loss—to trust in God, who can do all things to deliver the client from death or bring such peace and comfort to trust Him to do what is right and work it out for his or her good. This may keep the client from making an irresponsible decision that hurts him or her and possibly others.

In Abraham's case, notice that he slipped up two times under the same pressure and temptation. At the very least, it is a reminder to counselors that believing clients may slip back into old habits from time to time. It is not a good idea to drop them because of it.

(Genesis 21:9–10) Sarah saw Ishmael mocking Isaac. Then she approached Abraham, being emphatic about sending the bondwoman away with her son, because she did not want him to be heir with Isaac, her son. Underneath the anger at Hagar and her son was a fear for Isaac, her son, not being the sole heir to Abraham's fortune; also, hurt and pain. It was a loss of significance as well as security. This can best be described as a fear rooted in perceived loss. She was bent and determined to do something about it even if it was cruel and extreme and could end in the death of the two of them.

More than one example shows the power of perceived loss, particularly the loss of significance, resulting in causing pain and suffering to others by the person who attempts to find a solution to it. Ungodly solutions often result, bringing more pain. Loss multiplies loss. Perceived loss can cause hostility and aggression. This was category II, loss caused by your own sinful choice.

(Genesis 22) God tested Abraham's faith by commanding him to offer up his only son, Isaac, as a sin offering on the top of Mount Moriah. Abraham followed through, and just before the knife came down, an angel stopped him and pointed toward a ram whose horns were caught in a thicket and told him to sacrifice the ram instead of Isaac.

This is not just a story about great faith, which it is, but points to the Lord Jesus, God's only Son, as our sin offering. He is pictured as the ram caught in the thicket, not Isaac. Isaac is a picture of ourselves who justly deserve to be destroyed for our own sins and are released before judgment falls on us. Jesus took our place on the cross, so we could be released from certain eternal punishment.

Looking at it from a Christian counseling perspective of secondary loss, it is also about Abraham. In the past, he had failed twice when confronted with his own mortality salience in resorting to deception instead of faith, once with Pharaoh and then with the king of Gerar. Both cases are about a perceived loss of his safety. Isaac was dear to his heart, the child of his old age, the one whom God had chosen to have the continuation of the covenant made with Abraham, and the one whom God said would continue his line until his descendants were like the stars of the sky and the sand of the sea.

This is not only about his life, but it might just as well have been when talking about his precious son, his only son, Isaac. When confronted with this situation, Abraham had a choice to make. He could sacrifice Isaac, and there was the perception that he would die and not come back. This would be perceived loss. God did not say he would resurrect him. That would be an assumption Abraham could make. Or he could run with Isaac as fast as he could from that place, screaming "No!" to God. In the past, perceived loss had its way, and bad decisions were made. This time, Abraham said "No!" to perceived loss, the loss of his only son, and walked by faith. The decision paid off. God delivered Isaac, and it became part of the Scripture for God's people to ponder over the ages. Isaac's genogram would be interesting.

The counselor should encourage faith as an intervention for perceived loss. The counselor should realize that the right decision for the client may be very hard to make, and empathically connecting to the client at this time is a therapeutic assistance.

(Genesis 24:1–4) Abraham had brought up Isaac to be a God-fearing, covenant-keeping young man of marrying age. They had lived in an ungodly environment, and he shivered over the thought that Isaac could marry an unbelieving, idol-worshiping Canaanite woman. So Abraham sent his servant to his people and his country to find a wife for Isaac and bring her back.

There was spiritual growth in Abraham. He faced perceived loss once again. This was a perceived loss of security for his family line. Instead of acting out of character and making a wrong decision, he showed his maturity by doing the right thing: sending his servant to bring back a wife for Isaac from the right people. This should encourage the counselor, because people do and can change for the better. There may be clients who are suffering, because they have a loss of security, safety, or significance from those they have bonded with, such as a spouse or a child. Christian parents are concerned that their children who have grown up in church would marry unbelievers. Their perceived loss would be category VII, loss caused by the actions of another. The counselor would be wise in investigating this possibility.

(Genesis 25:31–34) Esau despised his birthright and demonstrated it by selling it to his brother Jacob for a pot of lentil soup and some bread, simply because he was hungry. Jacob saw the value of the birthright. Esau did not. He did not recognize its value until it was too late. Some people do not recognize loss until it is too late. They may despise relationships, husbands or wives, children, or friends, opportunities or blessings and regret it later on in life. People make decisions that they have not thought out, and they do not realize what further loss they will bring because of a bad decision. Esau had a loss of significance and security.

The counselor needs to carefully help the client to recognize the depth and the seriousness of potential loss in their particular life situation, because loss multiplies itself. The category of secondary loss for Esau was category II, loss caused by your own sinful Choice.

(Genesis 26:1–6) When famine strikes, the survival instinct kicks in. Isaac had some serious decisions to make about where to move and how to get food. Maybe he thought of going into Egypt as Abraham did. Perhaps, in Isaac's mind, it was surprising when God spoke to him and told him not to go into Egypt but to enter the land of Gerar.

In Isaac's situation, God was gracious and intervened, guiding Isaac and his people to safety and security. Isaac faced perceived loss of safety with the famine, but God guided him and helped him. The loss was category III, loss from living in a sin-cursed world. This is good news for the counselor who has a believing client. The implication is that when there is perceived loss, the client can trust

God to guide him or her to safety. Counselors at appropriate times need to ask God for direct intervention. Whether or not it is with the client or not is up to the judgment of the counselor. There are times when it is not wise to pray with a client who is hearing voices without first helping him or her to learn to discern the voice of God from the voice of the devil.

(Genesis 26:7–11) Isaac gave in to the same fear that his father Abraham did before him. Whether generational problems or a bad example, it is hard to say. He told the men in Gerar who were interested in Rebekah that she was his sister. When the king discovered it, having already learned the hard way through Abraham's folly, he simply put out a death threat on anyone who touched Isaac's wife. Isaac's perceived loss of life and safety made him act in a deceptive way out of his normal character. The perceived loss would be category I, loss caused by another's sinful choice. A genogram would demonstrate this family trait, and the counselor might use it to great effect. Transgenerational problems can be recognized as patterns, and the possibility of a demonic cause should not be ignored.

(Genesis 26:34–35) When Esau made a choice to leave the covenant community of faith and marry a Hittite woman, it broke his parents' hearts. The Scripture describes Isaac and Rebekah in "a grief of mind." The Hebrew text describes it as "a bitterness of spirit." This was a major loss for both parents. The noun for "bitter" is also a word for "deadly, pernicious, or poison." The context and the word indicate a heart-crushing emotional experience, a heaviness of sorrow, a brokenness.

The word also describes the viper's poison in Job 20:14 and Deuteronomy 32:32. The KJV uses the word "gall." This was not perceived loss, as if it might or might not happen. It is loss that really occurred. They were experiencing extreme sorrow, and what made it more irritating was that they raised him the right way. His choice was eternally significant, because it meant that he was walking away from God and his salvation. In addition, the security and safety of the covenant line was at stake. The parents suffered from loss of significance, security, and safety.

The mother, Rebekah, seemed to experience a deeper pain and disappointment than Isaac. Bitterness is often marked by resentment. This unbearable pain was a loss that would soon be demonstrated in actions almost as intense as the stinging sorrow. The counselor needs to remember that loss leading to bitterness is a dangerous place for the client to remain in. Physical health is endangered, broken fellowship with God can occur, and relationships with people will suffer, sometimes long after the apparent cause occurred. Anger at God can occur, which can create a circular pattern of pain, fueling anger and embracing the lie of the enemy. Both Isaac and Rebekah experienced category I, loss caused by another's sinful choice.

(Genesis 27) Bitterness and the resentment is like the poison that destroys good character. Rebekah concocted a plan to give Esau what he deserved. He did not want to be part of the covenant community of faith, so he does not need his father's blessing. Jacob would get it. She encouraged Jacob to deceive his father by putting hairy deer skin on his arms and rub the smell of the outdoors and game on him, so his near-blind father would think it was Esau. He stole Esau's blessing by a conspiracy with his mother. When Jacob was concerned about a curse coming upon him, his mother said the most foolish thing. She took that curse upon herself. Loss can cause deception, bitterness, resentment, and cynicism. The counselor must be sensitive and alert to those with deep loss at the slightest sign of bitterness creeping in. As seen in this story, deep loss, if not treated appropriately, can have dangerous repercussions on the client and others in relationship with him or her. Bitterness can cause spiritual blindness, and the counselor needs to prayerfully consider how to break the lie that keeps the person in bondage.

(Genesis 32) Jacob was afraid to meet his brother Esau after many years had gone by, because he fled from his home under a death threat after stealing the blessing. In this narrative is perceived loss of life—i.e., safety. The family trait showed how Abraham and Isaac failed to handle it in the right way. This time Jacob made a right decision to call upon God to be his deliverer out of Esau's hand. It demonstrated that Jacob was an intrinsic believer, because TMT has shown that when mortality salience confronts a person, they automatically seek comfort in their worldview (Wisman and Goldenberg, 2005). Jacob prayed and was delivered from Esau.

The counselor must give the believer encouragement to rest in his or her Christian worldview, seek the Lord, and have faith on His promises. If the unbeliever will not show an interest in the Christian Gospel, then the counselor can encourage the client to seek solace in doing things for the community or family, perhaps joining an organization where the person's name will be remembered, giving the person a sense of immortality. The sense of perceived loss in the case of the unbeliever can be treated by a Christian counselor with the PCT. The Gospel cannot be forced upon anyone. The Spirit must draw the person to the Father (John 6:44). Several categories could be in view here. Jacob's perceived loss could be from the possibility of his brother's actions for revenge, category I, loss caused by another's sinful choice or category VIII, loss caused by your own choice. He got himself in this position with his brother to begin with, and there was potential for the deaths of his loved ones—category VI, loss of a loved one. The Christian counselor, when the Gospel is refused, can give care, concern, and comfort and reduce the pain by wise counsel.

(Genesis 34) Simeon and Levi talked the male inhabitants of the city of Shechem into becoming circumcised, and, when they were in the most pain, slew them by the sword. This murder plan came about because Hamor defiled their sister Dinah in the field. They saw Hamor as treating her like a harlot. They were outraged and perceived that their sister lost honor and respect. This way of looking at it translated into loss of significance for themselves and their family and resulted in a murderous response that was carefully premeditated. This sense of loss resulted in evil decisions. The sons of Jacob had experienced category I, loss caused by another's sinful choice. After this tragic event, the family of Jacob lost significance within the region by getting a bad reputation among the inhabitants. Jacob's sons then suffered category II, loss caused by your own sinful choice. Jacob suffered loss of significance and safety, category I, loss caused by another's sinful choice. God gave them guidance and direction to resettle somewhere else safer after this incident.

Loss can result in violence and even murder. Homicidal or suicidal thoughts, and even plans, should be evaluated by the counselor and dealt with soon and appropriately.

(Genesis 37:4) The giving of the coat of many colors and assigning Joseph overseeing responsibility to report on the brothers' work, as well as his dreams, led to recognition that Jacob loved Joseph far more than he did the other children. Joseph, being young, lacked discretion and tact and inflamed the attitudes of the brothers against him by the very act of wearing the gift, causing him loss of relationship with his brothers, which was category VIII, loss caused by your own choice—not sinful. The brothers felt the loss of love and rejection from the father. They resented Joseph more and more. This loss caused the other sons to consider murder before putting Joseph in a pit. As the progression grew worse, they settled on selling Joseph as a slave that eventually brought their younger brother into Egypt. They had to cover themselves by a lie, so they told their father that the boy was killed by a wild animal; they presented the bloody coat as evidence.

This is another example of loss of love from the father and perceived rejection, loss of significance, which leads to murderous thoughts and an outrageously wicked response against Joseph. Loss can be dangerous. Notice that they stripped him of the coat of many colors, the symbol of the father's love (v.23). They sold their brother for a slave's price, putting emotional distance between him and them. They were deaf to his pleading. It was not right away, but as time went on, the brothers suffered from a loss of significance, which was category IV, voluntary loss for secondary gain. Living a lie never helps one's personal significance. They made a premeditated decision to gain revenge on a brother whom they viewed as robbing them of their significance in their father's eyes. Therefore, the original loss of significance that the brothers felt before they sold Joseph was category VII, loss caused by the actions of another—i.e., the giving of the coat to Joseph.

Joseph suffered far more loss than his brothers. Joseph's loss would have destroyed a person without a strong godly worldview. His tremendous loss included: loss of father, brothers, family, friends, freedom, love, safety, security, and significance. These are all the important things that a human being needs to remain mentally healthy. These were stolen from him in one day, category I, loss caused by another's sinful choice, and category VI, loss of a loved one.

(Genesis 39:11–41:57) After regaining to some extent his safety, security, and significance in Potiphar's house as chief steward, Joseph was betrayed by Potiphar's wife, was unjustly charged with attempted rape, and lost it all again by being sent to prison. The same loss experience happened a second time. Joseph only survived this with no emotionally permanent damage because he had a relationship with the living and true God. His worldview supported the stress and pain, giving him stability. His religion was intrinsic, not extrinsic. Even in prison, God supported his emotional state, keeping him from depression. Good character, concern for others, altruism, and quality leadership is demonstrated. God's gift of dream interpretation brought him from the prison to the palace of Pharaoh where he received, in the temporal world, security, significance, and safety once again. When the temporal was taken away, the reason Joseph survived was because he found his true significance, security, and safety in God. None of the things in the temporal world were ever substitutes for what he had in God. No one could take those things away from him.

(Genesis 43–50) God made sure that Joseph would reconcile with his brothers. He made sure that they faced Joseph and he faced them. When Benjamin arrived in Egypt, they had to go back and bring the father after Joseph revealed himself to them. For many years after the family settled in Egypt and right after Jacob died, the brothers were afraid that Joseph would take out his revenge on them. Joseph let them know that they were forgiven and said that he would look after them.

Forgiveness and possible reconciliation is of primary importance for a counselor to help the client.

Chapter Eleven

PCT and Posttraumatic Stress Disorder

Anger is one of the most difficult problems in veterans who suffer from posttraumatic stress disorder (PTSD). The purpose of this chapter is to clarify the better assessment testing instruments for counselors, differentiate the disorder from similar ones, and show the diagnosis and treatment for the disorder for counseling purposes using PCT. The method is to evaluate research focused on the various aspects of posttraumatic stress disorder (PTSD) and anger in Vietnam veterans and veterans of the Iraqi and Afghanistan wars. Treatment insights have been gained from research and scholarly articles that address the broader problems with anger and PTSD in a counseling setting. These treatment insights are included in the evaluation from a biblical perspective utilizing PCT.

Standard Tests Used for Diagnosing PTSD

Some testing instruments are more prominent and commonly used more than others among the various researchers. Primary tests for assessment are the Clinician-Administered PTSD Scale (CAPPS), used by four research studies (Brown, Antonius, Kramer, and Hirst 2008; Shea 2009; Taft, Street, Marshall, Dowdall, and Riggs 2007; Maguen et al. 2010); the State-Trait Anger Expression Inventory (STAXI), used in seven studies (Forbes et al 2004; Jakupcak et al. 2007; Marshall et al 2010; Morland, Greene, and Strom 2007; Shea 2009; Taft et al. 2007; Novaco and Chemtob 2002; Beckham et al. 2002); the Mississippi Scale for Combat-Related PTSD, used in one study (Chemtob, Hamada, Roitblat, and Muraoka 1994); the Novaco Anger Scale, used one time (Novaco and Chemtob 2002); the Minnesota Multiphasic Personality Inventory Posttraumatic Stress Disorder Subscale, used in one study (Chemtob et al. 1994); the Mississippi Scale Anger Aggression Index, used in one study (Novaco and Chemtob 2002); the Alcohol Use Disorder Identification Test, used in one study (Maguen et al. 2010); the Conflict Tactics Scale, used by two studies (Marshall et al. 2010; Taft et al. 2007); the Beck Anxiety Inventory, used by one study (Taft et al. 2007); the Beck Depression Inventory, used by one study (Brown et al. 2008); the Minnesota Multiphasic Inventory II, Antisocial Practices Scale (MMPI-II ASP), used in one study (Marshall et al. 2010); and the Mississippi Scale Anger Aggression Index, used in one study (Novaco and Chemtob 2002).

The most commonly used testing instrument was STAXI. This inventory contains the trait scale and the state scale and is the expanded version of those two original scales. Spielberger, in his online resume, has spent many years on anxiety and anger, explaining that these two are flight/fight responses. His interest in police stress and personality led him to work on anger in the 1970s through the present (Robyak 1986; Spielberger 2009). Internal consistency for state and trait anger is from 0.93 to 0.95 (Shoshani and Slone 2010). It is used to determine susceptibility to heart disease (Borteyrou, Bruchon-Schweitzer, and Spielberger 2008). Beckham et al. (2002), through the studies on cardiovascular responses to anger in PTSD vets, indicate that heart disease is a potential threat to those with high anger and PTSD.

The Novaco Anger Scale has a high internal consistency of 0.94 and a test/retest reliability of 0.84 to 0.86. It has a good concurrent and predictive validity. It assesses cognitive, arousal, and behavioral aspects of anger and has a second part that assesses the intensity of anger in descriptive anger-provoking situations (Novaco and Chemtob 2002).

The MMPI-II ASP was used by Marshall et al. (2010). This test was used with STAXI, Conflict Tactics Scale (for measuring partner aggression), and the subscale that pertained to Physical Assault. Since anger in PTSD affects the social network of clients, all of the anger and antisocial measuring instruments can be helpful, because they look at the complexity of the emotion from different angles, giving enough information to come to a confident conclusion about the anger in a specific individual even though some of the ground covered could be repetitious.

Differentiation of the Disorder

The American Psychiatric Association, DSM-IV-TR (2000) lists the differences between several other disorders that could cause confusion of the diagnosis. PTSD differs from adjustment disorder (AD) because PTSD requires an extreme, life-threatening stressor. AD can have a stressor of any severity. If PTSD-like symptoms occurred before the stressor happened, then a PTSD diagnosis must be ruled out. When a person is exposed to an extreme stressor and symptomology fits another disorder, then it may be diagnosed as the other disorder with PTSD added to it, if the situation is appropriate. Acute stress disorder (ASD) is different from PTSD, because the ASD symptoms occur and resolve within a four-week time period. PTSD usually begins showing up after one month. Obsessive-compulsive disorder (OCD) is differentiated from PTSD by the fact that inappropriate, recurring, intrusive thoughts that are not connected to a traumatic event occur. Flashbacks must be distinguished from psychotic hallucinations and delusions of schizophrenia, substance-induced disorders, and mood disorders with psychotic features.

Diagnosis of the Disorder

The American Psychiatric Association DSM-IV (2000) lists the diagnostic criteria for PTSD as witnessing a traumatic event in which one saw others, and oneself, threatened with harm or death. The response was intense fear, helplessness, or horror. The traumatic event is reexperienced through dreams and intrusive, recurrent, and distressing recollections of the event, including images, thoughts, or perceptions. Sometimes there is acting or feeling as if the traumatic event is actually recurring. These are dissociative flashback episodes that can involve hallucinations, illusions, and reliving the experience. These may occur on awakening or being intoxicated. When there is an internal or external cue symbolizing the event, it can trigger intense psychological distress. There may also be physiological reactivity that resembles or symbolizes an aspect of the traumatic event. This can occur on exposure to internal or external cues. Avoidance of stimuli associated with the trauma and a numbing of general responsiveness (not present before the event) are indicated by at least three of the following: efforts to avoid thoughts, feelings, or conversation associated with the trauma; efforts to avoid activities, places, and people that arouse remembrance of the trauma; inability to remember an important part of the trauma; strongly diminished interest or participation in important activities; a feeling of detachment or estrangement from others; a restricted range of affect, which means being unable to have loving feelings; a sense of a shortened future, meaning not expecting to have a career, marriage, children, or a normal life span. There are persistent activated symptoms not present before the traumatic event. These are seen in difficulty falling or staying asleep, irritability or outbursts of anger, difficulty concentrating, hypervigilance, and exaggerated startle response.

The length of time for the symptoms is more than one month. The disturbance causes clinically significant distress or debilitation in social, occupational, or other important areas of functioning.

Treatment of the Disorder

Brown, Antonius, Kramer, and Hirst (2008) show a helpful insight for counselors, stating that veterans with PTSD not only have higher anger and aggression than their non-PTSD counterparts but also make their trauma part of their autobiographical life story. It is part of who they are. A robust body of literature has shown that anger is a core component of PTSD.

Beckham et al. (2002) showed that veterans with PTSD had physiological reactivity, specifically higher heart rates and higher diastolic blood pressure readings; they were also quick to feel anger and anxiety when reliving self-chosen anger memories from trauma than those without PTSD. Counselors need to be aware that heart disease is a potential threat to those suffering from PTSD and must make that concern a part of the counseling treatment.

Veterans with PTSD are prone to demonstrate anger, hostility, and aggression. When reports of anger by the spouses were compared with non-PTSD veterans' spouses, there was no demonstrable difference. There was no increase in reported anger from the PTSD veterans' spouses. This was surprising to the researchers (Calhoun, Beckham, Feldman, Barefoot, Haney, and Bosworth 2002). Counselors need to consider that this could possibly be an indicator of ongoing domestic violence, where fear of retribution could suppress the need to state how much anger is occurring in the home life.

Anger in PTSD veterans is a major treatment problem for counselors. A clinical framework is suggested for understanding the regulatory process of anger and how it can be treated. Novaco has three domains of framework for anger. They are cognitive processing of environmental circumstances, conjoint physiological arousal, and behavioral reactions. These are intermeshed with the Chemtob information processing model of PTSD and its dysregulation of the survival system. It is triggered by external life-threatening events or the perception of them. Its activation occurs when it reaches a dynamic threshold reflecting the threat, the expectation of it, and engagement of it, which may not be a conscious act. Once triggered, the survival mode preempts any other cognitive activity that could indicate it is not what it seems to be. It rapidly reorganizes information processing activity to cope with the threat.

There are specific cognitive biases that are giving primacy to pattern matching: a tendency to react quickly, requiring less information regarding the threat, and a threat confirmation bias leading to quicker identification of the threat. There is also a substantial load put on the person's ability to optimally regulate arousal, leading to its impairment. When there is no threat, normal cognitive processing suppresses survival mode. The preemptive quality of survival mode causes a loss of self-monitoring, so the shift into survival mode is not consciously recognized. The context-inappropriate activation of survival mode makes it maladaptive in PTSD patients.

The important thing for the counselor to realize is what happens next. There is a positive feedback loop of confirmation bias that validates the engagement of survival mode. As the identification of the threat in the environment is confirmed, it increases physiological arousal. The activation of anger structures increases to full survival mode. The urgency prevents top-down regulation. As anger increases, inhibitory controls decrease and are overridden. The anger and aggression increases the symptomology of PTSD, and it becomes a continuous feedback loop. In addition, survival mode tends to be self-confirming and self-sustaining, and PTSD patients paradoxically often seek reexposure. This is why combat veterans report more anger and aggression than non-PTSD veterans (Chemtob, Novaco, Hamada, Gross, and Smith 1997).

As stated above, according to Chemtob et al. (1997), the PTSD patient detects the threat, and anger and aggression are activated. As that occurs, the threat system is activated and implies a vicious self-confirming cycle. The counselor, in treatment of this person, should help the patient develop anger regulatory skills by segmenting anger to dysregulate the survival system. This is done by teaching the patient to disrupt the cycle early in its activation system. The client learns to detect disconfirming evidence. Mitigating circumstances need to be recognized. In other words, there was no hostile intent. Training the client to self-monitor will enable a reframing of the episode. If this chance is missed, and the activation level triggers into survival mode, then the chance of self-regulation goes down.

The anger system has three domains: arousal, cognition, and action/behavior. Under normal situations, the anger system is highly coherent. Anger cognitions bring about arousal that energizes motor scripts for anger and aggression (the plan for responding to the threat). The system can be activated by any of the domains. Also, each domain can inhibit the others, preventing precipitating action. For example, the cognition system evaluates the threat and determines a fight-or-flight response and a motor script for dealing with it. Military training enables a person to react aggressively to a threat. High arousal may be there, but the person may be unable to react. Trauma, training, and experience can influence the coherence of these subsystems.

There is a gating function that ties the anger system to the threat system, so that action is done differently, even resulting in overriding the inhibitory structures, and action with regard to an extreme threat becomes automatic. There is the presence of a gating function for each domain. Trauma, for a long duration, resets the normal pattern of internal anger regulation to reflect and continue the activation conditions provoked by the traumatic event.

The shift into survival mode is often unconscious, but the threat is received associatively. Therefore, the counselor, realizing that the client unconsciously has a sense of immediacy to act upon the context-inappropriate cognitive distortions that perceive a threat, must first educate the client about the phase shift into survival mode. Automatic anger activation is a part of the phase shift. Clients are aware of it. Vietnam vets sometimes call it jungle mode. Education can help them to learn to recognize their personal anger pattern and to self-regulate it. It is important for the client to realize that at one time, that anger had a purpose, but now it has become partially dissociated. It is important to reattach the anger to its functional context. This enables the client to reclaim a number of adaptive elements to reinstitute regulatory controls. At the same time, the patient begins to recognize context-inappropriate use of survival mode and the joined anger and aggression. Anger is usually thought of as a passion that takes over the personality of an individual. Instead, the client is given conceptual tools to understand the anger subdomains and the experience while focusing on change. Segmenting anger puts it into its proper survival context and helps to reestablish regulatory controls.

The counselor, in treating the PTSD veteran, helps the patient to monitor the cognitions experienced in perceived threats as well as anger provoking situations; identify signs, duration, and intensity of arousal; recognize the role that angry cognitions play as responses to sensing danger; and learns to distinguish impulsive actions from more controlled actions. The counselor helps the patient to work on reachable goals, so that it brings hope and keeps the patient from seeing the problem as too big to change. Biofeedback for relaxation can help the patient to gain control over hyperarousal. Anger component analysis can help the patient to focus on specific dysfunctions.

The so-called "ball of rage" patients, before being counseled for anger control, are so angry that they need to learn how to distinguish between angry and non-angry states, first of all. They also require an angry-free zone within the treatment context before structured anger management can be done (Chemtob et al. 1997). Vietnam veterans are described as an angry group of people (Chemtob et al. 1994). External factors may also increase hostility. For example, some of the anger may not come from traumatic combat experiences, but in how they perceive the government's handling of the war, or the treatment they received from protesters meeting them at the airport and calling them "baby killers," and sometimes spitting on them. Those who remember the climate in our country also remember how veterans refused to walk in public with their uniforms on for fear of abuse. Operation Iraqi Freedom and Operation Enduring Freedom veterans were not treated like that when they came home from combat. Therefore, PTSD treatment may be accompanied by less comorbidity.

The DSM-III connects impulsivity with PTSD in contradiction to this research. Chemtob et al. (1994) state that there is no connection between impulsivity and anger in PTSD veterans. The DSM-IV also describes the PTSD patient as having impulsive behavior (American Psychiatric Association, DSM-IV-TR, 2000).

Forbes et al. (2004) confirm other studies in stating that anger is the most common problem in PTSD veterans, as reported by the persons themselves, their spouses, and clinicians. Forbes et al., in contrast to Chemtob et al. (1997), say that the activation of anger—since anger is a normal emotion—does not have the status of being a problem. It is the duration, intensity, frequency, and mode of expression that makes it maladaptive. Forbes et al. imply that the problems affect a wide range of social networks. This is confirmed by Kuhn, Drescher, Ruzek, and Rosen (2010), where aggressive driving was compared to veterans without PTSD. Those with PTSD from the Iraq and Afghanistan wars were more aggressive than other veterans and seldom used seat belts. The PTSD aggressive driving is two to ten times higher than the general U.S. population. What Forbes et al. (2004) claim that the expression is a problem for self and others but the activation of anger is not a problem is not true, because what comes out in expression begins with contextually inappropriate cognitive distortions. In treating the PTSD patient for anger, hope must be given, and brief therapy can deal with the behavior problems. But without dealing with the underlying distorted schemas, you are only treating symptoms and cannot get to a permanent cure.

Jakupcak et al. (2007) discuss subthreshold PTSD in veterans. This is not defined. If it is subthreshold, it is not appearing. Therefore, how do you know it is there in the first place? One either does have PTSD or does not. This appears to be splitting hairs. Medical doctors use a similar idea in speaking about someone having a precancerous condition. Either one does have cancer or does not. The fact that someone may turn out to have PTSD symptoms over time does not mean he or she could be labelled as someone with PTSD if they do not meet the criteria for it. The researchers do make a true statement that early treatment is important, because the anger and the PTSD will increase over time. PCT, because of its spiritual component, is a better alternative to the CBT approach to treatment.

Counselors who treat PTSD veterans for anger need to realize the impact of killing on mental health. Maguen et al. (2010) believe it is important to recognize that both direct killing and indirect killing are significant predictors of PTSD symptoms, including anger. This study involved Iraqi war veterans from the U.S. Mental health assessment and treatment should address reactions to killing to assist in readjustment after a deployment. In 2004, 77 percent to 87 percent of soldiers directed fire at the enemy. Approximately 48 percent to 65 percent reported being responsible for the death of an enemy combatant. Over 2,797 soldiers were involved in the study. Soldiers reported anger symptoms, and results showed that direct and indirect killing remained significant. Younger age, lower education, and female gender were significant predictors. Relationship problems came about as a result of killing in combat. Taking a life in combat is a powerful ingredient to developing mental health difficulties and psychosocial problems. It was demonstrated that killing is a significant predictor of anger.

This experience of killing may also be associated with moral injury and changes in spirituality or religiosity. Some may experience profound shame and guilt. Counselors must convey that in the therapeutic relationship, it is a safe place to explore the impact of killing a human being. Sometimes the counselor may discover that insensitive friends and family may cause them to refrain from speaking about it. There may be fear of judgment and a lack of understanding. Good counseling can prevent the damage done from secrecy, stigma, and shame (Maguen et al. 2010).

Counselors will be glad to know that this study showed small to medium reductions of trait anger, state anger, and physical aggression by using cognitive behavioral therapy along with anger management group therapy. Shea (2009) also indicates effectiveness in using cognitive behavioral therapy. The study by Marshall et al. (2010) builds upon the work of Novaco and Chemtob (2002). Physical aggression, anger, and PTSD lead to diminished social support over time. This is a vicious cycle that seems to exacerbate the symptoms.

Counselors may discover a high degree of comorbidity between personality disorder and PTSD. Antisocial personality disorder reduces the therapeutic benefits of treatment due to withdrawal from the process and resistance. These characteristics are potential predictors of treatment resistance. It was found that during anger management group therapy (AMGT), higher levels of antisocial characteristics were responsible for less reduction of trait anger and physical aggression.

When counseling the PTSD veteran for anger, multicultural sensitivity and awareness are important. Morland, Greene, and Strom (2007) did a study that showed ethnic differences in symptomology for PTSD. There is a need for more studies in this area for counselors to benefit from in the future. This study stimulates the appetite for more information that is not here. It confirmed former studies indicating that combat veterans with PTSD exhibited more anger than veterans without PTSD. The value of this research is that it shows some relationship between ethnocultural differences of PTSD and anger expression. Preliminary findings suggest that Native

Hawaiian-Pacific Island veterans scored higher than Asian American veterans on specific anger cognitions, reaction to provocation, and total anger scores. They also scored higher on anger behavior than Caucasians.

Clients who were veterans with PTSD and a high degree of anger and aggression need to be assessed by the counselor for domestic violence and/or partner abuse. Taft, Street, Marshall, Dowdall, and Riggs (2007) suggest in their findings that there is a potential mechanism for the association between PTSD symptoms and relationship abuse. There is a correlation between high levels of PTSD symptoms and high levels of trait anger, as well as state anger and anger reactivity following a trauma cue. Trait anger was also associated with physical assault and psychological aggression. This lines up with civilian studies of the comorbidity of anger and abuse among men. Trait anger mediates aggression and may cause the person to phase shift into survival mode in different situations. Counselors need to develop interventions for abuse activity among PTSD veterans. Cognitive processing therapy (CPT) techniques are recommended for this population dealing with abuse. CPT targets faulty cognitive processes and core beliefs that may underlie abusive behavior. Anger management approaches may help. Other targets of treatment can be depression, substance abuse, and relationship. Risk factors need to be examined to understand the complexity between PTSD, anger, and abuse. Trait anger may be casually related to PTSD and partner abuse. Counselors need to be aware of maladaptive cognitive and affective processes that occur during anger arousal and in dyadic interactions (Taft et al. 2007).

Novaco and Chemtob (2002) discovered that some of the anger of Vietnam veterans with PTSD appears to have come from postwar experiences. They also indicated that these people had fewer personal friends than non-PTSD veterans. They posit that because military training facilitates and mobilizes anger and aggression, combat-related PTSD is more highly related to anger than other forms of trauma. Various studies have determined that anger is fairly equal between men and women. The DSM-III and the DSM-IV both indicate that anger is the fifth highest symptom of PTSD from out of the seventeen symptoms attributed to it.

Threat perceptions and anger schemas are reciprocally influenced by one another. The detection of threat carries an urgent priority and quickly engages anger. The link with anger and PTSD carries several implications about the way it is activated. When symptoms occur, a coping response preempts alternative evaluations and alternative action plans of the triggering event. This causes the thinking process to move the system toward confirmation of the expected threat. The preemptive nature of the threat schemas and the strong arousal suppresses the inhibitory controls of aggressive behavior.

This threat-anger response system is a feedback loop. The more the threat is perceived, the more there is anger and aggression. And the more there is anger and aggression, the more readiness there is to perceive the threat. At the entry into survival mode, it is harder to regulate. They stress that it is vital to interrupt the cycle at an early point. The counselor needs to help the client recognize disconfirming evidence of a threat. This could include the detection of mitigating circumstances. Trained self-monitoring recognizes a lack of hostile intent. Therapy can help the client to reframe the event before the cycle moves forward. In PTSD, there is an intensified refractory, an unmanageable physiological activation that exceeds the general population. Significant attention should be given to the arousal system (Novaco and Chemtob 2002). This is in contradistinction from Forbes et al. (2004).

Anger is one of the strongest problems a veteran with PTSD will face. Since anger disrupts social relations, PTSD patients have the potential of having it interfere with overall functioning, social support, therapy treatment, involvement of the judicial system, and partner abuse.

Many people believe that letting out one's anger (nonviolently) is the best way to handle anger. This is a myth. Latest studies have shown that it is not true. Venting rage only increases its intensity. In the U.S., one in three murders is committed during an argument.

As the previous studies have shown, anger is now considered a significant risk factor for heart disease. Low levels of the neurotransmitter serotonin are associated with anger. The amygdale part of the limbic system in the brain appears to be responsible for processing anger. Animals that have that brain region damaged apparently cannot recognize or express hostility. Heredity can also play a part in how easily people get angry. People with excessive anger from PTSD are sometimes treated with selective serotonin reuptake inhibitors (SSRIs). Anger is far too complex for these drugs to be the entire solution. An integrated approach using cognitive behavioral therapy (CBT), learning new ways of solving problems and communicating wants and needs, relaxation techniques, and calming imagery can make great improvements in anger management. Using CBT, people usually get much better in eight to ten weeks and have maintained the improvement over several months (Harvard Mental Health Letter, 2002).

Concluding Discussion and Overview of Treatment

The diagnosis from the American Psychiatric Association DSM-IV (2000), in contrast to research on PTSD in veterans (Novaco and Chemtob indicate anger to be the strongest problem a PTSD veteran will face), plays anger down, not highlighting it. Chemtob et al. (1994) demonstrated in their research that in contradiction to the DSM-III, impulsivity was not connected to PTSD in veterans. The American Psychiatric Association DSM-IV also links impulsivity with PTSD. Although the DSM-IV is generally very helpful, it is not infallible as research points out. The DSM-IV is useful in differentiating other disorders.

Very often the same names appear repetitively in different articles. The ones that stand out are Chemtob et al. (1997) and Novaco and Chemtob (2002) for understanding the activation of anger, the domains of anger, and the implications for counselors in interrupting the cycle as early as possible and reframing with cognitive behavioral therapy. An integrated approach is the best, seeking a medical opinion as well. With extremely angry clients, SSRIs may be necessary for a time combined with CBT. Relaxation techniques may be helpful.

Awareness of the impact of killing is something the counselor must keep in mind. Comorbidity with anger and PTSD may include depression, alcohol, and substance abuse, as well as personality disorder. Due to the wide range of PTSD anger influence over almost every social network, spouse abuse needs to be evaluated. CAPPS and STAXI, along with the Beck Depression Inventory, are good assessment tools. The goal is to enable patients to find what they do not like, change what they can, and accept the things that they cannot change (Murphy 1980). It almost sounds like the serenity prayer.

Evaluation from a Biblical Perspective

One of the issues with anger and PTSD in veterans is the matter of killing an enemy combatant. Looking at the tremendous impact that killing has on the soldier in terms of mental health, the bottom line is it comes from the fact that the life taken was made in God's image (Genesis 1:28–29, KJV). Anger can come from killing a human being, but a biblical point of view offers the client who is willing to receive biblical counseling much help and hope. It gives the counselor confidence in being able to help. The client, for optimum mental health, must be treated as a psychosocial-spiritual being (Thomas and Sosin 2011). This point of view can straighten out the contextually inappropriate cognitive distorted schemas and can help in an intervention to short-circuit the vicious feedback loop of anger and aggression in a veteran suffering from anger in PTSD.

A Christian worldview accepts the fact of killing in just wars. The Old Testament describes Israel being led by God into battle. The New Testament supports the idea of serving in the military and fighting for one's country as an honorable thing. Jesus never told the Roman centurion (Equivalent to Major) to leave the Roman army (Luke 7:1–10, KJV). God ordained the government to use the sword to punish the evildoers (Romans 13, KJV). God blessed King David and helped him to kill Goliath, the enemy in battle (1 Samuel 17, KJV).

The Christian counselor must empathically and gently deal with the impact on the mental health of the soldier who has killed in battle and suffers from PTSD. The spiritual help from the Scripture assuring that God understands, forgives, and can set free the person from guilt and shame is a powerful intervention that can untwist cognitive distortions, replacing them with peace and truth.

From a PCT perspective, the counselor must deal empathically with the person who is suffering from PTSD, because of the terrible loss that affects the soldier's safety, significance, and security involving category I, loss caused by another's sinful choice; category II, loss caused by your own sinful choice; category VI, loss of a loved one; and category VII, loss caused by the actions of another. The last category may have taken place when the soldier was sent into a war by one's government via the draft. PTSD has more categories of secondary loss than any other emotional problem people face.

Loss is caused by sending people off to war. This is loss and trauma combined. The feedback loop that intensifies anger, survival mode, and rage, where the inhibitory controls are overridden, needs to be broken before the local environment becomes hostile in the perception of the client. Suggestions for doing this involve identifying the loss and pointing out that PTSD is a protective mode to deal with the loss. Cognitive restructuring includes recognizing that God is transcendent over all, and safety, security, and significance are in Him. PTSD comes in the situational realm where the lie is believed, that the environment is hostile, when the trigger occurs. The existential consists of the memories that live again—sights, sounds, and even smells—triggering this continuous feedback loop that gets more intense as it continues. Exposing the lie and recognizing that it is a lie is a first step to breaking the cycle. The triggers can be reframed by cognitive instruction based on Philippians 4: thinking on the things that are right, and true, and beneficial, not harmful. For example, one treatment intervention used on a veteran of the Iraq and Afghanistan wars who was disturbed by the smell of diesel fuel that acted as a trigger was to practice thinking about the good things that diesel fuel was used for, apart from his combat experiences where people died as a result of explosive devices on highways. This flooding worked.

When loss is dealt with empathically, the protective device of PTSD symptoms will not be necessary any longer. Significance ought to be found in the transcendental, while security and safety rested within the situational and existential realms in God's presence.

When there is healing in the spirit and soul, there is less chance of a lack of health in the body.

There is a lasting effect in the mind of a soldier who has killed a human being in wartime that is connected with anger and PTSD. PCT recognizes that the loss experienced when another human being is killed during war is from category VIII loss, the loss from your own choice. Killing in war is not always sinful, as is clear in the Old Testament. People make choices all the time that may not be the wisest and then experience loss apart from fighting in a war. The perception of the act of killing in war is what the PCT counselor must confront, and the use of the MCLT is very helpful in determining how deeply the loss is felt.

Chapter Twelve

PCT and Sexually/Physically Abused Children

Several approaches to treating sexually and physically traumatized children have been examined, and the conclusion is that it is better for the child and the parents involved if a multimodal approach is utilized. Art, play, group play, cognitive behavioral therapy (CBT), trauma-focused therapy, domain analysis, cognitive stage level assessment, parent-child interaction therapy, family therapy, posttraumatic stress disorder (PTSD) assessment, and even psychopharmacological interventions can be integrated in the counseling. In certain cases, containment in a residential short-term psychiatric facility may be necessary when the acting-out arrests the counselor's ability to treat the child. Skillful counseling in an integrated manner has good outcomes. An integrated Christian approach with all of these therapies can be used in treatment. PCT can integrate with these interventions and assist in helping the troubled child who has been sexually and physically abused by understanding and treating the loss at the bottom of the issues.

Treating Sexually and Physically Abused Children

Understanding how to treat sexually and physically abused children is vital for counselors, because domestic violence and child abuse are becoming more prevalent in the presenting issues in the therapeutic environment. Making children witnesses and victims of violence has significant societal impact (Borrego, Gutow, Reicher, and Barker 2008). In building upon the works of previous researchers, the hypothesis that the best treatment is an eclectic treatment is demonstrated. The practical implications for clinicians are in the combination of various therapies that meet the needs of sexually and physically abused children. Child counseling is different from adult counseling in that the counselors are more prone to suffer from grief and vicarious trauma more than they would be in adult counseling.

Recommendations for Counselors

There is truth to the adage, "Physician heal thyself" (Luke 4:23, KJV). Cunningham (1999) warns that counselors need to guard themselves from picking up secondary trauma in dealing with highly emotionally charged situations regarding abused children. The Scriptures give ample direction to protect the Christian counselor from this kind of transference (e.g., "shield of faith" in Ephesians 6:16 and the power of the indwelling Holy Spirit in Acts 2). The vicarious traumatization of the counselor can lead them to go through a grief process. The Christian counselor who relies on the teachings of the Word of God can weep with the weeping without debilitating consequences, and this is very much a part of PCT.

Van Velsor (2004) contributes insights regarding the counselor who does not have much experience in treating abused children. The counselor should realize that counseling skills must be adapted to children by using microskills. Treatment involves behavioral tracking, where the counselor tracks the behavior verbally by reflecting the content and feeling of the child, revealing that the counselor is paying attention, rather than trying to force a conversation. This approach requires sensitivity, remembering that each child is uniquely different in gender, culture, and individuality.

Assessing for PTSD

Assessing for posttraumatic stress disorder (PTSD) is a necessity when counseling abused children. Counselors need to be alert to the fact that children who witness the physical or the sexual abuse of their mothers are at risk for PTSD. Even if not abused, children suffered half as much emotional deficits as their counterparts who not only were witnesses but were also abused. Some of the symptoms are depression, withdrawal, aggression, tantrums, running away, having no friends, fearfulness, and failing grades in school. The child's inner resources to deal with life-threatening events are inadequate, and these come out in trauma symptoms of repeated nightmares, recurring thoughts, reenactment through play, and avoidance, withdrawal, loss of developmental skills, hyperarousal, irritability, difficulty sleeping, and hypervigilance.

Children sometimes feel that they were responsible for the beating of the mother. There is guilt, self-blame, and seeing the world as unpredictable and full of known and unknown dangers. These coincide with the chronic assaults and terror of the mother. All of this can exacerbate PTSD in the child who feels very vulnerable. Physically and sexually abused children display a multitude of different symptoms, showing how broad the impact is on the entire personality. PTSD evaluation should take place during the time of the assessment (Lehman 1997).

Looking at the PTSD in a child who sees the physical and sexual abuse on the mother from a PCT perspective reveals that the child is suffering from category I secondary loss—loss caused by another's sinful choice. In addition, when the child is made to feel that it is their fault that this occurred, then the child suffers from category II, loss caused by your own sinful choice, and category VII, loss caused by the actions of another.

Neo-Piagetian Developmental Theory

Ivey and Ivey (1990) suggest a developmental counseling approach to assessing children, integrating neo-Piagetian developmental theory. It assesses the cognitive level of the client without requiring much time in its implementation. The counselor orients the questions to the varying cognitive levels that demonstrate differences in the child's speech. This combination of levels enables the counselor to develop a comprehensive treatment plan. For example, the preoperational (ages four to seven) is called the late sensorimotor stage. The goal is to understand the problem as the child understands it. The child may communicate the story at several developmental levels in the same conversation. Four ways to assess developmental level at the preliminary cognitive assessment are the following stages or levels: sensorimotor, where the goal is to describe what was seen, heard, or felt; concrete operations, where the event is described in a linear description; formal operations, where repeating patterns are talked about, or one's thoughts and feelings are examined; and the dialectic/systemic, where concepts are being put together. The family can be brought to see the total context of the problem. After assessing the cognitive level of the child, conceptualization of interventions can be matched with the level of the child. In order to prevent a boring counseling style, and to build a more solid foundation, drop back a level, say, from concrete to sensorimotor. The counselor should remember to match the conversation with the changing developmental level of the child that can vary in one conversation. Basing the counseling on a sensorimotor stage and concrete stage can bring out information and patterns. A developmental counseling therapeutic approach gives the counselor a baseline for analyzing the complexity of each child. The usefulness of this therapy is reflected in the developmental constructs that can be discovered within five or ten minutes.

PCT can integrate this approach in determining the perception of loss incurred, depending on the age of the child. The older the child, the more appropriate is the Miller Crisis Loss Test (MCLT). It also increases the communication between the counselor and the child, enhancing the therapeutic environment.

Play Therapy

Van Velsor (2004) indicates that in play therapy, the counselor will be looking for thematic pattern in the play, as well as the symbolism that represents aspects of the traumatic event or events. Part of the counselor's goal is to redirect aggressive play into appropriate directions. Davies (2011) suggests that during the assessment, risk and protective factors should be noted.

Treatment for the physically abused preschool child includes play therapy, which allows the counselor to see into the inner world of the abused child with careful attentiveness through their fragile defenses. The traumatized child may have difficulties in distinguishing inner fantasies from external realities. Sometimes, during play therapy, the confusion between fantasy play and reality results in the child transferring his or her anger and aggressiveness toward the counselor, and may include throwing toys around the office. Counselors can make comments like, "I know what it feels like to want to crash things together," or "Wow, that's a strong feeling." The child could be encouraged to find a safe way to represent his more troubling experiences (Schiller 2008).

Group Play Therapy

It is important for the counselor to realize that there are immediate and long-term effects of abuse on preschool children. Symptoms may be anxiety, fear, and depression, and may include physical effects, such as eating problems, aggressiveness, antisocial behavior, sexual behavior problems, boundary issues, sleep problems, poor self-esteem, feelings of guilt and blame, and developmental delays. As in all abuse victims, PCT would look for what substitutes the child would utilize to make up for the loss of safety, significance, and security that came from people who should have been trusted.

Group play therapy is an effective treatment for several reasons. Practicing healthy relationships with other group members, learning about abuse in others, and realizing that others have had the same experience help the children work through secrecy issues. Isolation, being different, vicarious learning, and feeling comfortable enough to work through the results of the abuse when ready are some of the reasons why group play therapy is successful.

Counselors should be knowledgeable of how the dynamics and effects of sexual abuse in preschool children play out in group therapy. Aggression, withdrawal, hypervigilance, sexual behavior, reenactment of the abuse, dissociation, regressive-nurturing behaviors, conflict, and boundary problems are symptoms dealt with in group play therapy. Appropriate interventions should be used to address them.

Screening is important. Children must be within one-year age difference, similar size and development, and not suicidal nor self-mutilating nor aggressive to others without remorse. Group size should not be more than three or four children. One intervention for aggressive behavior is to reflect the meaning behind the aggression by saying, "You would like to tell him to leave you alone and stop being so mean to you." When the aggressive behavior becomes unsafe, limit setting is important to establish and can be done by telling the child that you do not approve of biting, and that they all need to be safe in the playroom. Redirection by telling the child to punch the clay or draw an angry picture is another intervention. Children who are passive and withdrawn should be encouraged to use words to ask for help, or be reminded that it is okay to say, "No." Reduce hypervigilance by telling the child that he or she feels safe when he or she knows what everyone in the room is doing. Since a child in this situation has lost significance, safety, and security, these interventions fit in with a PCT understanding of the root of the problem.

Obviously, limit setting in a nonpunitive way is important when children act out in sexual behavior. For example, when a child touches another's genitals, telling her or him that you can be close to someone and even like them without touching the private parts of their body is one way to intervene. Sometimes children reenact sexual abuse in the group using dolls. Dissociation is avoiding the painfulness of the abuse that makes them appear like they are playing in a trance. It is like leaving the scene of the accident. The counselor should not snap the child out of it. Instead, narrate what the child is doing, especially if it is in play.

Regressive-nurturing behaviors become evident when the child starts acting like a baby. Validating the child's feelings by narrating the play, the counselor should say, "The baby feels safe when you hold her and take care of her." Safety is what the child lost and needs to be reinstated into the child's life. Coach children to resolve conflict; learn to share and use conflict-resolving strategies. These children need to learn appropriate boundaries. Boundaries are not respected in dysfunctional families, so children may try to take adult roles with other children by aggressiveness, being passive with aggressive children, or hugging and kissing others inappropriately (Jones 2002).

The Parental Component in Treatment

Almost all of the approaches to treating children involve a parental component. Very often families are forced to come to counseling by the justice system. They are reluctant participants at best, probably because they were involved in the entire dysfunctional environment or abusive event. Kindsvatter, Duba, and Dean (2008) assert that giving family members hope for change is a way to get them invested in the counseling process. Recognizing family subsystems (as advocated by the structural model) by questioning the goals of each member also includes them in the counseling process. Instead of trying to grasp all the data revealed in the session, it is wiser to attempt to focus on a reachable and reasonable goal for change and follow up on that theme. When meeting the family with the child, try to discern their subsystem boundaries. After perceiving the boundaries, the counselor may consider rearranging the seating to put psychological distance between certain members of subsystems.

Hyman, Gold, and Cott (2003) have shown that children who were sexually abused show greater self-esteem and lower depression through the stress buffering support of parents not involved in the abuse, even more than peers. When circumstances allow it, advice from parents has been shown to keep children from developing PTSD symptoms. God designed it so that parents have a tremendous influence on their children and can provide their significance, security, and safety in their lives. It is not surprising that they can prevent PTSD in their children by their support.

Synthetic Model of Personality Development and Treatment

Weitzman (2005) encourages the use of the synthetic model of personality development, presenting a comprehensive view of the abused child. Using this approach, the counselor must distinguish between single episodes of trauma and long-term abuse trauma. The single episode, like a natural disaster, dog bite, or car accident, is similar in affect as a one-time sexual abuse episode or physical abuse.

The developmental factor shows how trauma can impact a child. At an early age, trauma can constrict the personality functioning, implanting itself deep within the child's personality to create massive character distortions. Both single episodic trauma and chronic and severe abuse can create this distortion. Long-term abuse has more far-reaching effects on the child's development and brain structure, because trauma creates developmental deviations. Older children may suffer from PTSD, but damage is not done to foundational neurological and psychological forces. Research has discovered that trauma can cause victims difficulties with affective regulation, memory storage, and hyperarousal. Joseph (1998) has demonstrated that prolonged stress can damage the hippocampus in the brain, producing amnesia. Berliner, Hyman, Thomas, and Fitzgerald (2003) add to this information by proving that a traumatized child's memory has less sensory detail and coherence, but has more impact and meaning than the positive experiences. Peterson and Biggs (1997), in the same line of thinking, states that children who have been traumatized have trouble answering specific questions. Therefore, it is not surprising that learning in school may be negatively impacted. Therefore, this memory aspect is something that the counselor should be looking for, especially with school functioning.

Weitzman (2005) says that a very young child when abused will have greater problems with cognitive, social, and emotional growth. The reason is that older children have the ability to self-soothe. Over the years, many models of human development in psychology have focused on different aspects of the personality. They describe what aspects must be completed by the child to move on smoothly into adulthood, and from this perspective, they have described traumatized children as having problems with attachment, ego functioning, and self-disorders.

Until recently, the different models have looked at the child from only one perspective. This is a solipsistic point of view, being imprisoned within the circle of one's own ideas. The child's problems are complex, and the clinician has been tempted—by the sheer volume of models—to ignore some important symptoms and focus only on others, depending on the model chosen, to the detriment of the child. This is why an integrative model of personality is important.

The major developmental theories of personality can be categorized into four areas of the functioning of the personality. These are the parallel partners of self, ego, drive, and object. Self is associated with self-esteem, self-regulation, body-self integrity, and self-agency. Ego is associated with ego adaptations, ego defenses, defects, cognition, and learning. Drive is associated with sexuality, sensation, impulse, aggression, conflict, and anxiety. The domain of object is associated with attachment-seeking, internalization, differentiation of objects, and mental representations as they are relived in the present life of the child. The issues which each domain encapsulates are treated accordingly. None of the domains should be looked at as more important than another. The psychological issues of each domain grow and develop as the child grows.

This multiperspective approach allows for understanding the damage done across the entire spectrum of the child's personality in abuse and trauma-related situations. A black object is better seen from a white background. Therefore, to be contextually clear, it is important to recognize that a healthy young child in the domain of self is naturally buoyant. There is plenty of self-affection and a natural curiosity of the world, which comes from positive caregiving. As the child develops a more realistic understanding of self and appreciation of others, disappointments, frustrations, and limitations are integrated in a healthy way. This is the result of living in a caring, loving home. The self is a work in progress, and trauma at a young age can cause it to wither away. PCT would then view that this self, and perhaps a lack of self-regulation manifesting in negative behavior, has originated from the need for significance replacement, which has withered away from the trauma. Hostile experiences can dim the joy and lead to self-doubt, shame, worthlessness, and self-defeat. Physical and sexual abuse can lead to distortions of body image and sensation. Life-threatening experiences can move the locus of control outside of the child's body and lead to helplessness, passivity, and lack of initiative.

The domain of ego is mainly about the child adapting to the world around him and having a capacity for controlling his own impulses and needs. It is about thinking, judging, coping, and using language and symbolic communication. How others respond to the child's communicated needs is the unfolding of cognitive schemata. In abusive environments, novel learning experiences can be stopped because of fear, fear of failure, and shame. Abused children are not encouraged to learn problem-solving strategies and communication skills as ways to resolve conflict. Abusive homes lack structure, routine, and consistency, and do not encourage internal controls in the child. Repressive homes, where children are rigidly obedient, cause children to develop false-selves. This type of environment causes cognitive impairments, verbal deficits, and impulsiveness that reflect the illogical unpredictability of the environment.

Ego defenses are radicalized and have to work overtime. Denial, projection, displacement, identification with the aggressor, and other defenses can make exaggerated claims on the ego to protect it from danger or disintegration. Dissociation and out-of-body experiences permit the sexually abused child to leave the scene of the crime. A lifestyle of psychological defense and being identified with the aggressor can lead to various maladaptive behaviors in order to survive. Ego-impaired children tend to avoid school, show learning disabilities, shy away from new experiences, and stay away from team sports, because they might show their vulnerability. Object domain is about relationship. In healthy children, an empathic bond takes place that forms secure and warm relationships. A template is formed for all future relationships, because the child is able to internalize positive integrated mental representations of the self and others. Children naturally grow into reliability, consistency, and warmth. There is a capacity of ambivalence toward others and an ability to integrate the good and the bad into a balanced whole. They have a strong identification with their parents and adopt core values, beliefs, and styles of coping. As the parent takes pleasure in their growing independence, the child learns autonomy through supportive interactions. Trauma in the object domain creates attachment disorder and an arrest in relationships, intimacy, and basic trust. If dependency needs are frustrated too often, it can lead to dependency, conflicts, or psychopathic detachment. Chronic abuse can cause the child to become cold and detached. If the abuse happens after the dependency needs have been fairly well established and then disrupted as an older child, the child can develop borderline personality characteristics. When early relationships are disrupted by abuse, the child develops little tolerance for ambivalence in relationships, and, as a result, intimacy and attachments become a problem. Drive domain is about biologically-driven impulses. A healthy family develops healthy sexuality, intimacy, and assertiveness in a child. Trauma in the drive domain leads to impulse control problems, overactivity, excitability, distractibility, and overstimulated sexual and aggressive urges. This can lead to sexual acting-out and overdetermined drives for sexual gratification in place of real love. There can also be a preoccupation with power and control through defensive-aggressive domination. This has been one of the causes that drive sexual offenders.

There are treatment implications for traumatized children who have been harmed in several domains. Some domains may not be injured, while others can be severely injured. The ego may develop outside the sphere of object relations and result in a person who appears to function well yet complains of depression and emptiness. By evaluating domain impairments, the counselor can get an idea of the degree of psychological damage done and can account for a wide variety of symptoms that are put in an intelligible framework. This approach helps the counselor to treat the child from a broader perspective and to use a larger number of different intervention tools. A girl whose ego is mostly intact can respond to cognitive tools that can intervene in helping her with the acting out of erotic impulses (drive domain disturbance). Problem-solving skills can be learned by using self-observation, keeping a log, and looking for triggers, as well as verbalization. An ego-impaired child cannot draw on those resources, and if his drive domain is causing him to run rampant with sexual acting out, he is harder to treat than the former girl described whose ego is intact.

There are various tools that can be used, such as empathic mirroring, limit setting, containment, and confrontation of destructive defenses. The child whose typical coping style is to act out in a destructive way can be intervened by confrontation and containment. The disordered behaviors are not tension-reducing mechanisms. In order for these children to attend to internal feeling states, they require external containment and holding environments. Some children have been so affected by trauma that all four domains have been affected and may require specific interventions. At times, they may require residential treatment, because it is a holding environment. As a result of acting-out behavior, they need external structure that enables the various domains to be treated.

Children injured in the self-domain will need a treatment approach that repairs problems like self-esteem, affective regulation, and body integrity. At times, physical therapy that enhances body-image distortions might help. Teaching to self-soothe is another technique. Counselors need to be ready for flexibility in treatment style as well as techniques, because children with multiple domain impairments shift domain states during treatment. A child who suddenly becomes extrovert and inquisitive can benefit from an informative and directive style. A child who is suddenly defiant needs limit setting. Another child may begin to question competence and requires a simple task that brings about success. This synthetic approach can use play therapy, music, and art therapy, or cognitive therapy, depending on the child's needs. Children who have suffered from abuse and reflect a wide variety of symptoms can easily be diagnosed by the DSM-IV-TR in a variety of categories. The problem is that the DSM-IV-TR is too simplistic to deal with the complexity of children suffering from trauma. As a result, the counselor only has a grasp of part of the problem. The same thing can be said by deriving interventions from a single model. This is why domain functions are so comprehensive in treating children with trauma. A broad PTSD approach also enables a counselor to respond to shifting domain states. The counselor has to approach the traumatic past at some point. Cognitive and behavioral, recreational, educational, and other interventions can be woven into a treatment plan to help children function more effectively. This synthetic approach demands much from the counselor and can take years to make significant differences, but treatment outcomes are likely to be enhanced. There is no reason why this multiperspective approach cannot be included with a PCT application.

Parent-Child Interaction Therapy in Treatment

Sometimes foster parents feel overwhelmed at the complexity of the issues that foster children display, making living with them very frustrating. Often children have gone through a large number of placements where they have virtually worn out their welcome, because nothing that the well-meaning foster parents do brings about needed change in the behavior of the child. Many of these children are sent to child counselors by the Department of Children and Families. A substantial amount of these children have suffered physical and sexual trauma. In this context, Timmer, Urquiza, Herschell, MacGrath, Zebell, Porter, and Vargas (2006) recommend using parent-child interaction therapy. Foster parents need to have their parental skills enhanced, and the child needs a good outcome.

Parent-child interaction therapy (PCIT) has empirical support behind it for treating abused children with disruptive behavior. The multiple placements of children make them at risk for more mental health issues. Attachment problems, defiance, noncompliance, and aggression cause family conflict, and the children do it for at least two reasons. The behavior helps them to feel comfortable in organizing their environment, and they have patterned their behavior from the family of origin. Inconsistent and dysfunctional patterns of parental behavior cause abused children to have an impaired ability to develop healthy social relationships. Placement disruption is often due to attachment problems.

PCT counselors would explore loss issues with children who have disruptive behaviors. Very often the behavior is a substitute to defend against loss. It comes out of a dysfunctional worldview. Helping the child to understand that their significance, safety, and security are in God can help an adolescent deal with the loss. Communication must be on the level that younger children can understand. Parents can be helped to understand where the disruptive behavior is coming from and how to pray for, and with, the child.

PCIT is unique in that it provides the mechanism to change the dysfunctional parent-child relationship through strong, positive, parent-child interaction. PCIT's structure is two phases that consists of child-directed interaction (CDI) and parent-directed interaction (PDI). This is preceded by relationship enhancement and behavior management (REBM) concepts, where these are explained to both child and parents. The following six or eight sessions are coaching sessions for parents. The counselor uses verbal cues as the parent interacts with a child who is playing with age-appropriate toys. The main goal is to provide effective parenting skills for the parents in managing their child. Parents are coached in giving positive attention to their children, especially when the child is exhibiting positive behaviors. They are also coached to eliminate statements that promote negative interactions, like being critical or threatening. PCIT is a good approach for strengthening families, especially foster families.

Rational Cognitive Emotive Behavioral Therapy in Treatment

Prather and Golden (2009) propose a rational cognitive emotive behavioral approach to helping abused children based on the premise that perception and learning history guide all behavior and therefore traumatically induced behavior would be the same. This approach is suitable for formerly abused children who have been placed in foster care or were adopted. Traumatized foster and adopted children often act out to control their environment. Therefore, caregivers are not viewed as a source of safety, and hyperactive and aggressive behaviors are likely to occur. They have a profound lack of trust and a distorted sense of security. They often lack impulse control, are emotionally distant, and fail to develop secure attachments. The idea of caregivers not being viewed as a source of safety comes from the loss that the child has encountered and fits well with PCT.

Until recently, the problem with attachment theory is that there is no solid, tried-and-true method of treatment. Prather and Golden (2009) offer a different approach and believes that altering the fixed statements or language of abused children will lead to dramatic changes in the quality of family and external relationships. This proposed treatment is better than nondirective approaches, and the rationale behind it is brevity integrated with attachment theory and rational cognitive perspectives. The reason given for the brevity of treatment is that children can change quickly. The reciprocal role of emotion and thought in causation of behavior and the encouragement of rational thinking and behavior change are central premises of this approach.

The need for safety in the first five years of a child's life is primary for physical survival and emotional needs. When those needs are not met, the child experiences trauma. Attachment is broken and coping behaviors are used: lying, manipulation, and intimidation. In order to have their needs met, other people are often looked to, apart from the foster parents. These foster parents are lied to and often manipulated if naïve. It is relatively easy to get over on new parents, especially when they are encouraged to earn trust and believe their children. These children are masters of surveillance. No matter how diligently the caregivers monitor healthy behavior and not reinforce inappropriate behaviors, children are constantly being reinforced by the outside world. No matter how the caregivers model appropriate behavior and tell the children why they should not act that way, the children will not believe them, because those warnings do not appear to be coming true, such as, "People won't like you. You will lose your friends, and you will get in trouble."

Some kids are good at lying, while others simply just do not believe the caregivers. The children will ignore the parents and go with strangers, because they will reinforce their behavior. Sometimes there is an emotional shutdown, a refusal to feel or think or believe anything the caregiver says, because it reminds them of the trauma. The avoidance prevents the children from correcting their cognitive distortions. Avoidance is a symptom of PTSD. When the caregivers attempt to correct them, their response is almost a happy or neutral state. They do not seem to feel normal shame, sadness, guilt, or embarrassment when being corrected. Research indicates that reinforcement maintains problem behavior. Therefore, unlearning and relearning healthy cognitive and emotional reactions requires learning verbal and motor behavior in the scope of parental interaction.

RCEBT sees a triadic interaction between behavioral, emotional, and cognitive factors, and also the environmental influences, which are interlocking and bidirectional in the way they affect each other. Social interaction is necessary for reinforcement to take place in treatment. In part, RCEBT is based on behaviorism and solution-focused therapy. Treatment involves shifting attention away from problem talk, normalizing language, and focusing on times when the parent-child relationship works. They are taught and rewarded in a safe environment in how to compete with negative thoughts.

Ten distinct steps of treatment are proposed. They are in three categories: rational or solution-focused, cognitive emotional, and behavioral. The goal is to provide the parents with positive behavior change, teach interpersonal skills, and learn greater control over themselves and their relationships. The ten steps are: determining and normalizing thinking and behaving, evaluating language, shifting attention from problem talk, describing times when the attachment problem is not occurring, focusing on how family members successfully solve problem attachment behavior, acknowledging unpleasant emotions, identifying cognitive and emotional connections in behavior, encouraging previously abused children to experience or own negative thoughts and feelings, rewarding positive behavior change in themselves and in relationships, and encouraging and rewarding thinking and behaving differently.

This approach focuses on the impact that the child's negative thoughts have on causing behavior. It is different from traditional attachment therapy in that it helps individuals solve unattachment behavior and uses interventions that compete with negative interactional patterns in and outside the family. Since behavior is affected by outside influences, this approach uses interventions to compete with the negative factors that originally influenced behavior. The thinking is that if they change the language and behavior, then they will feel good about themselves, which, in itself, is another reinforcement.

PCT's triadic structure of the mind, will, and the emotions interact at this juncture. What must be done is to override the outside negative factors that originally influenced the behavior. Helping the child to forgive those who brought about the loss will enable him or her to rise up in significance and be able to drop the behaviors that create unattachment.

Trauma-Focused Therapy in Treatment

Golden, in the same article, disagrees with Prather and Golden (2009) in that he thinks that changing speech will not change behavior. In his proposed trauma-focused therapy, counselors cause the children to revisit the traumatic experiences and are helped to understand that these events were outside of their control, which led to the feelings, thoughts, and behaviors they experienced. Empathy regarding their painful experiences is part of the counseling. Children learn to tolerate the uncomfortable feelings. They are encouraged to hold on to situation-appropriate negative feelings, assisting them in changing their behavior. As a result, children can learn to express emotions appropriately through modeling, shaping, prompting, and reinforcement.

Cognitive Behavioral Therapy Combined with Multimodal Interventions

James and Mennen (2001) recommend cognitive behavioral therapy combined with multimodal interventions for abused children with multiproblems. Pre-post studies have shown significant improvement in child abuse victim's symptoms of PTSD, sexualized behaviors, depression, self-esteem, and externalized and internalized problems using cognitive behavioral therapy, music therapy, group therapy, and multifaceted therapy. It is equally important for physically abusive parents to be treated as well as the child in physical abuse situations. Children often have problems with aggression, social and interpersonal competence, and developmental deficits. Physical abuse and neglect go hand in hand. Traditional psychotherapy has not been very effective in treating parents concerning neglect. What is recommended is a more promising approach of multiservice interventions that work best for sexually and physically abused children, and combining behavioral and social support with concrete case management from social workers.

There are more benefits to short-term goals with opportunities to practice them for neglectful parents. In cases of sexual abuse, no particular symptom has shown up for everyone, so no particular intervention works across the board. Child abuse is an experience, not a disorder. It is an experience of loss of innocence, trust, safety, significance, and security. Traumatic symptoms could come from a dysfunctional family life or a traumatic event. Abusive parents are often involuntary clients, and the record is that many do not finish an entire course of treatment. Cognitive behavioral therapy seems to work best for long-term successful outcomes, probably because it looks into the root causes called schemas.

The CATS Consortium (2007) learned lessons to be shared. The lessons from the traumatized children and adolescent treatments and service (CATS) project after the 9-11 terrorist attacks are useful for child therapists to keep in mind. The most significant lesson to be learned is that there is a significant population of children and adolescents who need trauma treatments beyond crisis counseling. CBT was utilized during CATS, and there appears to be good outcomes as a result. There was a high incidence of PTSD symptoms as would be expected. The value of this article is that CBT is used in trauma treatment and is a natural fit for trauma abused children, particularly from a PCT perspective.

Copping, Warling, Benner, and Woodside (2001) combine cognitive behavioral therapy with attachment therapy and parent training to form a synthesis of interventions to treat both parent and child in a comprehensive model. That development can be hindered by trauma and PTSD is manifested. Psychoeducational sessions are important to help the parents and child to understand how trauma works and to understand principles of attachment and cognitive behavioral therapy.

Caregivers need to understand and learn how to use power in the family. They need to be challenged in their interpretation of the oppositional behavior of their child. It is important to disengage the caregiver's conflict with the child. Charts, articles, or written homework assignments are given. Diagrams can show automatic thoughts and reveal the underlying schemata by the salient points of the caregiver's thoughts, feelings, and behaviors as a child and as an adult. Once the dysfunctional thinking is identified, it can be altered. The same is done with the child. The child can create stories using a sand tray, which may reveal his thoughts, feelings, and actions, culminating in a diagram that reveals the child's story. The counselor should identify the coping strategies used by the child and the child's perception of his or her safety. The child's attachment to the caregiver can be assessed using the sand tray technique.

After assessment is done, the shame and guilt the child experienced—the imbalance of affect and cognition in the child—is revealed, the loss of a significant relationship is shown, and the attachment relationship to the caregiver will all be hopefully recognized. When there is some improvement in the home, then the behavior choice program (BCP) is used by the caregiver to resolve any further behavioral problems with the child. It initially causes the caregiver to modify his or her behavior. Then it helps the caregivers and the child to understand the emotional forces that drive the child's behavior. The choice of behaviors rests completely on the child.

Smith, Yule, Perrin, Tranah, Dalgleish, and Clark (2007) concluded that CBT use with individuals who experienced trauma-related PTSD works well for children. Trauma-focused CBT includes anxiety components of coping skills and also works with parents. One difference of treatment is that children who have experienced chronic sexual abuse need a different treatment than children who have experienced a one-time traumatic event. Ten sessions were found to be adequate for improvement. Children need to be exposed to the trauma memory by talking, writing, or drawing. This would be integrated with cognitive restructuring distorted thoughts. When cognitive distortions are identified and modified, then PTSD symptoms are ameliorated.

Cohen, Berliner, and Mannarino (2003) use CBT that is trauma-focused, along with psychopharmacological treatments for child crime victims. No single treatment is always appropriate for all children. Psychoeducation puts things in perspective for parents and children.

Crisis intervention is a supportive intervention used immediately in the aftermath of a stressful event. It is like psychological first aid. Play therapy with crime victims has been a means of enhancing the communication of trauma-related issues. Psychoanalytic techniques are used to explore and resolve conflicts about the abuse experience. These are individual sessions, largely nondirective and interpretive, that sometimes takes place over many months. Different styles of family therapy focus on different needs. Physically abused children need a style focusing on enhancing cooperation of family members, parent training, dealing with coercive behaviors, teaching communication skills, and working on problem-solving abilities. Traumatic bereavement therapy based on modified adult grief interventions is utilized for children who were witnesses of homicides. CBT interventions were developed for children who were victims of sexual and physical abuse. They include psychoeducation, some element of exposure, cognitive exploration and reframing with regard to causation and responsibility for the event, coping, relaxation skills, limit setting for sexually inappropriate behavior or aggressiveness, safety education, and problem-solving skill-building components.

All of these models have a parent-treatment component. Group approaches tend to lessen stigma. Children who suffer from PTSD and depression should probably be treated with selective serotonin reuptake inhibitors (SSRI), which are especially popular because of mild side effects. A child suffering from panic and hyperarousal symptoms might be treated with an adrenergic blocking agent. CBT has the most empirical support for treating sexually abused children. It seems to be superior to all other treatments, especially for PTSD symptoms. Counselors should be looking for avoidance coping that is not always revealed to adults and is not on the surface. Even though a child appears to be functioning well enough, cognitive distortions involving guilt or self-blame may be going on under the surface. PTSD screening should be done.

PCT should work well with sexually abused children because of similarities to CBT. The difference is looking at the trauma as loss; in fact, a specific category of loss that can relieve the child of guilt or self-blame. PTSD symptoms, as seen in the chapter on PCT and PTSD, can be relieved as the loss is dealt with, bringing healing and hope.

Art Therapy

Birch and Carmichael (2009) encourage drawing as an intervention from a Jungian perspective for treating abused children. Art brings issues to the surface and accelerates the counselor's ability to help with the child's problems. Drawing can be used diagnostically as well as treatment intervention. The goal is to cause the child to value himself and gain self-empowerment. This makes for change. Art can provide insight into the child's sense of self-worth. The counselor can bring direction to the child by the following: "I wonder what it would feel like for you to be in this drawing? Tell me a story that goes with the picture. Give me a moral that goes with this picture or story. Give me three feeling words that go with this picture. Tell me what happened before this picture. Tell me what is going to happen after this picture." Serial drawing is used over a period of time. Children can be asked to draw a rosebush. A child who needs defenses may draw a fence around it. The need for security and stability in life is often expressed by the roots and root structure, which are emphasized. When the thorns and the full-blooming flowers are drawn, it reflects a maturity that takes the good with the bad. The fullness of leaves and flowers reflects the fullness in the child's life. If just buds are drawn, then great changes are expected in the child's life. A dead bush and broken limbs reflect hopelessness, despair, or depression. Ask the child what the weather is like for the rose bush. It may reflect what the child thinks of the environment—cold or warm. Children may be very literal and concrete, just drawing what they have seen, so there must be careful consideration before jumping to conclusions. Jungians direct thought processes through guiding questions and do not interpret the drawing for the child. They trust the unconscious to make sense of the metaphor. The counselor may suggest that the rose bush is stronger than it looks. Journal drawing is another technique where the child collects a picture journal instead of using words. PCT fits well with art therapy since the counselor is looking for loss, and this will be expressed by the child in drawing.

Conclusion

Counseling children is the surgeon doing a heart transplant in contrast to the doctor who pulls out a splinter. It requires sensitivity in the fullest sense of the word. Discriminating insight is needed as all the skills of listening and looking are on high alert. The Christian counselor is more capable of doing all of this without the secondary vicarious trauma and grief. This requires far more expertise than the counselor who focuses on only one approach.

It appears that multimodal therapy (all of the above descriptions of treatment) for multiproblem children is the most efficacious treatment for parents and children. Physical and sexual abuse is not an emotional problem; rather, it is an experience. The combination of family therapy, play therapy, drawing therapy, group therapy, CBT, trauma-focused therapy, grief therapy, rational emotive cognitive behavioral therapy (RECBT), domain analysis, treatment for PTSD, neo-Piagetian developmental theory for assessing cognitive stage levels, parent-child interaction therapy (PCIT), and PCT can be integrated for each unique child who needs to be treated for abuse. CBT and PCIT are empirically supported treatment modalities with good long-term outcomes. When all domains are injured, it may be appropriate for a child to go to a residential center for containment, so that he or she can be medicated and the domains can be treated separately. Another alternative is to have a physician treat the child with SSRI or an adrenergic blocking agent for a short period of time.

If a Christian family that is open to the Word of God is the client's family, then all of the above, along with the Scripture and prayer, should be utilized. If not, then with informed consent, prayer and scriptural principles can be included. Families need hope and children can change quickly. Counseling children is therefore, in view of the treatment opportunities available, a challenging and rewarding calling. The terrible truth of the tragic loss of a child's significance, security, and safety from physical and sexual abuse requires the integration of various interventions, but they all have elements that fit well within the PCT parameters.

Chapter Thirteen
PCT and the Homeless Population

I n visiting two separate Christian homeless shelters one hundred miles apart, one in Alabama and one in Florida, I was able to observe the difference in structure and atmosphere. The first event at the Alabama shelter was an evening meal with both men and women present. The formal structure of this particular shelter was uncomfortable for the people participating in that they only had thirty minutes to enter, sign in, eat, clean up, and leave. The atmosphere was more like a corrections facility, very rigid, and I found easier access to the homeless population on the street outside the shelter.

In contrast, the Florida shelter's atmosphere was lighthearted, pleasant, and friendly. Even a service dog and a few kittens were being enjoyed by the homeless as they sat and talked. After touring the facility, I spent the next few hours in the day center and the courtyard and had the opportunity to talk and meet many of the homeless, both men and women, who seemed to enjoy the visit with someone new. This facility is larger in terms of the people served at mealtime (800 a day) as opposed to about fifty at the Alabama facility. I was invited back as many times as I would like to come and take part in any aspect of the shelter's functions without an appointment.

My observations regarding this population of people are that most of their situations stemmed from economic loss, which, according to PCT, usually stems from category III, loss from living in a sin-cursed world. Sometimes it came from criminal victimization, which fits well with category I, loss caused by another's sinful choice. Schizophrenia is another reason for being homeless. This fits with category III, loss from living in a sin-cursed world. Terrible trauma, both physical and emotional, came from a variety of losses that differed slightly in situations.

Expectations and Reality

A surprising percentage of the homeless were highly educated and qualified men and women in unusual circumstances and not the stereotypical homeless person who is either an addict, alcoholic, or mentally ill. I met several people with master's degrees, including an M.S.W. and a master in biochemistry. Outside the shelter, there was a new Lexus convertible that belonged to one of the homeless clients. The director informed me that they had a former CEO of a large corporation in Arkansas at the shelter and a man who owned a million-dollar house on the beach, as well as doctors who have and do use the shelter facility when their lives bottom out.

The homeless are often embarrassed about sharing their present situation with others, because people will stereotype them to be lazy, drug addicts, alcoholics, crazy, and generally bad characters whom one should avoid (Shier, Jones, and Graham 2010). This was not what I found to be reality. They were quick to want to talk about their situations and had no embarrassment. They were also willing to admit to their shortcomings, mistakes, and habits that put them in the position they are in at the present time.

A definition of a person who is homeless is someone who lacks a fixed, regular, and adequate nighttime residence (PBS 2009). I was surprised to find out that some of the people I met at both facilities had a fixed, regular, and adequate nighttime residence but could not afford to eat for various reasons, so they utilized the homeless shelter for meals and a place to go in the daytime.

Emotional Impact

One man, in particular, made a great impact on my thinking regarding the plight of the homeless in America. Before he ended up at the Florida shelter, he was then a full-time employee for Alabama Power and Light, the main utility company. One night, when he stepped outside his apartment, he was struck from behind by a man with a hatchet, splitting his skull open in three places. He did not know the man, but the man was high on drugs and did not know what he was doing or probably thought he was somebody else.

Medicaid did not pay for the proper surgical repair of this man's brain, and, as a result, he is going deaf, his speech is deteriorating, and he has lost almost all of his teeth due to nerve damage. He suffers from severe migraines and has lost an enormous amount of weight because of constant vomiting. This man's plight touched my heart. He needs more than a shelter. He needs an advocate who will help him get the needed brain surgery to correct the mistake, and people who will care about him. He worked his whole life, is not homeless due to anything on his part, but is homeless because he is a victim of category I, loss caused by another's sinful choice. Yes, the perpetrator is spending life in prison, but this man is spending his life homeless with no hope. He received prayer, encouragement from the Word, and a chance to have some of his questions about God answered. The other situation that touched me emotionally is finding out that at this shelter, there are 900 school-age children who are homeless in the county. The hidden homeless are all around us, and we cannot keep our blinders on any longer.

During our forty-six years of marriage, there have been several times when my husband and I and our eleven children were in circumstances that would have left us homeless if it were not for God's intervention and Christian family who were willing to take us in at certain critical times in our lives. My home, as I was growing up, was always a haven for those who were hurting in one way or another, and our home throughout these years of marriage and raising children has been a place that continuously takes in those who are endangered or rejected by society for various reasons. Even the children whom we have adopted were endangered both here in America and in other countries. Jesus tells us that when we give even so much as a drink of water in His name, we do it unto Him (Matthew 25:35–40). Just because I have food and drink and shelter, safety, significance, and security does not mean I have the right to turn my back on those who lack these things if God puts them in front of me. We cannot rescue every hurting person in the world, just as I could not rescue every orphan in the world, even though God says we should care for the orphans, but I was to rescue those he put in front of me. The homeless I saw at these meetings needed food to eat, and the shelter was providing that need. Just bread alone will not meet some of the needs I saw and heard about, but the bread that will cause them to truly live is every word that proceeds from the mouth of God (Matthew 4:4).

The homeless have the same needs that we who are not homeless have—the needs of safety, significance, and security. The spiritual flavor and atmosphere in the Florida shelter was so apparent. When I walked through the front door, I saw several staff members in a huddle around the front desk, and one was leading a devotional, just talking about how the Bible applied to his life. Walking through the men's section, a man was sitting on the couch, reading the Bible out loud to himself. Passing through the day center, there were approximately a dozen people watching a religious broadcast on the large-screen television.

When I went into the courtyard, sitting down at a picnic table under a large umbrella was an elderly woman. A walker was beside her, and all her belongings in a bag were hanging from it. She brought a Bible to the table, sat down, and said she was trying to find a verse that would encourage her that the Lord would be with her. I was able to direct her and encourage her to read Psalm 91. The man whose head was split with the hatchet wanted to know how to forgive completely and if God had let this happen to him for a purpose. He also shared that when he was just a little child, his father was murdered by a gunshot to the head. And now he wondered if there was some connection between the way his father died and his near-death experience. This man had suffered loss of safety, security, and significance. I was able to explain to this man what Jesus says about forgiveness, as well as how to break off generational curses, and pray for him for the miraculous healing he believed he needed.

PCT is broad enough to help the homeless community as well as many others. The lack of security, safety, and significance comes from loss in the lives of these people, and educational level did not matter. Loss multiplies loss, and much of their psychopathology can be traced back to a major loss event in their experience.

Chapter Fourteen

PCT AND DEPRESSION IN OLDER WOMEN

It is interesting to note that symptoms for dementia and depression can be two sides of the same coin, because they are similar in many aspects. Major depression in aging women is not of high interest for counselors coming out of graduate programs today as evidenced by a university advisor who informed me that the course in gerontology counseling was no longer offered as a graduate elective because of a lack of interest. Major depression in aging women is also not an unusual subject, except for the fact that Kasen, Chen, Sneed, and Cohen (2010) discovered that early stress exposure to women under sixteen was a correlate to subsequent major depression disorder in elderly women. This research brings out what PCT emphasizes: that loss may bring about dysfunctional thinking, no matter how old the person who suffers from it is, and that loss multiplies loss.

Most empirical models for late-life depression focus on recent stressors as a causality. Women throughout their life span have risk factors that can lead to depression. Kasen et al. (2010) demonstrated the truth of their hypothesis: that adversity in childhood or negative life events (NLE), including marital stress early in adulthood, were all risk factors that led to possible late-life major depressive disorder (MDD). Empirical evidence supports the idea that PCT is applicable to a client in this situation.

Without recognizing other risk factors, it was shown earlier that high NLE doubled the odds of late-life MDD, of which other studies are in agreement. High stress exposure has long-term consequences for depression, and the Kasen et al. (2010) study suggests that stress burden may be cumulative over the life span. Late-life depression can lead to physical illness and a poor prognosis, and cognitive function declines.

This relatively new idea that late-life depression in older women is a result of a cumulative process of NLE over a lifetime fits well with the PCT understanding that loss multiplies loss. The loss of significance, safety, or security in earlier life experience builds into the danger to physical health and perhaps a decompensation of cognitive functioning.

Research to determine predictors of dementia and cognitive decline on a population sample of women ages seventy to seventy-nine were done over a five-year longitudinal study (Brayne, Best, Muir, Richards, and Gill 1997), with a conclusion that simple cognitive tests were found to be the most efficient method of the detection of dementia. Vascular lesions and apolipoprotein e4 may be the link for high-risk dementia. A very important factor is self and informant awareness of the problems with cognition. In itself, it is not a reliable identifier of coming dementia, because depression can cause these problems as well. The counselor needs to listen very carefully to self and informant awareness, both at the primary care level as well as in the clinical setting. Brayne et al. emphasize that the presenting problem may well be from depression and not dementia. Sensory impairments, sight, hearing, and stroke should not be lumped in together with cognitive evaluation, but need to be examined separately. Cognitive function is the best way to identify dementia due to the fact that it is the main indicator of the underlying pathology leading to dementia (Brayne et al. 1997).

All too often, women in general are not always accurately diagnosed at the primary care level by medical doctors, particularly male, because of gender bias. This has personal relevance for me, because it has helped me understand a situation that I encountered where this gender bias almost cost me my life. Many male medical doctors, looking at my age and the fact that I had eleven children whom I homeschooled, made a mental health diagnosis when I complained for eleven months of extreme pain and pressure in my head and neck, especially when bending over. The solution I was given was that I had too many children, and I should just stop bending over. Eleven months later, I was dying due to a completely blocked superior vena cava with four inches of clotted blood and twelve inches of clotted blood in all the branches above the heart. I was given just hours to live. I now have a stent and am on blood thinner due to male doctors with gender bias.

Older women do not fare much better. An example of this is with my own eighty-five-year-old mother who is legally blind, being given a cognitive test that required her to see numbers and arrows on small clocks. Brayn et al. are correct by saying that sensory impairments should not be lumped in together in making cognitive evaluations. In their study, older women with visual impairment improved, showing adaptability, which is in itself a sign of high cognitive functioning. My personal experiences plus research warns me to be very careful of distinguishing depression from dementia, and not to take the quick and easy way of making a diagnosis only on recent stressors.

If presenting problems mimic one another between dementia and depression, and, all too often, if diagnosis is only based on recent stressors, MDD can be misdiagnosed as the onset of dementia. The importance of a genogram cannot be overemphasized, which would pick up on NLE before sixteen and throughout the life. Referrals for checking for lesions and other measures should be done (Brayne et al. 1997), as well as cognitive testing, to attempt to rule out biological disease.Knowing that NLEs in early life can have such cumulative impact in later life makes it very important for younger women to take advantage of interventions, and perhaps counseling, before they get old. This is where PCT can absolutely apply in discerning the loss and its consequent affects. PCT can aid in its focal points of considering loss that can prevent misdiagnosis between dementia and MDD. I believe that elderly women can easily be misdiagnosed, especially emphasized by Brayne et al. The fact linking both articles is that MDD can be confused with dementia and vice versa. Both articles point out a tremendous need for multicultural sensitivity in counseling elderly women.

Now that I am caring for an old-old woman, the importance of correct diagnosis is a big concern and takes this information out of the theoretical realm and moves it into the realm of the heart. These two articles are definitely very different sides of the same coin, and with all the contextual connectors is one elaborative topic. If the loss is the focus of treatment, and not the symptoms, then the outcome should be much better.

Chapter Fifteen
PCT: Cognitive Behavioral Therapy and Family Counseling

Cognitive behavioral family therapy (CBFT) continues to grow as a chosen form of counseling therapy in the world. Research continues to show empirical support for its theories and its interventions. Frank Dattilio, Norman Epstein, and Donald Baucom have expanded its reach in new and more comprehensive understanding of the field of marriage and family counseling. Understanding family schemas intergenerationally provides good outcomes for the client, as well as their relationship with family members. It incorporates reinforcement principles from behavioral therapy but goes beyond behavioral therapy by adding a cognitive component. CBFT is a natural fit in which it is possible to integrate a Christian worldview and PCT. Both perspectives are meta-analytical and cognitive. CBFT provides helpful interventions that can be expanded upon by creative Christian therapists to encompass a spiritual component in an otherwise good theory. PCT, in utilizing the idea of schemas underlying behavior, looks for loss components that are compensated for in dysfunctional (nonbiblical) thinking in family relationships.

Cognitive Behavioral Models of Family Therapy

There are various approaches to marriage and family therapy, but the most effective for its flexibility and integrative potential is cognitive behavioral family therapy (CBFT). As a result of its structure, its comprehensiveness, and focus on cognition (Dattilio and Epstein 2005), it is easily integrated into a Christian worldview. The understanding of family schemas (Goldenberg and Goldenberg 2008) that CBFT presents is not foreign to the Scripture, which speaks of the sins of the fathers being passed down to the children. Dysfunctional thinking is viral and transmitted through unconscious assumptions about others, one's family, and how it relates to the world.

Early family therapy pioneers like Bowen, Jackson, Wynne, Boszormenyi-Nagy—all having been trained in psychoanalytic counseling—have rejected the person as the problem and instead have looked at the dyad or triad. Boundaries, enmeshments, disengagements, and subsystems, as Minuchin contributes; fusion, symbiosis, and triangles, as Bowen suggests; or relational ethics and family loyalty, as in Boszormenyi-Nagy, all have one thing in common: they look beyond the individual to a system.

Pioneers in the field of family counseling were led to a behavioral approach by experimental psychology, B.F. Skinner, and learning theory. In trying to eliminate problematic behavior in the client, they noticed that family members stimulated the maladaptive behavior in the client. Richard Stuart, a social worker, Gerald Patterson, a psychologist, and Robert Liberman, a psychiatrist in the 1970s, attempted to manipulate certain behaviors in the client by telling certain family members how to behave, so as not to reinforce the maladaptive behavior of the client. This kind of reinforcement was the beginning of behavioral parent training. Prior to these efforts, the family was regarded as simply part of the general environment. Behavior therapists adopted a teacher-coach model. Operant and classical conditioning was used as interventions in behavior therapy. A contingency contract was added for couple therapy—a written schedule for exchanging reinforcing behaviors, later utilized in family therapy. Couples in conflict in the 1980s were treated by adding a cognitive component to the behavior therapy. This was the realization that attitudes, thoughts, beliefs, attributions, and expectations also influenced behavior. These were successfully applied to family therapy, and so, cognitive behavioral therapy was born. This has more empirical evidence to support it than any other therapeutic approach.

Aaron Beck, a Philadelphia psychiatrist, and Albert Ellis, a New York psychologist, offered the earliest cognitive approach to couples counseling. Ellis approached it by saying that it was not the events of people's lives that is the most disturbing thing, but the twisted flawed interpretation of the events. Ellis suggested that cognitive restructuring would change the negative thoughts. Beck said that family interactive patterns were involved in the clients' negativity about themselves. There were underlying core beliefs and attitudes about life and people called schemas, which were formed through unfortunate life events. Cognitive distortions then led to a distortion of reality. Beck's approach to therapy was to disconfirm the negative automatic thoughts ("I'm worthless") by providing the client with experiences in the session and out of it that would attempt to alter the negative schemas. The therapist and the client can work together, so that the client will learn new methods of changing the dysfunctional behaviors in the future.

Beck's ideas, when applied to families, involve exposing the family's schemas, which are about why certain things happen to the family and its members. The schema of the family is its core beliefs and attitudes. The therapist's goal is to change the dysfunctional beliefs, attitudes, and attributions, and to restructure the schemas resulting in reduced dysfunctional behavior.

These ideas were initially received as too simplistic when originally presented, but by the 1980s, cognitive interventions were well received. Currently, the major figures in this field are Frank Dattilio (University of Pennsylvania School of Medicine), Norman Epstein (University of Maryland), and Donald Baucom (University of North Carolina). It is interesting that Albert Ellis changed his rational emotive therapy to reflect the influence of Beck by renaming it rational emotive behavioral therapy (REBT) (Goldenberg and Goldenberg 2008).

Dattilio (2005) has used cognitive behavioral therapy (CBT) not only for couples but for family therapy. Cognitive behaviorists do not see clients as the behaviorist did—pushed around by outside forces, nor being driven by inner drives as in traditional psychotherapy. Instead, clients are expected to self-regulate and to self-direct in order to change behavior. Integration of the psychodynamic and systems-oriented family therapies with behavioral techniques might be involved with CBFT. It is an attempt to change conscious thinking patterns justified by empirical research. Its emphasis is on data-based decisions and regular monitoring. Smith and Schwebel (1995) have made an effort to develop a cognitive behavioral family perspective by integrating with a systems approach and behavioral family therapy (BFT). Integration will expand the ability of therapists to describe what the family is doing and how it responds to change. Combining the reinforcement interventions of behavioral therapy with the homeostasis and cybernetic understanding of systems theorists with the addition of CBFT, and their understanding of how individual members of the family think, along with understanding family schemas, integration is a powerful way of adding to the therapeutic understanding of family therapy.

The CBFT approach uses the circular concept from systems thinking, which describes the interaction of the family members, not only using the reinforcement reciprocal principles from behavioral therapy but going beyond by explaining that when behavior of the individual upsets the family balance, a cost-benefit analysis is used to resist change so that homeostasis is maintained. In resisting change, the family members fall back upon the principles found in the family schema. In order to gain a complete understanding of the reciprocal circularity of family members, each member's cognitions must be examined in the light of the family schema.

Most cognitive behavioral family therapists today find that the form and frequency of a client's behavior are developed from the preceding and following events of each family member's behavior, making family involvement in therapy very important. Family units change as a result of the changes in cognitions of the members. Family homeostasis is maintained by favorable cost-benefit ratios, and families will not tolerate for long unfavorable cost-benefit ratio. It is noteworthy that families will generate tension as members go through life-cycle development (Smith and Schwebel 1995).

Both cognitive behaviorists and behavioral therapists use similar techniques during the assessment, such as considering preceding and following behavior of family members after the client's words or actions that represent maladaptive behavior. The presenting problem, explicit identification of problems, and resulting consequences, according to Beck, are the same for both approaches.

Dattilio (2005) noted that cognitive behavioral therapists assess the client at three levels: the most accessible level of automatic thoughts, the underlying assumptions, and at the schema level. On the other hand, a behavioral assessment uses two levels for the assessment: a problem analysis and a functional analysis, which examines the interpersonal environmental factors that precede and follow a maladaptive behavior. Family members need training to bring about positive interaction and improved behavior. The cognitive behavioral family assessment is in contrast to the assessment from behavioral therapy. The CBFT includes a functional analysis of inner experiences: thoughts, attitudes, expectations, and beliefs. They are less linear in their approach. In order to get this data, three forms of clinical assessment are used: direct observations of family interactions, individual and joint interviews, and self-report questionnaires. In cases of adult relationship problems, the Relationship Belief Inventory (Eidelson and Epstein 1982) or Fincham and Bradbury's (1982) Relationship Attribution Measure might be used. Role playing is used to check on progress on targeted behaviors. Automatic thoughts are probed. Direct observation may uncover communication problems.

Behavioral therapy in family therapy is likely not to include the entire family in all sessions. The individual's symptomatic behavior is examined, and individually oriented treatment is usually given. Only after failure occurs with the individual that the family may be brought in, but only until that phase is over. Then it goes back to the individual. Behavioral family therapists are linear, not circular, in their concept of causality (Goldenberg and Goldenberg 2008).

James, Cushway, and Fadden (2006) have done research that examines the difficulty of getting the engagement of families in counseling. Most families do not want to be involved in the therapy. There is withdrawal and resistance, yet BFT, in the authors' minds, appears to desire family engagement as a team affair with the therapist. This runs counter to the impression given in Goldenberg (2008).

As CBT became more popular in the 1980s, they argued that a strict behavioral therapy approach is too linear. Rather, cognitive, behavioral, and affective factors influence conflict in couples. Therefore, problem-solving techniques are not enough to stave off conflict in the long-term (Byrne, Carr, and Clark 2004). It requires more than immediate problem solving, and CBFT can accomplish this by restructuring schemas that affect automatic thoughts and emotional responses to other people. Fraser (2003) has come up with an eclectic approach for family therapy in that she has combined the CBT approach with behavioral therapy and the systems approach of Bowen and others. This approach always desires the family to be involved, with the therapist taking the position as a coach of the team. She attempts to integrate the cognitive, behavioral, and affective factors, as well as identity boundaries, and then fusion everything into one approach.

Dattilio (2005) emphasizes that not every family counseling theory is easy to integrate with CBFT. There are too many different starting points that make it difficult to integrate. Romero, Donohue, and Allen (2009) describe a case study using home-based BFT on a mother and children with presenting problems of drug abuse, neglect, and domestic violence. The results indicated that symptoms were ameliorated in all areas. What is obvious is that these were problem-oriented symptom relieving interventions, and the long-term results were not apparently researched. The superiority of CBFT is that it deals with schemas, not just symptoms, and is better in the long term for positive results. PCT, along with CBFT, is more circular than linear and looks back to past events so as not to just treat presenting problems.

Behavioral therapy is quite different from CBFT, especially in the way the assessment is done: two levels in behavioral therapy and three levels in CBFT. It also appears that behavioral therapy was good enough in its time, but it has been eclipsed by CBFT. Behavioral therapy is linear in causality, and CBFT is circular. Dattilio (2006) stands on the shoulders of giants of the past to bring CBT to the next level of a deeper family therapy understanding. The intergenerational family schemas are helpful in exploring a client's family background and are powerful antidotes against ingrained family schemas, especially in domestic violence situations.

Dattilio is thankful for Aaron Beck's heavy emphasis on schemas and indicates that attention must be given to intergenerational family schemas that can be positive or negative. Intergenerational family schemas can be identified through the use of genograms, which reveal schemas and their origins and the automatic thoughts that develop as a result. Regarding the loss of identity and security in an intimate partner violence (IPV) situation, Dattilio suggests challenging the long-standing family schema by showing the potential risk involved, identifying the erroneous information that supports the schema, accentuating the impact of such beliefs over time, building self-concept and self-esteem skills, and facilitating empowerment by homework assignments that build self-reliance and self-esteem. The therapist should emphasize the fact that people have a choice as to how they want to be loved and how much they are willing to endure (Dattilio 2006).

Our worldview integrates well with CBFT. One particular aspect of CBFT is its emphasis on family schema, particularly intergenerational family schemas. Our personal experience in knowing Dr. Cornelius Van Til, professor of apologetics at Westminster Theological Seminary, and learning his presuppositional apologetics made us appreciate underlying belief structures that influence attitudes toward life and the presuppositions beneath arguments. Theological similarities with a presuppositional approach resembles Aaron Beck's concept of schemas. God made man to interact with other people, the environment, and most importantly, with Himself. We are not animals that are simply a bundle of neurons that respond only to classical and operant conditioning. Men and women are of value because they are made in the image of God. The larger focus of CBFT fits well with the big picture that PCT presents of man and his family and environment. A Christian worldview is a macrounderstanding of man and his world, and CBFT is the same in that regard. Unintentionally supporting the idea that a Christian worldview can integrate with CBFT, Dattilio and Epstein (2005) say that it is not always workable to integrate CBFT with solution-focused therapies. The reason for this is that CBFT is not content with the quick fix in a superficial way. PCT, in conjunction with the work of the Holy Spirit, can help clear up unbiblical thinking by utilizing some of the interventions that CBFT offers and not just treat the presenting symptoms.

In relationship with others, the family is something that God created and was not an evolved formation. The Bible emphasizes speaking the truth in love to others, teaching a cognitive approach to problems. For example, "Let a man examine himself" (1 Corinthians

11:28) is an invitation to consider your cognitions. Exposing the lies in schemas takes the power away from automatic thoughts, making it easier to restructure how people think. Moving people from intergenerational lies to the truth of right family relationships is a noble and God-honoring endeavor, at the least, suitable for common grace, and, at the most, bringing individuals and even whole families to a saving knowledge of the Lord Jesus Christ.

The way God sees family is this: a united group of people in various stages of human development that respects one another, respects identity boundaries, communicates in love, builds one another up, and seeks to help the weak for the glory of God. The family has the highest priority for caring for one another, which is over neighbors, friends, coworkers, and even church. In that sense, they are close. They are also open and are influenced by culture, traditions, mores and norms, civil government, and other external influences.

Unfortunately, families rarely treat one another like the above ideal, and sometimes they need therapists to counsel them to bring the client and the family to a better relationship. Sin has created a dysfunctional pathology. The cure is in Jesus Christ. Better mental health is achieved when there is more truth and love functioning and less lies that influence members of families. Emotions are not ignored in CBFT as some have mythologized (Dattilio 2005). Emotions are complex reactions to how we think we are doing in life. Strong emotions are connected to family schemas, and, with a number of family members in a session, interventions can be used to soothe upset members. I would explore the cognitions connected to the strong emotion, so that emotional intensity can be lessened and clearer thinking can occur. For example, a teenager may be angry because the parent refused to let her go to a party. By asking questions, it is discovered that she is really angry because she thinks she will be rejected by her friends if she does not attend (Dattilio 2005).

Therapists involved in family therapy sometimes have difficulty getting families to participate. One reason is that family members may think the therapist is blaming them for the client's maladaptive behavior. Another reason is that there is a circling of the wagons when family homeostasis is threatened either by outside forces—a perceived threat from the therapist—or within the family from the client's behavior. Doing counseling from a CBFT Christian perspective gives the therapist an opportunity to do a spiritual approach in order to get cooperation from the family. CBFT therapy clears up cognitive misperceptions by using educational interventions in its approach. Therefore, family teaching from the beginning—before resistance happens—about the biblical perspective of God's plan for family members in assisting the family member client can get family participation and may clear up some misunderstandings about attribution.

Beginning with God's family relationships from the Scripture, the ideal family of God, member responsibilities within the Church, and ending with how it applies to the client's family is the way to proceed. Genesis 12:3 indicates that families who have the faith of Abraham shall be blessed in a spiritual and covenant relationship with God. Psalm 107:41 shows that the blessing of the poor is the children. Jeremiah 31:1 reminds us that God is the God of families, His people. Ephesians 3:15 describes all the people of God as a family.

The Greek word used in Ephesians 3:15 for family, is *patria* (Vine, n.d.). The inference is that they are descendants from a common father. Family consists of a concrete group of people. The family that comes for counseling is part of a specific and special fellowship that by nature of the term "family" necessarily excludes others (Rienecker and Rogers 1980). Thus, being part of a family is a God-given privilege, because He goes out of His way to put the lonely people in families (Psalm 68:6). Therefore, it is the family's responsibility to learn how to be the kind of family that pleases God. Examining what they have always taken for granted is a good place to start.

A good intervention for couples therapy that can be built upon from a Christian counseling perspective is Sullivan and Baucom's (2005) Relationship-Schematic Processing (RSP), which was designed to measure the degree to which individuals process information in a romantic relationship. A coding system was designed to assess the behavior. Research determined that wives showed a more frequent and higher quality RSP than their husbands. Husbands were more satisfied when wives engaged in more frequent and higher quality RSP. Wives were more satisfied when husbands engaged in higher quality relationship processing.

This is about relationship talk. Studies have shown that there are gender differences. Men do not enjoy talking about relationship.

Women do. Sullivan and Baucom (2005) expand on this relationship processing. Relationship schema people organize their perceptions of the world into relationship or nonrelationship categories. For example, the husband comes home from work, sits down on the couch, and turns on the news to relax. The wife thinks he is mad at her, because he does not talk to her about his day or her day. He thinks it feels good to relax and watch television. They both are involved in the same event but process it in two different ways. The wife organizes the event in terms of relationship; the husband does not.

There are four types of relationship-schematic comments that reflect underlying relationship processing. Internal-individual is the first type, which focuses on the dynamics between the two people. For example, "I hate it when you ignore me!" The second is called internal-couple. This focuses on the functioning of the couple as a unit. "We fight a lot less since we worked out our finances." The third is external-individual. This addresses interactions between one partner in the couple and the outside world. "When I see you talking to your coworkers, I just feel jealous." The fourth is called external-couple. This focuses on the interactions on the couple as a unit and the outside world. "I'm going to be really upset if we go to your parent's home for the holidays again." The therapist marks down what was said in a particular category. They also must add a relational or emotional meaning to the relationship talk. For instance, "I see you all the time when you started working at home." This is not regarded as a relationship-schematic comment until the emotional component is added on. "I see you all the time when you started working at home. This is the best thing that has happened to our marriage." This construct evaluates the quality of relationship processing.

Many times couples process relationship information but do not communicate it in a constructive way. The husband tells his wife in the seventh month of her pregnancy that she ought to start working out and getting some hobbies. She already has two toddlers. The husband processes relationship information in terms of his romantic ideas but does not consider some very relevant information. He engages in **RSP** but not very well. The therapist should be able to observe for dysfunctional beliefs and to get a general idea of the quality of **RSP** from listening to their story.

This was a research project, not an intervention. Sullivan and Baucom (2005) encourage the use of **RSP** and will send the coding manual to therapists for specific analysis, although the coding is complex and would take time for the therapist to get familiar with its formulations. It does seem easy to grasp and, without the code, would generally give the therapist an idea of how well they are doing in **RSP**.

In looking at it from a Christian worldview, it might be worth the effort to consider other categories in evaluating the quality of the couple's relationship with each other and with God. The spiritual-internal-individual is the first to be utilized. The frequency and quality, either positive or negative, focuses on the spiritual dynamics between the two. "I appreciate that you pray for me." "I hate it when you preach at me." The spiritual-internal-couple is another category. This looks at the spiritual functioning of the couple as a unit. "We fight less since we started to go to church." The third category is spiritual-external-individual. This focuses on interactions between one partner in the couple and the spiritual activities in the outside world, or church and Kingdom, fellowship, meetings, and serving in the community through the church. "I would rather you stay home with me on Sunday morning instead of going to church, because it is my only day off." Spiritual-external-couple comments are about interactions in the couple as a unit and the outside world. "I am going to be really unhappy if we go to that spiritual church retreat again this year." The problem with CBFT RSP is that it is not designed with a spiritual component emphasis. Using this as an intervention, with emphasis on spiritual component, can get at the root of sinful pathology and spiritual schemas that may be the underlying distortions and cognitions putting stress in the couple's relationship, and would fit well with PCT's emphasis on loss and safety, significance, and security in the transcendental, situational, and existential aspects.

Man is a spiritual being with either a good or a bad relationship with God, which will influence a marriage in a good or a bad way. All in all, CBFT has enough similarities to a biblically-based approach to marriage and family counseling and not enough differences to be disqualified. Referring to dissimilarities means that it was not conceived with the presupposition to glorify God. Common grace has given precious insights to its founders. Some interventions are grist for creative integrating, and the cognitive approach that takes in all cognitions and schemas is an appropriate approach for big-picture, biblically-based Christian counseling.

Parenting problems are very much a part of the challenges facing therapists involved in family therapy. Parenting schemas are important for the therapist to identify and analyze for possible change if it is a maladaptive one, too rigid, or too simple. Azar, Nix, and Makin-Byrd (2005) have presented information on parenting schemas and how to change them. Parenting schemas have elements of what the caregiving role is about, beliefs about personal functioning in that position, knowledge of children, how kids develop and how they should act, and thoughts about one's own children. Schemas help people to predict another's behavior.

Parents' schemas are shaped by their own parents, friends, and people who have influenced them in the past. The schemas are not deterministic but can change through circumstances. Adaptive parenting requires flexibility in changing the schemas. Problem schemas also contain negative emotions. They tend to be either too controlling or lack structure. Absolute control over children reflects a person who has little control in relationships in general. The perception of low personal control or inadequacy often results in an unsafe home environment. Parents who believe that their children's injuries are due to fate are less likely to take remedial action. Those who are poor and are subject to catastrophic events beyond their control are less likely to intervene. Abusive parents and neglectful parents have distorted expectations of the abilities of children to care for themselves.

With this problematic schema, I would ally myself with the parents in terms of the challenge of raising children. Since there is much negative emotion with the situation, I might move to the concept that children are gifts of God and use Psalm 127 as an illustration of structuring for parents. This and other Scriptures would gradually expose the lies undergirding their distorted family schema that has brought them to the place of mandatory counseling. Younger parents might be helped by explaining that even infants can see, hear, and understand emotional communication.

The principles that the CBFT Christian counselor can use should create a safe place where parents can feel they can trust the counselor. Prayer is helpful in creating a trusting therapeutic atmosphere. Activate maladaptive schemas, so parents can understand what motivates their behavior, and use the Scripture to do this. Educate the parents as to how their actions bring about the loss of safety, security, and significance, as well as introducing new elements so that their parenting skills can become more complex and competent. Provide the parents with new strategies that will help them to become more competent as caregivers and give relief to certain stressors. All of this must be done with extreme sensitivity. The counselor must convey to the parents that his or her desire is to help them with an understanding of the emotional baggage they carry before challenging family schemas. This is an appropriate match for a Christian counselor who loves his neighbor as himself. Worthington (1999) reminds counselors that hope must be instilled in difficult relational counseling, and where this is missing, there is loss in that area. The same advice applies to couples counseling in the area of marriage and especially in the area of parental counseling.

PCT sees the linkage between God, the family, and the environment. The triadic structure of Father, Son, and Holy Spirit is linked to the triadic structure of the transcendental, the situational, and the existential. The family and its relational problems are intertwined with loss in the significance, safety, and security and the need for replacement in the dysfunctional schemas, which are interrelated to family relationships. All of the CBFT information offered here can be of great assistance in implementing PCT in family therapy.

Chapter Sixteen
PCT and Human Sexuality

Integration of human sexuality and the Word of God involves the incorporation of both scientific research and systematic theology. Both Greek words *theos* and *logos* combine to define "theology" as God's word (Vine, n.d.). Systematic theology applied to human sexuality in the counseling context asks the question: "What does the whole Bible say about sex?" (Grudem 2000). General principles, in addition to applied principles about specific sexual issues, bring the macro to the micro in theology of sex. It is a counseling-sensitive context that will aid the counselor in sexual therapy. Foundations are meant to be built upon. It is a place to start what will give direction and confidence for counselors to bring hope to people who stumble in the darkness and hurt themselves and others. Being foundational, it unites human sexuality with God's purposes for giving mankind a satisfying and meaningful life.

One of the most difficult things to talk about is sex. It is harder to talk about problems with sex when one is personally involved in the problem. It is not an easy thing for counselors to deal with either. So much mythology and distorted thinking has surrounded this subject like no other. The Church has been just as guilty of twisted thinking as the world and sometimes even worse (King 2012). A personal theology of sex should be empirically validated and biblically validated. There appear to be three focal points in the Scripture that are connected to human sexuality, which are Creation, Fall, and Redemption. Sex before the Fall was good and part of all creation. Sex after the Fall reflected the selfish state of the heart, and sex in Redemption involves our stewardship and struggle between self, others, and God and His purposes. Unity, as opposed to the sinful results of disunity, is the goal of human sexuality (Thomas, n.d.)

Sex is declared good by God as part of His order in creation. Gender and sex is ordained by God and part of creative goodness (Genesis 1:25–28, 31). It is also part of the marriage relationship (Genesis 2:20–25). The woman was taken out of the man, so that the man by intercourse goes into the woman, symbolizing giving himself totally to her in love (Thomas, n.d.). Along with everything else, human sexuality has been harmed by sin from the fall of man (Genesis 3). Man, who still is the image of God after the Fall and therefore responsible for the actions of his life to His Creator, has distorted human sexuality into something for his own autonomous ends (Romans 1:18–32).

For the Christian who has been redeemed by Christ, all of life is to be used to glorify God and is to live a holy life, and this includes the sexual experience (1 Corinthians 10:31, 1 Peter 1:15–16). The sexual experience involving body, soul, and spirit from a Christian worldview opposes the evolutionary model stating that sexuality is something only physical and emotional in nature (King 2012). Rosenau (2002) points to Ephesians 5:28–29, 31 as pivotal in a marital sexual relationship where nurture and care surround the sexual relationship. This also indicates that sexual relations are not for oneself alone, but for the other. Sex, therefore, from a PCT perspective, is an affirmation of human significance, safety, and security in one's experience; the opposite of a loss experience. Theology, in order for it not to be ivory-tower thinking, must apply God's Word to all of life, specifically to sexual counseling.

The following is a beginning of integration of the Bible with empirical support on topics that a counselor will have to interact with based on a theology of sex. It is not exhaustive but illustrative and practical as far as it goes. Topics are in alphabetical order to make it easier to refer back to for future counseling.

Aging brings another set of dynamics regarding sex. Direct stimulation of the penis will bring about erection rather than mental stimulation. Ejaculation is less strong, but with less ejaculations, endurance can be longer in intercourse. Testosterone replacement is only effective with men who are low in testosterone, not those with normal levels that decline with aging (Rosenau 2002). Viagra can force relational problems for some couples. It is not about the penis; it is about relationships, which Viagra cannot fix (Rosenau 2002).

PCT is about relationships; therefore, it can be effective in helping people with sexual problems. If there was loss in relationship, it will show up in the sexual relationship in a negative experience. Human sexuality is often like a photographer's dark room where negatives show up. Sexuality is like the check engine light that shows up on the dashboard of a car, letting the driver know that there is something wrong somewhere. If there is a problem in the relationship, it is reflected in the quality and frequency of sex, or a lack of both.

Sexual problems are not always caused by relationship problems. As people age, sexual dysfunction appears to be pain in women as the most frequent complaint. Counselors need to examine the biological, psychological, relational interaction, and the social factors. These things determine sexual health in the elderly (Bitzer, Johannes, Platano, Giacomo, Tschudin, Sibil, Alder, and Judith 2008). The spiritual attitude of the elderly coming for sexual counseling is critically important to assess their situation. Although the Scripture speaks of honoring the aged for wisdom (Fifth Commandment, Exodus 20), it does not say that every fool (unbeliever) becomes wise just because they get old. Dumb and immoral people when young stay dumb and immoral when old. Assessing the spiritual worldview will show whether a person is forgiveness-oriented or not, or caring for the other as oneself or not.

Body image problems can be exacerbated by the gnostic view that the body is evil and the spirit is good. Some people distort what Paul is speaking about in Romans 7:18, 22–23. Paul was not influenced by Greek dualism, and this can be shown by two ideas. First, if God created the world, then it would be an evil act, which contradicts God's comment that it was all "very good" (Genesis 1:31). Second, Paul nowhere condemns sex in marriage. The body itself is destined to share in the glory of the redemption of Christ (Romans 8:23, 1 Corinthians 6:20). King (2012) points out that a good body image is important for good sexual functioning.

The media constantly bombards people with unrealistic standards of what is a sexually attractive body type, which most people cannot live up to. In reality, personality, smell, voice, taste, and the way of showing care for one another in sexual ways are more important than being overweight or underweight. This is pointed out again by Ephesians 5:28–31, where respect, loving care, and nurture bring about oneness in the relationship. When there is a lack of these things, there is loss and its accompanying dysfunctional thinking and behavior.

A study regarding body image and human sexuality was done involving women who had breast cancer and mastectomies. Sexual intercourse was not a source of pleasant feelings, and the conclusion was that body image deeply changed after breast cancer. Physical feelings were extremely reduced. The perception of body image was more influenced by the fear of dying than external sexuality (Maggioni 2007). After the loss of significance comes the loss of safety and security.

Caring for a wife after birthing a child is sometimes not understood by husbands who are unaware of what is going on in their bodies. He becomes somewhat aware, especially if she has had an episiotomy, and he cannot have sex for about six weeks (King 2012). There is a huge drop in estrogen and progesterone hormones. There is a flabby belly skin, stretch marks, a loose vagina, and an emotional impact on the woman who may wonder if she will ever look like she did before she was pregnant. There can be a loss of significance. Women can have three levels of depression after childbirth: postpartum blues (first two weeks), postpartum depression (afflicts 15 percent), and postpartum psychosis (affects one in a thousand). Environmental factors can also cause emotional upset: financial pressures, lack of sleep, middle-of-the-night feeding schedules, lack of family support (King 2012), and a husband who still expects a clean house and dinner on the table and the usual love and affection without understanding his wife's needs. Understanding is probably more important at this time than when she was pregnant. Understanding and help in many areas (Ephesians 5:28) will go a long way to having a good relationship during this time of transition. These are all losses, and awareness of them goes a long way in encouragement.

Counselors must recognize risk factors predictive of postpartum depression. Postpartum blues occur in 15 to 85 percent of mothers in the first ten days after childbirth, peaking on the fifth day. Although in most cases it does not need intervention, it is a risk factor for subsequent postpartum depression. Other risk factors are antenatal depression, previous depression before pregnancy, and premenstrual dysphoria (Pearlstein, Howard, Salisbury, and Zlotnick 2009).

Disabilities can become a challenge for a satisfying sex life. People occasionally have temporary disabilities, which may be physical in nature. Make adjustments in lovemaking. Even holding and caressing may replace intercourse. When both people have disabilities, there is sometimes a prejudice against the other's disability. It calls for maturity and wisdom. Learning new lovemaking techniques is not always pleasant and easy. It requires patience. Without knowledge, marriages have been traumatized and have failed. It is also important to realize that certain medications have side effects that will lower libido, such as blood thinners and blood pressure medication, as well as antidepressants (Rosenau 2002). Love, mutual care, and understanding is needed and taught in the New Testament (1 Corinthians 13).

People with disabilities have just as strong sexual desires as those without disabilities. Research indicates that people with disabilities realize that they have different bodies that do not work like everyone else, which leads to a lack of sexual satisfaction and frustration. Sexual positioning, lack of bowel and bladder control, erection problems, lack of penile sensation, or sensation in other areas of the body are barriers for people to enjoy sex (Taleporos and McCabe 2001). These can become challenges instead of barriers with Christian counseling. The reframing of thought with biblical thinking is part of PCT.

Expectations that are unmet in the sexual relationship in marriage sometimes lead to marital conflict. About half of all married couples have experienced problems with sex because of the different expectations they both had about it. There are different desires, different assumptions, and differences in preferred kinds of behavior (King 2012). Meditating upon the meanings of the different words for love in the New Testament can open up deeper understanding. *Astorge* means without natural or family affection (2 Timothy 3:2; Romans 1:31) (Thayer 1974). *Storge* means the affection that family members have for one another (Thayer 1974). *Agape* is the love by the Father that unselfishly sent the Son to the cross. *Agape love* wants the husband to desire that the wife be everything she can be in her life development and sexual satisfaction. It is also true for the wife to desire that of the husband. *Phileo* is the word for friendship (Thayer 1974). Husbands and wives should be each other's best friend (Rosenau 2002). These words have the common theme of reaching outward for the benefit of another.

Fornication is a word for sexual immorality, sometimes adultery. The problem of extramarital affairs is not an uncommon sexual problem for counselors to attempt to grapple with for their client's benefit. Adultery strikes at the foundation of the commitment, trust, and comfort of marriage. As Rosenau (2002) reminds us, the roots of adultery are a series of poor choices. He indicates that there are five phases to an adulterous relationship: inception, prediscovery, discovery, recovery, and resolution. What is lacking is a biblical forgiveness that is necessary for a good outcome.

Christ does not demand divorce in an adulterous situation even though He permits it (Matthew 5:32). If a marriage makes it to the recovery stage, there is a good chance it will be resolved, and future intimacy will blossom (Rosenau 2002). He suggests preventive steps. Commit to never having an adulterous relationship. Do not keep sexual secrets, especially from your mate. Keep your sexual fantasies focused on your mate. Do not reveal pain and frustration to a third party of the opposite sex, because it creates bonding. Do not grow intimate friendship with persons of the opposite sex without tight boundaries. Do not spend unaccounted time with people of the opposite sex. Be clear on what is appropriate behavior with persons of the opposite sex. Pay attention to your guilty feelings. Do not counsel someone of the opposite sex without another person in the same area of the building. Never think that it cannot happen to you.

Gender problems of identity and role can face the counselor in our day and age. Gender difference is an important way in which people view themselves. The genders of male and female are being viewed as a social construction that is opposed to a biblical view of male and female being created by God (King 2012). Gender dysphoria can occur when a child was born and the attending physician made the call as to what gender the child really was, especially when the genitalia were deformed. The problem comes in when the decision was incorrect.

Biology has been shown to have a far more influential role than was previously believed. Consider the sad story of a set of twin boys. Due to a surgical mistake, one of the twins lost his penis when circumcision was done at eight months of age. After much deliberation, at the doctor's urging, the parents decided to raise the child as a girl. At the time, it was believed that children are psychosexually neutral until the genitals develop. When the boy was one and a half years old, his name was changed from Bruce to Brenda. Surgery was done to make the genitals look more female. The parents dressed the child in girls' clothing. They gave him girls' toys and encouraged girl interests and activities. The doctors and parents considered all of this sexual reassignment a great success as the child assumed a female gender identity. The other twin brother assumed his male identity. This was in 1975. Thousands of other children were given sex reassignment surgery because of this supposed ground-breaking success. This was based on the idea that gender difference was based on the appearance of the genitals. If it was ambiguous looking, then it was an optional decision to choose a gender based on how the surgical alterations could be changed.

In the case of Brenda, the psychiatrist following her development noticed many problems. She was having a hard time embracing a female identity as a woman. She rejected girls' toys and clothing and chose a more masculine look and identity. She imitated her father. She tried to urinate standing up. Upon entering adolescence, she became depressed and suicidal. Ultimately, the parents were forced to tell this child the truth about the sex reassignment surgery. The initial reception of this news enabled this girl named Brenda to finally make sense out of all his urges, stating that being raised as a female "did not feel right." He felt that he finally understood who he was at last. Brenda changed his name to David, after the biblical person who fought and defeated Goliath. He chose to have a mastectomy. Then he received male hormone shots. Surgery was done to partially restore his penis. Later on, he married and adopted his wife's children.

This sounds like a happy ending to a sad story. It is too bad that it did not end happy. David Reimer suffered from depression. You wonder how much it had to do with the loss of his identity, which is the category of loss incurred from the actions of another. He ultimately committed suicide. How many of the other children raised in the opposite gender also suffer from depression (King, Bruce M., *Human Sexuality Today*, 7th edition, 2012, p. 203–204).

Christian counseling from a PCT perspective can be of great help. Assuming they have discovered the truth about themselves, they must be encouraged to realize that God knows them for who they really are on the inside and values them because they are made in His image and have significance. Raising them as the opposite sex was unsuccessful, because fetal hormones are released, altering the brain, resulting in dysphoric feelings (King 2012). This is loss of category VII, loss caused by the actions of another, i.e., the doctors and parents who made the decision of gender.

Homosexuality is a sexual interest in the same sex (King 2012). The gender identity stays the same, but the sexual attraction is to the same sex. Many people who are gay, whether lesbian or gay men, are more on a continuum of sexual interest between the same sex and opposite sex and are called bisexual (King 2012). Psychotherapy from a non-Christian worldview attempts to make the gay people comfortable with their sexual orientation (King 2012).

Romans 1:18 and following teaches that its roots go back to worshiping the creature rather than the Creator and therefore is a sin with terrible consequences. It is a choice and is not biological in nature. There is a relationship between sexuality and worship. In Ephesians, Paul speaks about marriage, and then the idea that it is a living illustration of Christ and the Church. There is an intimate unity between those who have sexual relations, and there is a relationship of union with Christ between Him and His Bride, the Church.

Homosexuality, whether male or female, is a distortion of that relationship, which is characteristic of primary loss. The new birth can change the heart's desire and give the person the desire to change, but there must be continued therapy to change entrenched habits. Theology in line with the Bible would integrate the counselor with the mind of God in such matters, bringing compassion, understanding, concern for the client's well-being (without approving of the sin), and empathy into the therapy.

Incest within families may be understood better by looking at the family dynamics and the profile of the incestuous father. In the home, the father is the all-powerful person. He is authoritarian. Those outside the home may view him as even shy or normal. He establishes fixed, hard gender roles for every family member. They are rigid with external boundaries that keep the family separated from the outside world, closed. Boundaries become blurred and he makes sure that all emotional needs are met in the family. The family becomes increasingly isolated. Independent thoughts and feelings are viewed as destructive. Overdependency on one another begins to happen. The mother does not protect her children. As incest occurs, they feel a sense of abandonment and fear. Children who grew up in this dark world often repeat the process when they get a family, thinking that what is familiar is normal (King 2012).

The Bible condemns incest in Leviticus 20, but in the NT, in the Corinthian church, the guilty man who was turned over to Satan but repented was received back into fellowship (2 Corinthians 2:7). A theology of sex consistent with the Scripture would emphasize forgiveness in the area of sexual sin.

If any passage of the Scripture could be chosen to exemplify a theology of sex, it is Ephesians 5:22–33. The apostle Paul shows us the behavior of relationship that undergirds and strengthens the sexual relationship. In addition, he points out that sex itself, apart from procreation, is an illustration of Christ's relationship with His Bride, the Church. It is clear that He never acted selfishly in His behavior toward the Church. He never harmed her. This is foundational for any theology of sex, and counselors need to remember this passage above all.

Conclusion

A man noticed beside a farm house what appeared to be a man pumping an old hand pump. He was pumping furiously up and down, never slowing, never getting tired. The man walked over to see what was going on and realized that it was a wooden figure painted like a man. The hand was wired to the pump and the elbow was hinged. The water kept pouring out, but not because the figure was pumping it—the water was pumping the man. When you counsel for God and produce good results and outcomes, realize that it is because the Holy Spirit is working through you, not your efforts that are giving results. All you have to do is to keep your hand on the handle.

PCT is designed to keep your hand on the handle. As long as the counselor humbles himself before the Holy Spirit who gives the insights and directs the counselor, then God gets the glory. When that happens, the counselor is blessed, and it is not work. It has been said that when someone enjoys what they are doing, then it is not work. The same can be said for a PCT counselor. It is the authors' desire that others may build upon what we consider a small beginning in assisting the field of Christian counseling.

The Scripture was not meant to be chained to a pulpit, but to live and breathe in the public arena. This purpose, among others, requires a biblical presuppositional base in counseling and doing science in general. Integrating empirical research and the Scripture in Christian counseling has led to this latest approach called paraklasis counseling theory (PCT). The strong, biblical, triune foundation, coupled with loss and its biblical basis, gives strength to Christian counseling that far exceeds the proof-test methods of the past. PCT is not exclusively limited to counseling Christians, as demonstrated in this book, because loss is universal and mankind was created in God's image. PCT is not necessarily a brief therapy, but what has been observed in actual counseling is that it can get to the root of problems quicker than other approaches, as it touches the emotional core of people.

Chrissie Hynde, from the rock group the Pretenders, wrote a song called "I'll Stand by You." The words describe PCT aptly. God stands by His people in their darkest hour. When they come to the crossroads of life and find decisions painful, He will be there. The Holy Spirit is the Paraklasis, the One who stands by us and supports us with the grace, insights, wisdom, and comfort of God. He encourages us when no one else can. In relying on Him rather than our great skill and counseling education, we stand in awe when He changes people and renews failing marriages. People begin to value one another, relationships change for the better, and loss that underlies terrible problems is repaired. Thank God!

REFERENCES

Adams, J. 1986. *How to help people change.* Grand Rapids, MI: Zondervan Publishing House.

Aland, K., M. Black, C. Martini, B. Metzger, and A. Wikgren. 1975. *The Greek new testament.* New York: American Bible Society.

Allison, K., I. Crawford, R. Echemendia, L. Robinson, and D. Knepp. 1994. Human diversity and professional competence: Training in clinical and counseling psychology revisited. *American Psychologist.* doi:10.1037/0003-066X.49.9.792

American Psychiatric Association. 2000. *Diagnostic and statistical manual of mental disorders* (Revised 4th ed.). Washington, DC: Author.

Anderson, N. 2000. *The bondage breaker.* Eugene, OR: Harvest House Publishers.

Arch J. and M. Craske. 2006. Mechanisms of mindfulness: Emotion regulation following a focused breathing induction. *Behavior Research and Therapy* 44:1849–1858.

Arndt, J., J. Greenbert, S. Solomon, T. Pyszczynski, and L. Simon. 1997. Suppression, accessibility of death-related thoughts, and cultural worldview defense: Exploring the psychodynamics of terror management. *Journal of Personality and Social Psychology* 73(1):5–18.

Azar, S., R. Nix, and K. Makin-Byrd. 2007. Parenting schemas and the process of change. *Journal of Marital and Family Therapy* 31(1):45–58.

Backus, W. and M. Chapian. 2002. *Telling yourself the truth*. Grand Rapids, MI: Bethany House.

Bath, D. 2010. Separation from loved ones in the fear of death. *Death Studies* 34:5, 404–425.

Beckham, J., S. Vrana, J. Barefoot, M. Feldman, J. Fairbank, and S. Moore. 2002. Magnitude and duration of cardiovascular response to anger in Vietnam veterans with and without posttraumatic stress disorder. *Journal of Consulting and Clinical Psychology* 70(1). doi:10.1037/0022-006X.70.1.228

Berliner, L., I. Hyman, A. Thomas, and M. Fitzgerald. 2003. Children's memory for trauma and positive experiences. *Journal of Traumatic Stress* 16(3), 229–236. Retrieved from EBSCOhost.

Bernal, G., M. Jimenez-Chafey, and M. Rodriguez. 2009. Cultural adaptation of treatments: A resource for considering culture in evidenced-based practice. *Professional Psychology: Research and Practice.* doi:10.1037/a0016401

Betz, N. and L. Fitzgerald. 1993. Individuality and diversity: Theory and research in counseling psychology. *Annual Review of Psychology* 44:348–81.

Birch, J. and K. Carmichael. 2009. Using drawings in play therapy: A Jungian approach. *Alabama Counseling Association Journal* 34(2), 2–7.

Bitzer, J., G. Platano, S. Tschudin, and J. Alder. 2008. Sexual counseling in elderly couples. *Journal of Sexual Medicine* 5(9):2027–2043. doi:10.1111/j.1743-6109.2008.00926x

Borrego, J., M. Gutow, S. Reicher, and C. Barker. 2008. Parent-child interaction therapy with domestic violence populations. *Journal of Family Violence* 23:495–505. doi:10.1007/s10896-008-9177-4

Borteyrou, X., M. Bruchon-Schweitzer, and C. Spielberger. 2008. The French adaptation of the STAXI-2, C. D. Spielberger's state-trait anger expression inventory. *The Encephale-Revue De Psychiatrie Clinique Biologique Et Therapeutique* 34(3):249–255. Retrieved from http://www.serialssolutions.com

Brayne, C., N. Best, M. Muir, S. Richards, and C. Gill. 1997. Five-year incidence and prediction of dementia and cognitive decline in a population sample of women aged 70–79 at baseline. *International*

Journal of Geriatric Psychiatry 12(11):1107–1118. Retrieved from http://web.ebscohost.com.ezproxy.liberty.edu

Brown, A., D. Antonius, M. Kramer, and W. Hirst. 2008. Anger, aggression, and PTSD among Iraq and Afghanistan combat veterans. *Anger, Aggression, and PTSD among Iraq and Afghanistan Combat Veterans.* Retrieved from http://www.psycnet.apa.org.ezproxy

Brown, F., S. Driver, and C. Briggs. 1983. *The new Brown-Driver-Briggs-Gesenius Hebrew-Aramaic lexicon.* Christian Copyrights.

Brown, K. W. and R. M. Ryan. 2003. The benefits of being present: Mindfulness and its role in psychological well-being. *Journal of Personality and Social Psychology* 84:822–848.

Brown, K. W., R. M. Ryan, and J. D. Creswell. 2007. Mindfulness: Theoretical foundations and evidence for its salutary effects. *Psychological Inquiry* 18:211–237.

Byrne, M., A. Carr, and M. Clark. 2004. The efficacy of behavioral couples therapy and emotionally focused therapy for couple distress. *Contemporary Family Therapy: An International Journal* 26(4):361-387. doi:10.1007/s10591-004-0642-9

Calhoun, P., J. Beckham, M. Feldman, J. Barefoot, T. Haney, and H. Bosworth. 2002. Partners' ratings of combat veterans' anger. *Journal of Traumatic Stress Disorder* 15(2):133. Retrieved from http://www.EBSCOhost.com

Carlyle, K. and A. Roberto. 2007. The relationship between counseling self-efficacy and communication skills of volunteer rape crisis advocates. *Communications Research Reports* 24(3):185–193. doi:10.1080/08824090701438994

Cayleff, S. 1986. Ethical issues in counseling gender, race, and culturally distinct groups. *Journal of Counseling and Development* 64.

Cervantes, J. and T. Parham. 2005. Toward a meaningful spirituality for people of color: Lessons for the counseling practitioner. *Cultural Diversity and Ethnic Minority Psychology.* doi:10.1037/1099-9809.11.1.69

Chemtob, C., R. Hamada, H. Roitblat, and M. Muraoka. 1994. Anger, impulsivity, and anger control in combat-related posttraumatic stress disorder. *Journal of Consulting and Clinical Psychology* 62(4). doi:10.1037/0022-006X.62.4.827

Chemtob, C., R. Novaco, R. Hamada, D. Gross, and G. Smith. 1997. Anger regulation deficits in combat-related posttraumatic stress disorder. *Journal of Traumatic Stress* 10(1):17–36. Retrieved from http://www.EBSCOhost.com

Churchill, Winston S. 1948. *The gathering storm.* Boston, MA: Houghton Mifflin.

Clinton, T. and G. Oshlschlager. 2002. *Competent Christian counseling* (Vol. 1). Colorado Springs, Colorado: WaterBrook Press.

Cloud, H. and J. Townsend. 1999. *Boundaries in marriage*. Grand Rapids, MI: Zondervan.

Cohen, J., L. Berliner, and A. Mannarino. 2003. Psychosocial and pharmacological interventions for child crime victims. *Journal of Traumatic Stress* 16(2):175–186. Retrieved from EBSCOhost.

Colbert, L., J. Jefferson, R. Gallo, and R. Davis. 2009. A study of religiosity and psychological well-being among African Americans: Implications for counseling and psychotherapeutic processes. *Journal of Religion and Health* 48:278–289. doi:10.1007/s10943-008-9195-9

Cooper, S., K. Stark, D. Peterson, A. O'Roark, and G. Pennington. 2008. Consulting competently in multicultural contexts. *Consulting Psychology Journal: Practice and Research*. doi:10.1037/0736-9735.60.2.186

Copping, V. E., D. L. Warling, D. G. Benner, and D. W. Woodside. 2001. A child trauma treatment pilot study. *Journal of Child and Family Studies* 10(4):467–475. Retrieved from EBSCOhost.

Corsini, K. (speaker). n.d. *Back to the blueprint*. [Movie]. Lynchburg, VA: Liberty University.

Crabb, L. 1977. *Effective biblical counseling: A model for helping caring Christians become capable counselors*. Grand Rapids, MI: Zondervan.

Cunningham, M. 1999. The impact of sexual abuse treatment on the social work clinician. *Child and Adolescent Social Work Journal, 16*(4), 277-290. Retrieved from http:EBSCOhost.

Dennis, M. 2009. Suicide and self-harm in older people. *Quality and Aging* 10(1).

Dermer, S., S. Smith, and K. Barto. 2010. Identifying and correctly labeling sexual prejudice, discrimination, and oppression. *Journal of Counseling and Development* 88(3):325-332, 7 pgs.

Dattilio, F. 2005. The restructuring of family schemas: A cognitive-behavior perspective. *Journal of Marital and Family Therapy* 31(1):1-13. Retrieved from http://proquest.umi.com.ezproxy.liberty.edu

Datillio, F. 2006. A cognitive-behavioral approach to reconstructing intergenerational family schemas. *Contemporary Family Therapy: An International Journal* 28(2):191–200. doi:10.1007/s10591-006-9-005-z

Dattilio, F. M., N. Epstein, and D. H. Baucom. 1998. *An introduction to cognitive-behavioral therapy with couples and families.* New York: Guilford Press.

Datillio, F. and N. Epstein. 2005. Introduction to the special section: The role of cognitive-behavioral interventions in couple and family therapy. *Journal of Marital and Family Therapy,* 31(1):7–13. Retrieved from http://proquest.umi.com.ezproxy.liberty.edu

Davidson, B. 1970. *The analytical Hebrew and Chaldee lexicon* (p.517). Grand Rapids, MI: Zondervan.

Davies, D. 2006. *Child development,* (3rd Edition). New York, NY: The Guilford Press.

Dooyeweerd, H. 1984. *A new critique of theoretical though.* Ontario, Canada: Paideia Press Ltd.

Eidelson, R. J. and N. Epstein. 1982. Cognition and relationship maladjustment: Developmental of a measure of dysfunctional relationship beliefs. *Journal of Consulting and Clinical Psychology* 50:715–720.

Entwistle, D. N. 2010. *Integrative approaches to psychology and Christianity.* Oregon: Cascade.

Fillit, H. and R. Butler. 2009. The frailty identity crisis. *Journal of the American Geriatrics Society* 57(2):348–352. doi:10.1111/j.1532-5415.2008.02104.x

Fincham, F. and T. Bradbury. 1992. Assessing attributions in marriage: The relationship attribution measure. *Journal of Personality and Social Psychology* 62:457–468.

Forbes, D., G. Hawthorne, P. Elliott, T. McHugh, D. Biddle, M. Creamer, and R. Novaco. 2004. A concise measure of anger in combat-related posttraumatic stress disorder. *Journal of Traumatic Stress Disorder* 17(3):249–256. Retrieved from http://www.EBSCOhost.com

Fouad, N. 2006. Multicultural guidelines: Implementation in an urban counseling psychology program. Goldstein, R., & Gruenberg,

A. (2007). Major depressive disorder in the older adult: Implications for women. *Journal of Women and Aging.* *19*(1/2), 63-78.

Fraser, B. 2003. The common factors that connect all approaches to family therapy. *Australian and New Zealand Journal of Family Therapy* 24(4):225–227. Retrieved from http://web.ebscohost.com.ezproxy.liberty.edu

Friedrich, G., ed. 1977. *Theological dictionary of the New Testament, V.* Grand Rapids, MI: Wm. B. Eerdmans Publishing Co.

Garzon, F. 2008. *Pursuing Peace.* Maitland, FL: Xulon Press.

Glasser, W. 1965. *Reality therapy: A new approach to psychiatry.* New York: Harper and Rowe.

Goldenberg, H. and I. Goldenberg, I. (2008). *Family therapy: An overview,* (7th Edition). Belmont, CA: Brooks/Cole.

Goldstein, R. and A. Gruenberg. 2007. Major depressive disorder in the older adult: Implications for women. *Journal of Women and Aging* 19(1/2):63–78.

Granello, D. 2010. A suicide crisis intervention model with 25 practical strategies for implementation. *Journal of Mental Health Counseling* 32(3):218–235. Retrieved from http://ProQuest Psychology Journals.

Greenstone, J. and S. Leviton. 2002. *Elements of crisis intervention: Crises and how to respond to them,* (2nd Edition). Belmont, CA: Brooks/Cole.

Grudem, W. 1994. *Systematic theology: An introduction to biblical doctrine.* Grand Rapids, MI: Zondervan.

Hage, S., A. Hopson, M. Siegel, G. Payton, and E. DeFanti. 2006. Multicultural training in spirituality and interdisciplinary review. *Counseling and Values* 50(3):217, 18 pgs.

Hart, A. 1999. *The anxiety cure.* Nashville, TN: Thomas Nelson.

Harvard Mental Health Letter. 2002. Managing and averting anger. Retrieved from http://www.health.harvard.edu

Hawkins, R. (speaker) n.d. *Hawkins' model for guiding the counseling process.* [PowerPoint slides]. Lynchburg, VA: Liberty University.

Hayes, S. 2006. Acceptance and commitment therapy: Model, processes and outcomes. *Behavior Research and Therapy* 44:1–25. Retrieved from http://www.sciencedirect.com.ezproxy.liberty.edu

Herek, G. and L. Garnets. 2007. Sexual orientation and mental health. *Annual Review of Clinical Psychology* 3:353–375.

Hoagwood, K. 2007. Implementing CBT for traumatized children and adolescents after September 11: lessons learned from the child and adolescent trauma treatments and services (CATS) project. *Journal of Clinical Child and Adolescent Psychology* 36(4): 581–92.

Hung, L., G. Kempen, and N. De Vries. 2010. Cross-cultural comparison between academic and lay views of healthy aging: A literature review. *Aging and Society* 30:1373–1391. doi:10.1017/Soi44686X10000589

Hyman, S., S. Gold, and M. Cott. 2003. Forms of social support that moderate PTSD in childhood sexual abuse survivors. *Journal of Family Violence* 18(5):295–300. Retrieved from EBSCOhost.

Ivey, A. and M. Ivey. 1990. Assessing and facilitating children's cognitive development: Developmental counseling and therapy in a case of child abuse. *Journal of Counseling and Development* 68(3):299–305. Retrieved from EBSCOhost.

Jakupcak, M., D. Conybeare, L. Phelps, S. Hunt, H. Holmes, B. Felker, M. Klevens, and M. McFall. 2007. Anger, hostility, and aggression among Iraq and Afghanistan war veterans reporting PTSD and subthreshold PTSD. *Journal of Traumatic Stress* 20(6):945–954. Retrieved from http://www.EBSCOhost.com

James, C., D. Cushway, and G. Fadden. 2006. What works in engagement of families in behavioural family therapy? A positive model from the therapist perspective. *Journal of Mental Health* 15(3):355–368. doi:10.1080/09638230600700805

James, S. and F. Mennen. 2001. Treatment outcome research: How effective are treatments for abused children? *Child and Adolescent Social Work Journal* 18(2):73–95. Retrieved from EBSCOhost.

Jones, K. 2002. Group play therapy with sexually abused preschool children: Group behaviors and interventions. *Journal for Specialists in Group Work* 27(4):377–389. Retrieved from EBSCOhost.

Jones, S. and R. Butman. 1991. *Modern psychotherapies: A Christian appraisal.* Downer Grove, IL: InterVarsity Press.

Joseph, R. 1998. Traumatic amnesia, repression, and hippocampus injury due to emotional stress, corticosteroids and enkephalins. *Child Psychiatry and Human Development* 29(2):169–185. Retrieved from EBSCOhost.

Kabat-Zinn, J. 1990. Full catastrophe living: Using the wisdom of your body and mind to face stress, pain, and illness. New York, NY: Delacorte.

Kanel, K. 2007. *A guide to crisis intervention,* (3rd Edition). Mason, OH: Cengage Learning.

Kasen, S., H. Chen, J. Sneed, and P. Cohen. 2010. Earlier stress exposure and subsequent major depression in aging women. *International Journal of Geriatric Psychiatry* 25(1), 91–99. Retrieved from http://web.ebscohost.com.ezproxy.liberty.edu

Kindsvatter, A., J. D. Duba, and E. P. Dean. 2008. Structural techniques for engaging reluctant parents in counseling. *Family Journal: Counseling and Therapy for Couples and Families* 16:204–211.

King, B. 2012. *Human sexuality today.* Upper Saddle River, NJ: Prentice Hall.

Kittel, G., ed. 1976. *Theological dictionary of the New Testament, II.* Grand Rapids, MI: Wm. B. Eerdmans Publishing Co.

Kuhn, E., K. Drescher, J. Ruzek, and C. Rosen. 2010. Aggressive and unsafe driving in male veterans receiving residential treatment for PTSD. *Journal of Traumatic Stress* 23(3):399–402. Retrieved from http://www.EBSCOhost.com

Lehmann, P. 1997. The development of posttraumatic stress disorder (PTSD) in a sample of child witnesses to mother assault. *Journal of Family Violence* 12(3):241–257. Retrieved from EBSCOhost.

London, H. and W. Devore. 1988. Layers of understanding: Counseling ethnic minority families. *Family Relations* 37(3):310–314.

Machen, J. 1937. *The Christian view of man.* New York: The Macmillan Co.

Maggioni, C. 2007. Body image and breast cancer. *Journal of Psychosomatic Obstetrics and Gynecology.* Retrieved April 19, 2012, from http://proquest.umi.com.ezproxy

Maguen, S., B. Lucenko, M. Reger, G. Gahm, B. Litz, K. Seal, S. Knight, and C. Marmar. 2010. The impact of reported direct and indirect killing on mental health symptoms in Iraq war veterans.

Journal of Traumatic Stress 23(1):86–90. Retrieved from http://www.EBSCOhost.com

Marshall, A., E. Martin, G. Warfield, S. Doron-Lamarca, B. Niles, and C. Taft. 2010. The impact of antisocial personality characteristics on anger management treatment for veterans with PTSD. *Psychological Trauma: Theory, Research, Practice, and Policy* 2(3). doi:0.1037/a0019890

McMinn, M. R. 1996. *Psychology, theology and spirituality in Christian counseling.* Illinois: Tyndale House.

Miller, C. 2008. Crisis counseling in Silicon Valley. *The New York Times,* 158. Retrieved from http://EBSCOhost

Montgomery, F. and S. Newman. 2010. Traits of student leaders on a technical campus: gender differences. *College Student Journal* 44(2):437–447.

Morland, L., C. Greene, and T. Strom. 2007. Ethnocultural variations in anger expression in Hawaiian Islands combat veterans. American Psychological Association 2007 Convention Presentation. Retrieved from http://psycnet.apa.org.ezproxy

Morrish, G., ed. 1979. *A concordance of the Septuagint.* Grand Rapids, MI: Zondervan.

Murdock, N. 2009. *Theories of counseling and psychotherapy: A case approach,* (3rd Edition). Upper Saddle River, NJ: Pearson.

Murphy, K. 1980. A cognitive-behavioral approach to client anxiety, anger, depression, and guilt. *The Personnel and Guidance Journal* 59(4):202. Retrieved from http://www.seriassolutions.com

Murray, J. 2001. Loss as a universal concept: A review of the literature to identify common aspects of loss in diverse situations. *Journal of Loss and Trauma* 6:219–241.

Nam, S., H. Chu, M. Lee, and J. Lee. 2010. A meta-analysis of gender differences in attitudes toward seeking professional psychological help. *Journal of American College Health* 59(2):110, 7 pgs.

Neville, H., L. Spanierman, and B. Doan. 2006. Exploring the association between color-blind racial ideology and multicultural counseling competencies. *American Psychological Association.* doi:10.1037/1099-9809.12.2.275

Nezu, A. 2010. Cultural influences on the process of conducting psychotherapy: Personal reflections of an ethnic minority psychologist. *Psychotherapy Theory, Research, Practice, Training.* doi:10.1037/a0019756Niemiec, C., K. Brown, T. Kashdan, P. Cozzolino, W. Breen, C. Levesque-Bristol, R. Ryan. 2010. Being present in the face of existential threat: The role of trait mindfulness in reducing defensive responses to mortality salience. *Journal of Personality and Social Psychology.* doi:10.1037/a0019388. Retrieved from hhtp://psycnet.apa.org.ezproxy.liberty.edu: 2048/journals/psp/99/2/344.html

Novaco, R. and C. Chemtob. 2002. Anger and combat-related posttraumatic stress disorder. *Journal of Traumatic Stress* 19(2):123. Retrieved from http://www.EBSCOhost.com.

Paulson, B. and M. Worth. 2002. Counseling for suicide: Client perspectives. *Journal of Counseling and Development* 80:86–93. Retrieved from http://EBSCOhost.

Pearlstein, T., M. Howard, A. Salisbury, and C. Zlotnick. 2009. Postpartum depression. *American Journal of Obstetrics and Gynecology* 200(4):357–364. Retrieved from http://rx9h3hy-4r.search.serialssolutions.com

Peterson, C. and M. Biggs. 1997. Interviewing children about trauma: Problems with "specific" questions. *Journal of Traumatic Stress* 10(2):279–290. Retrieved from EBSCOhost.

Prather, W. and J. A. Golden. 2009. A behavioral perspective of childhood trauma and attachment issues: Toward alternative treatment approaches for children with a history of abuse. *International Journal of Behavioral Consultation and Therapy* 5(2):222–241. Retrieved from EBSCOhost.

Rainey, S. and J. Trusty. 2007. Attitudes of master's-level counseling students toward gay men and lesbians. *Counseling and Values* 52(1):12.

Rienecker, F. and C. Rogers. 1980. *Linguistic key to the Greek New Testament*. Grand Rapids, MI: Zondervan.

Robyak, J. 1986. Measuring states and traits: A dialogue with Charles Spielberger. *Journal of Counseling and Development* 65(2):89. Retrieved from http://www.serialssolutions.com

Romero, V., B. Donohue, and D. Allen. 2010. Treatment of concurrent substance dependence, child neglect and domestic violence: A single case examination involving family behavior therapy. *Journal of Family Violence* 25(3):287–295. doi:10.1007/s10896-009-9291-y

Rosenau, D. 2002. *Celebration of sex.* Nashville, TN: Thomas Nelson.

Ross, R. and H. McKay. 1979. *Self-mutilation.* Lexington, MA: D.C. Heath and Co.

Sandoval, J., A. Scott, and I. Padilla. 2009. Crisis counseling: An overview. *Psychology in the Schools* 46(3):246–256. Retrieved from http://EBSCOhost.

Sapp, M. 2006. The strength-based model for counseling at-risk youths. *The Counseling Psychologist* 34:108–117. doi:10.1177/0011000005282370

Schiller, V. 2008. Therapeutic work with a physically abused preschooler. *The Psychoanalytic Study of the Child* 63:83–110. Retrieved from http://liberty.summon.serialssolutions.com

Schimel, J., J. Hayes, T. Williams, and J. Jahrig. 2007. Is death really the worm at the core? Converging evidence that worldview threat increases death thought accessibility. *Journal of Personality and Social Psychology* 92(5):789–803. doi:10.1037/0022-3514.92.5.789

Schulte, D., T. Skinner, and D. Claiborn. 2002. Religious and spiritual issues in counseling psychology training. *The Counseling Psychologist* 30(1):118–134. doi:10.1177/0011000002301009

Seven states share $19.2 million from SAMHSA for hurricane aftermath crisis counseling aid. 2006. *World Disease Weekly*. Retrieved from http://EBSCOhost

Shea, M. 2009. Treatment of PTSD-related anger in troops returning from hazardous deployments. Retrieved fromhttp://www.psycnet.apa.org.ezproxy

Shier, M., M. Jones, and J. Graham. 2010. Perspectives of employed people experiencing homelessness of self and being homeless: Challenging socially constructed perceptions and stereotypes. *Journal of Sociology and Social Welfare* 37(4). Retrieved from http://web.ebscohost.com.ezproxy.liberty.edu

Shoshani, A. and M. Slone. 2010. Prevention rather than cure? Primary or secondary intervention for dealing with media exposure to terrorism. *Journal of Counseling and Development* 88(4):440–448. Retrieved from http://www.go.galegroup.com

Silva, A. and M. Klotz. 2006. Culturally competent crisis response. *Principle Leadership (High Sch Ed)* 5(6):11–15. Retrieved from http://MyWilsonWeb

Smith, B. G. and Schwebel. 1995. Using a cognitive behavioral family model in conjunction systems and behavioral family therapy models. *American Journal of Family Therapy* 23:203–211.

Smith, G. and A. Schwebel. 1995. Using a cognitive-behavioral family model in conjunction with systems and behavioral family therapy models. *American Journal of Family Therapy* 23(3):203–212. Retrieved from http://web.ebscohost.com.ezproxy.liberty.edu

Smith, P., W. Yule, S. Perrin, T. Tranah, T. Dalgleish, and D. Clark. 2007. Cognitive-behavioral therapy for PTSD in children and adolescents: A preliminary randomized controlled trial. *Journal of the American Academy of Child and Adolescent Psychiatry* 46(8):1051–61. Retrieved from http://vnweb.hwwilson.web.com.ezproxy

Snaith, N., ed. 1976. *Hebrew Old Testament.* London, England: The British and Foreign Bible Society.

Sohn, P. 2011. Crisis counseling a priority in tornado aftermath. *Chattanooga Times/Free Press.* Retrieved from http://EBSCOhost

Sosin, L. (speaker) n.d. Welcome to counselor professional identity, function, and ethics. Lynchburg, VA: Liberty University.

Spielberger, C. 2009. [Professional resume]. Retrieved from http://www.doctorbrunner.com

Sullivan, L. and D. Baucom. 2005. Observational coding of relationship-schematic processing. *Journal of Marital and Family Therapy* 31(1):31–44. Retrieved from http://proquest.umi.com.ezproxy.liberty.edu

Sue, D. 1991. A model for cultural diversity training. *Journal of Counseling and Development* 70.

Sue, D., P. Arredondo, and R. McDavis. 1992. Multicultural counseling competencies and standards: A call to the profession. *Journal of Multicultural Counseling and Development* 20(2):64–89.

Sue, S., N. Zane, G. Hall, and L. Berger. 2009. The case for cultural competency in psychotherapeutic interventions. *Annual Review of Psychology* 60:525–548.

Taft, C., A. Street, A. Marshall, D. Dowdall, and D. Riggs. 2007. Posttraumatic stress disorder, anger, and partner abuse among Vietnam combat veterans. *Journal of Family Psychology* 21(2):270–277. doi:10.1037/0893-3200.21.2270

Taleporos, G. and M. McCabe. 2001. Physical disability and sexual esteem. *Sexuality and Disability* 19(2):131–148. Retrieved from http://proquest.umi.com.ezproxy

Thayer, J. 1974. *Greek-English lexicon of the New Testament.* Grand Rapids, MI: Zondervan.

Thomas, J. n.d. *Toward an integrative theology of sexuality* [PowerPoint slides]. Retrieved April 10, 2002, from https://bb7.liberty.edu

Thomas, J. and L. Sosin. 2011. *Therapeutic expedition: Equipping the Christian counselor for the journey.* Nashville, TN: B and H Publishing Group.

Timmer, S., A. Urquiza, A. Herschell, J. McGrath, N. Zebell, A. Porter, and E. Vargas. 2006. Parent-child interaction therapy: Application of an empirically supported treatment to maltreated children in foster care. *Child Welfare* 85(6):919–39. Retrieved May 18, 2011, from ProQuest Medical Library.

Van Velsor, P. 2004. Revisiting basic counseling skills with children. *Journal of Counseling and Development* 82. Retrieved from EBSCOhost.

Vine, W. n.d. *A comprehensive dictionary of the original Greek words with their precise meanings for English readers.* Peabody, Massachusetts: Hendrickson Publishers.

Watson, P. and J. Ruzek. 2009. Academic/state/federal collaborations and the improvement of practices in disaster mental health services and evaluation. *Administration Policy in Mental Health* 36:215–220. doi:10.1007/s10488-009-0212-4

Weitzman, J. 2005. Maltreatment and trauma: Toward a comprehensive model of abused children from developmental psychology. *Child and Adolescent Social Work Journal* 22(3/4):321–341. doi:10.1007/s10560-005-0014-9

Wenk-Sormaz, H. 2005. Meditation can reduce habitual responding. *Advances in Mind-Body Medicine* (Fall-Winter), 21(3-4):33–49.

Wilmoth, J. and S. Smyser. 2009. The ABC-X model of family stress in the book of Philippians. *Journal of Psychology and Theology* 37(3):155–158. Retrieved from http://EBSCOhost

Wise, S. 2007. Ask the experts: Counseling sexual abuse survivors. *American Psychotherapy Association* (Summer) 18–20. Retrieved from http://EBSCOhost

Wisman, A. and J. Goldenberg. 2005. From the grave to the cradle: evidence that mortality salience engenders a desire for offspring. *Journal of Personality and Social Psychology* 89(1):46–61. doi:10.1037/0022-33514.89.1.46

Worthington, E. 1999. *Hope-focused marriage counseling.* Downers Grove, IL: InterVarsity Press.

Young, A. and N. Brumley. 2009. On-scene mental health services: Establishing a crisis team. *FBI Law Enforcement Bulletin* 78(9):6–11. Retrieved from http://EBSCOhost

Young, R. 1969. *Analytical concordance to the Bible.* Grand Rapids, MI: Wm. B. Eerdmans Publishing Co.

www.ingramcontent.com/pod-product-compliance
Lightning Source LLC
Chambersburg PA
CBHW070531160426

43199CB00014B/2242